The Empathy Fix

Keetie Roelen is a Senior Research Fellow and Co-Deputy Director of the Centre for the Study of Global Development at The Open University, UK. She has a PhD in Public Policy from the University of Maastricht in the Netherlands and has been working in the field of poverty, social policy, and international development for nearly two decades. She is also founder and host of the podcast Poverty Unpacked, a platform for exploring the hidden sides of poverty.

Her work has featured in media such as The Guardian and BBC World Service. She has spoken about how to address poverty to multiple audiences, ranging from government ministers and members of parliament to students and activists.

The Empathy Fix

Why Poverty Persists and How to Change it

Keetie Roelen

ALLEN&UNWIN

Published in hardback in Great Britain in 2025 by Allen & Unwin,
an imprint of Atlantic Books Ltd.

10 9 8 7 6 5 4 3 2 1

A CIP catalogue record for this book is available from the British Library.

Hardback ISBN: 978 1 80546 175 3
E-book ISBN: 978 1 80546 176 0

Printed and bound by CPI (UK) Ltd, Croydon CR0 4YY

Allen & Unwin
An imprint of Atlantic Books Ltd
Ormond House
26–27 Boswell Street
London
WC1N 3JZ

www.atlantic-books.co.uk

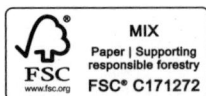

MIX
Paper | Supporting
responsible forestry
FSC
www.fsc.org   FSC® C171272

To Mum and Dad

CONTENTS

NOTE FROM THE AUTHOR

———

Before we dive in, it would be remiss of me if I didn't acknowledge the position of immense privilege from which I wrote this book. I have never lived in poverty, nor experienced the threat of finding myself in precarious living conditions. I'm incredibly lucky to have a safety net I can fall back on if things don't work out. Being middle-class and white has kept me from having to contend with struggles and disadvantages that are a daily reality for so many others, both close to home and further afield.

When it comes to poverty, my personal socioeconomic circumstances inevitably make me an outsider looking in. Yet, perhaps somewhat perversely, it's exactly my lack of lived experience that has made me acutely aware of the need for empathy as a foundation for fighting poverty. As an academic and policy researcher, it's my aim to contribute to the science of poverty and the practice of how to tackle it. But without first-hand insight into the struggle to make ends meet, it's impossible to make this contribution without trying to see the world through the eyes of those who have. Without the honesty and generosity of those at the forefront of living and fighting poverty – from the UK, the Netherlands and the US to Bangladesh, Ethiopia and Haiti – in sharing their stories and experiences with me, this blatantly obvious truth might not have come to me.

The perverse reality is that most of the knowledge generated about poverty and the policies that seek to address it are made by those who don't have lived experience. While it should go without saying that anyone working on this issue should do so from a place of humility and curiosity, it has been striking to witness the opposite on far too many occasions. It's these experiences that have impressed on me the importance of empathy. Empathy is crucial to bridge the divide and counteract the schism between them and us. To compel scientists, policymakers and politicians to come down from their ivory towers to engage with and include those who live in poverty. And for all of us to examine our roles in the condoning and perpetuation of injustice, and to fight against it.

INTRODUCTION

———

It's a dark December afternoon and I'm late for my video call. I'm hosting a conversation for my podcast, Poverty Unpacked, and I'm aware that my guests are waiting on the other end, probably with devices eating away at valuable mobile data. You'd think that after all that time working from home during the pandemic, Zoom hiccups were a thing of the past. Not on this occasion, though, and I feel more frazzled with every minute that passes. Cursing myself for my technological ineptitude, I finally manage to log on. Soon enough my guests start appearing on my screen. To my relief they look remarkably patient and reassuringly good-natured.

'Sometimes my daughter is absolutely freezing and begging me to turn the heating up. But it's just too expensive.' Brian, a single dad from London, is the first to respond to my question about what it's like to get by on a low income in modern-day Britain. Affable and considering his words carefully, he explains that he faces the impossible choice nearly every day of heating his home or buying dinner. 'People say we live in a rich country but there's millions of people that just haven't got enough money for basic needs such as food or heating.'

It's a bitterly cold day and my heart sinks realising that winter has only just begun.

Things have gone from bad to worse for Brian in the last few years. When we speak, in December 2021, benefit payments in the UK haven't increased in line with inflation, meaning he can afford less now than he did five years ago. Unexpected expenses, such as setting up an internet connection so that his daughter could continue her schooling during COVID lockdowns, hit him hard. A cost-of-living crisis not seen in the UK since the 1970s is creating an even greater squeeze.

'How it is possible that in one of the world's wealthiest countries, you're forced to forgo one basic good so you can afford another?' I ask. Sounding exasperated, Brian responds. 'Politicians talk a lot, but it never seems to actually come down to any firm actions. They make announcements of what needs to change but it never leads to people having enough money to be able to support themselves and their families.'

As a social scientist who has researched hardship and injustice for nearly two decades, I've had the privilege of talking with many people around the world about what it means to live on little. From far-flung corners of rural Africa and overcrowded low-income neighbourhoods in some of Asia's megacities to hidden pockets of suffering in Europe, I have sat with those who find themselves at the sharp end of deprivation and inequality. Together with colleagues I have collected information about reasons for slipping into poverty and efforts that can help break the cycle. Keen to transform learnings into positive change, I have participated in discussions about how to turn things around at the United Nations in New York, the European Parliament in Brussels, and government offices in Accra, Kathmandu and London. In all those years of listening to stories, analysing data and examining policy options, I kept returning to the same observation. Poverty may look different from one place to the next, but it also has one common denominator: it exists because we let it happen.

For Caroline, my other guest on the podcast, staying warm in the evening at her house in a small town in Northern Ireland means huddling in front of an open fire with her teenage daughter. She assures me there's nothing remotely romantic about this. Although Caroline has a job, her income isn't enough to make ends meet. She doesn't mince her words when sharing her thoughts about having to queue to receive a parcel from the food bank. 'Has our society become so inhumane that we think it's okay for people to have to beg for food?'

I don't need to be in the same room with Brian and Caroline to sense their weariness. The veneer of their friendly smiles barely disguises deep fatigue. Instead of sleeping, they spend their nights worrying about how to pay bills. Needing to weigh up the expense of getting to the hospital against the cost of a food shop inevitably takes its toll. Both struggle with stress and anxiety. The inability to provide for their children tugs at their self-esteem. 'I feel totally useless as a father not being able to support my daughter and keep her warm at home,' says Brian. I can hear the tremor in his voice.

It's not just the lack of money that makes things hard. 'It kind of feels like an *Oliver Twist* scenario sometimes. You're having to beg, you have to justify your pennies,' Caroline explains when I ask her about the support she receives. Brian weighs in: 'You get all these programmes on television, and they make it look as though you're just out to get money for nothing and get whatever you can from the government. But that's not the attitude of most people on low incomes.'

Caroline nods her head in agreement. 'People on a low income have a desire to want better for their children and themselves,' she sighs, 'but many of us struggle to attain that because we're stuck in a cycle of being devalued and undermined by the system. It just feels like it's an ever-growing cycle. How do you break that cycle?'

My conversation with my guests mirrors those I've had with many others who find themselves trapped on a low income. Brian and Caroline's experiences are unique, yet they are also emblematic of one of the biggest challenges of our time. After decades of success in reducing poverty, progress has stalled. We live in a world of unprecedented and unimaginable wealth, yet millions struggle to put food on the table.

In the UK alone, one in five people live in poverty.[1] Approximately 3.8 million people experienced destitution in 2022, almost two and a half times more than in 2017. Britain is the sixth largest economy in the world,[2] yet as many as one million children regularly find themselves going to bed hungry, having to sleep in an unlit or unheated house, or without a roof over their heads. These figures mirror the situation in other rich countries. Across Europe, more than one in five people are at risk of poverty or being socially excluded.[3] In the US, every tenth person experiences deep deprivation.[4]

Global figures are mind-boggling. Worldwide, 648 million people live in extreme poverty – roughly 8 per cent of the global population. This is based on a threshold of a mere $2.15 per day. Adjusted per country to reflect price differences, this amount is a pittance in richer as well as poorer countries. When using a slightly more lenient threshold of $6.85 per day, the number of people in poverty rises to a staggering 3.6 billion.[5] With just over 8 billion on this planet,[6] that's nearly half of us. Throw the globe's population in a giant bingo tumbler and almost every second person falling out is struggling to make ends meet.

This isn't to say there hasn't been any progress. Economic growth, medical advances and investment in public services are some of the factors that have contributed to widespread improvements in living conditions. Extreme poverty fell by almost two thirds between 1990 and 2018.[7] Malnourishment, measured by the proportion of children under five years who are too short for their age, dropped from 33 per cent in 2000 to 23 per cent in 2020.[8] And while two centuries ago almost half of all children died before their fifth birthday, this fell to 4 per cent in 2017.[9]

Sadly, today's picture looks anything but rosy. Crises such as the COVID-19 pandemic, war in Ukraine and the Middle East, a rise in the cost of living, and the ongoing climate catastrophe have left and continue to leave their mark. For the first time in decades, we are no longer witnessing progress in the fight against adversity and deprivation. In 2022, the proportion of children in extreme poverty globally was the same as it was in 2019.[10] In some countries, such as the UK, the number of poor children rose in recent years.[11] In others, such as the Netherlands, child poverty is set to rise if no action is undertaken.[12] Worldwide predictions suggest that stagnating poverty rates are a best-case scenario, but an increase in poverty is a real prospect.[13]

Let me be clear: we didn't end up here by chance. We got here by choice.

Widespread destitution and hardship don't exist because there isn't enough money to go around. Hunger and deprivation don't persist because the pie isn't big enough. It's because the size of its pieces and how they're distributed is outrageously uneven and incredibly unfair.

'We're all in this together' was the much-repeated adage during the COVID-19 pandemic. In reality, the opposite happened. Since the beginning of this decade, in the wake of an unprecedented global health crisis, a handful of business giants have expanded their already vast amounts of wealth at the expense of millions losing their jobs and livelihoods. Anti-poverty charity Oxfam estimates that the world's five richest men more than doubled their fortunes in the first few years since 2020.[14] At the same time, over half of the global population saw their wealth decline. Billionaires are now 34 per cent richer than they were at the start of the 2020s, yet the real incomes of hundreds of millions of workers declined in the face of high inflation and sky-rocketing cost of living. And while progress on poverty has come to a standstill, the number of millionaires is projected to nearly double in the next few years.

Never has the gap between rich and poor seemed so stark. As Richard Branson, Jeff Bezos and Elon Musk compete in their own billionaire space race, more and more families struggle to put food on the table. In many rich countries, job security is a thing of the past. Zero-hour contracts and the gig economy have pushed workers into a permanent state of precarity, often attaching themselves to multiple employers to make ends meet. Privatisation of public services and years of austerity have led to two-tier systems offering quality care and top-notch education only to those who can afford it. While the rich are able to accumulate wealth the size of a small country, increasing numbers of ordinary people are thrown into a life of socioeconomic insecurity.

In poorer countries such dynamics take place against the backdrop of centuries of colonial exploitation, continued wealth capture by rich countries, and international aid structures promoting models of socioeconomic development that, at their worst, make the poor suffer more than they already did. Structural adjustment policies, introduced by the powerful International Monetary Fund and the World Bank in the 1980s, have left a particularly harmful legacy. Rolled out across lower-income countries to promote economic growth and reduce public debt, they imposed austerity measures that made poor people pay for health care, schooling and other basic services.[15] These policies are alleged to have led to increased child mortality, greater child malnutrition and thousands of excess deaths from tuberculosis and other respiratory diseases.[16]

For most of us, the likelihood of experiencing poverty at some point in our lives is infinitely higher than taking a seat in a spacecraft and being catapulted into the atmosphere. Yet despite the schism between the rich and the rest of us deepening by the day, the wealthy are afforded superstar status, while the poor are treated as second-rate citizens. Like Caroline and Brian, those struggling to make ends meet are derided for the predicament they find themselves in and made to jump through endless hoops to access support that is ultimately insufficient. Instead of seeing inequality and hardship as a failure of our socioeconomic systems, fault is placed with those living on little.

It begs the question: Why?

Why do we find it acceptable that a handful of individuals can accumulate unfathomable wealth, yet so many are left to live hand-to-mouth? How have we come to idolise the rich, whose actions arguably do more harm than good, but ignore and denigrate people in poverty? Why do we ask those in hardship to prove their deservingness and make them grovel for basic support?

We suffer a collective empathy deficit, and it hurts us all.

A common response to the argument that we should try harder to create more just societies is that it's too expensive. Taxpayers feel hard done by when their hard-earned cash is doled out to those with little to live on, especially when faced with underdeveloped or crumbling infrastructure and underfunded and overstretched public services. Deprivation and hardship are brushed aside as someone else's problem, for others to deal with. Addressing poverty takes a back seat, other priorities deemed more urgent and worthy of investment.

This is a short-sighted attitude. Not only does it display a staggering lack of solidarity with those less fortunate, but poverty also comes at a price. There are immense human costs to living on little. The constant struggle to make ends meet affects physical and mental health, limits social connections and erodes dignity. Poverty reduces quality of life as much as it shortens life itself. But it doesn't merely affect those at the sharp end of disadvantage. There are social costs too.

In 2006, the *New Yorker* magazine ran a piece about 'million-dollar Murray'.[17] Murray was a well-known figure in downtown Reno, a city in Nevada in the US. A heavily built and wide-smiled war veteran, he spent most of his time on the streets drinking or hunting for vodka. When inebriated, he would become aggressive and difficult to handle. This resulted in frequent arrests for public drinking and disorderly behaviour, sometimes more than once on a single day. It wasn't unusual for Murray to be so badly intoxicated that he needed to be brought into hospital, where he would spend several days recovering. Despite all this, police officers and social workers spoke fondly of him, describing him as warm and generous.

There were moments when the front-line workers who knew Murray well thought things were finally taking a turn for the better. At one point he was enrolled in an alcohol addiction treatment programme and placed into accommodation. He got sober and found a job. He even managed to save a sizeable chunk of money. But when the programme came to an end, so did the regular check-ins by programme staff. Murray fell back into his old habits. Soon enough he was out on the streets again, returning to the cycle of drunkenness, arrest and emergency care.

This return to square one greatly frustrated the policy officers who responded to Murray's personal crises. For him to be arrested and patched up in hospital only to be left to his own devices until he inevitably ended up back in medical care struck them as both inhumane and unnecessarily expensive. Wanting to find out the cost of this revolving-door approach to Murray's struggles, the officers tracked down his hospital bills. Back-of-the-envelope calculations suggested they totalled $100,000. This only accounted for his most recent spell of homelessness. When the officers extrapolated the figures to a decade of Murray being homeless, they arrived at an estimate of $1 million. As they astutely observed, this shocking amount of money was used not to improve his life, but rather 'not to do something about Murray'.

Closer to home, in the UK, lack of support for those at risk of homelessness also contributes to higher bills for the taxpayer. During the COVID-19 pandemic, half a million renters across the country were unable to keep up with their payments. Anti-homelessness charity the Big Issue estimated[18] that by the end of 2021, tenants in the UK had accrued a total of £360 million in rent arrears. According to the charity's calculations, dealing with the fallout of homelessness for an estimated 225,000 people could amount to £2.6 billion per year. Measures in response to homelessness, including temporary accommodation, social support services, health care and criminal justice, all add to the expense. Preventing homelessness, instead of letting it happen, they say, could save the government an eye-watering £2.2 billion a year.

The social cost of poverty goes beyond today's taxpayers' bills. An equally important cost is the one of lost opportunity. Of what could have been. Take child poverty. Children growing up without being able to reach their full potential presents an enormous loss to society. From an economic perspective, it means lost productivity and forgone earnings. In the UK alone, the loss of future income due to children growing up in poverty is estimated to be more than £11 billion.[19]

There's no doubt that poverty is expensive. Not just for those living it, but for all of us. Yet we continue to stack the odds against people in hardship. Deeply ingrained in our collective consciousness is the belief that wealth is within reach for every one of us, if only we make smart choices and work hard enough. However, the truth is that opportunities for those caught in the web of deprivation and disadvantage are few and far between. Support for those who fail to move up the ladder is minimal. What's more, our societies firmly place the blame for their misfortune with the poor themselves. 'They don't want to work' or 'It's their own fault' are common refrains when confronted with the hardship and despair that so many must contend with.

Patience and understanding are thin on the ground for those having fallen on hard times. In a bid to protect ourselves from the distress of witnessing others' suffering, we have grown accustomed to turning a blind eye. We have become so attached to the idea that good fortune is the result of graft and grit that we can only make sense of misfortune by believing it's down to personal weakness. We pat ourselves on the back for our achievements and deride those who haven't quite made it.

Such exaggerated and false notions of the degree of personal responsibility in individual socioeconomic circumstance lead to toxic levels of blame and shame. Instead of trusting their intentions and capacities, we pursue, police and punish the poor for their predicament.

It's this lack of perspective that prevents us from seeing what life in poverty really entails, how the odds are stacked against those living on little, and why efforts to tackle it make things worse. Prevailing false narratives make us ignorant of the fact that low-income families in the UK pay more for their daily shop than those with money to spare. They stop us from understanding that when parents in South Africa use child grant payments for their own medical bills or a new outfit, this constitutes a wise investment rather than wasteful expense. Our collective lack of empathy makes it possible for pupils in the US to have their arms stamped when their parents are unable to pay for school lunches, for a high-skilled unemployed Australian worker to be asked to remove work experience from her CV and then find herself accused of fraud for doing so, and for poor villagers in Zambia to be presented with their own excrement when unable to build their own toilets. It's time to change the script. It's time for an empathy fix.

In this book, I propose a radical rethink of the way in which we understand poverty, what it means and how to break the cycle. It takes empathy as the starting point, breaking it down into three components – what I refer to as the three Rs – to ensure a meaningful approach to tackling poverty, and one we can all be part of.

First, we need to *relate* to the crisis that poverty constitutes, and understand its devastating consequences. Second, we must *realise* the reasons why anti-poverty interventions are often ineffective at best and detrimental at worst. Third, we need to *respond* in ways that respect the dignity, agency and voice of those at the receiving end of such interventions. Rather than treating poverty as a technical problem that can be solved through clever engineering, or considering it the result of a character flaw that requires a cracking of the whip, empathy allows us to see it as the human experience it is and to find humane solutions to tackle it.

Sceptics might argue that empathy is too fuzzy, or too soft, to offer a meaningful foundation for tackling a problem as large and intractable as poverty. This couldn't be further from the truth. Engaging empathy to address deprivation and disadvantage isn't simply about being kind. It demands meaningful involvement, a shift beyond virtue signalling or tokenistic conversations. It requires a willingness to be open to lived-experience experts' views and insights, even – or especially – if they're not in accordance with our own. Preconceived ideas, assumptions and judgements need to be left at the door. Empathy calls for deep and genuine listening, and truly hearing what people have to say. It demands being still and taking in, a far cry from the general tendency to voice opinion and make ourselves heard. And it involves action, a response to the injustice that is staring us in the face.

More than that, an empathetic response to poverty also demands self-reflection. It requires every one of us to look in the mirror and ask ourselves hard questions about our own role in perpetuating hardship and suffering. What attitudes do we hold about people in poverty? How do we speak about welfare recipients, and what do we do when passing someone sleeping rough on the streets? Where do we shop, and do they pay their workers a decent wage? How much tax are we willing to pay, and what policies do we support through our vote? If we're serious about creating a more equal world for all, and doing so from a place of empathy, we can't shy away from asking these questions and acting in accordance with our values.

The good news is, empathy is in our genes, and part of how we are wired. We all have the capacity to take perspective and create an understanding of how others experience the world. Many of us will engage our compassion and sympathy every single day in connecting with our nearest and dearest. There's no reason we can't do the same in relation to poverty. We're all able to feel the injustice suffered by those less privileged, and to find out why it persists.

Poverty isn't a problem out there, in someone else's world. It's a crisis within our own societies and communities. It exists and is condoned within the web of interconnected lives we're all part of. Every one of us is implicated in poverty's existence. Yet being part of the problem means we can also be part of the solution. Empathy can help us get there; we only have to tap into it.

1

GETTING TO GRIPS
WITH EMPATHY

'Come with me. I'll lead the way.'

Shakil turns around and starts walking. He waves his hand to indicate I should follow him. He moves quickly, turning left and right, disappearing into hidden openings I never would have known were there. I pick up the pace to make sure I don't lose him. Looking back, I see my colleagues are close behind.

We make our way through narrow alleyways and in between ramshackle houses. Shakil effortlessly avoids children chasing each other, rickshaws speeding down the street and old women carefully crossing the road. I'm clearly less adept at navigating this urban maze, apologising every time I bump into someone. Fortunately, Shakil regularly checks to see whether I'm still following him.

We zigzag some more until he suddenly stops in front of the entrance to a large building. 'We're here.' I look inside, but struggle to see much. It's dark, and all I can make out is a long corridor with doors on either side. I'm hit by a pungent smell, something chemical. It might be glue or paint. The fumes make their way to my lungs, and I can feel a coughing fit coming on. 'Let's go inside,' Shakil announces as he walks through the door. I hold my breath as best I can.

I'm in Dhaka, the capital of Bangladesh. With an estimated population of 24 million,[1] almost 1.5 times as many people as live in the entirety of my home country, the Netherlands, it's one of the most densely populated cities in the world. Once you find yourself in Dhaka, however, you don't need statistics to realise how crowded it is. One car journey across this city, invariably spent stationary in large volumes of loud traffic, is enough to understand that vast numbers of people reside here. It's no surprise I struggled to steer clear of Dhaka's residents as I tried navigating its streets.

The building we're about to enter is in one of the city's poorest neighbourhoods. Close to the majestic Buriganga river and part of Dhaka's historic Old Town, this used to be an industrial hub for leather production. Many of the large factories have now relocated to an area outside Dhaka, but the leather sector is still very much alive here. Small-scale tanneries and workshops keep churning out sturdy shoes, gloves and bags. Yet unlike previously, when most products were exported and sold in shops across Europe and the US, these businesses mostly serve the Bangladeshi market.

The absence of international scrutiny means that pay is low and working conditions are harsh. Producing leather goods has many steps, from washing and dehairing to dyeing and cutting, often involving chemicals and heavy machinery.

Protective gear is usually unavailable, making the work dangerous and harmful. The way in which the fumes triggered my
lungs after a single inhale is a sign of their toxicity. Still, a job
in the leather industry is an important source of income for
many of the area's residents, including children.

I follow Shakil and step into the corridor ahead. My eyes
quickly adjust to the low light, making it easier to avoid pieces
of leather strewn across the floor or knocking over waste
baskets positioned outside doorways. Taking quick glances
left and right as we walk down the passageway, I realise the
rooms on either side serve as family homes or workshops, or
sometimes both at the same time. Large beds, tightly packed
wardrobes, mountains of leather offcuts, heavy shears and
sewing machines are all crammed into the tiny spaces, often
no more than a few square metres in size. A woman standing
in one of the doorways smiles at me and nods by way of
welcome. She's an exception. Most of those in the building
go about their businesses without taking much notice of their
visitors. They have more important things to do.

Shakil turns left into a smaller hallway and then comes
to a halt in front of an open door. 'Here it is,' he says as he
points into the room. His face is filled with pride. He has just
guided us to one of the families he's been supporting over the
past year.

I put my head around the door frame to look inside. A
woman stands next to a bed that fills most of the tiny room.
'This is Raisa,' says Shakil. I smile and say hello, hoping
she'll forgive me my lack of Bangla language skills. She
returns my smile and gestures for us to enter her home. 'You

can go in. She would like you to go in,' Shakil translates. I take off my sandals, leaving them by the door, and step into the small space.

The room isn't much more than a rectangular concrete box. Next to the bed is a cupboard filled with crockery and clothing. Large pots and pans are stacked on top of each other on a shelf overhead. Blankets and sheets are neatly folded in a pile next to the cupboard. There aren't any windows to let in natural light, and a single bulb lights the room. It's stiflingly hot and humid in Dhaka at this time of year, and the room feels stuffy. A ceiling fan is whirring loudly, but it does little to cool the air. I can feel the sweat trickling down my back.

'Sit down, please, sit down,' says Shakil as Raisa points to the bed. It doesn't feel right to take a seat where the family sleep, but there isn't anywhere else to go. As I carefully perch on the edge of the bed, I feel stirring behind me. A young boy appears from underneath the brightly coloured covers. He lifts his head to have a look at what's going on before laying it back down and closing his eyes again. 'This is Raisa's son, her youngest child. He's not well,' explains Shakil.

My colleagues have now also entered the room and sit down next to me. A chair is brought in from elsewhere for Raisa to take a seat opposite us. Shakil remains standing, taking up position next to Raisa.

'Thank you for inviting us into your home,' I say to Raisa. 'We really appreciate it.'

I'm not sure she understands, but she gives me another smile and nods.

'Can you tell us a little about the support you've received from Shakil?' I ask. 'We're really interested in how you've been working together.'

One of my Bangladeshi colleagues translates the question. Raisa's face lights up, and she's quick to offer a response.

'Shakil has been coming to visit me regularly in the past months. At first, he came to ask me lots of questions about my family and how we live. I wasn't sure why he was asking all these questions. But then he kept returning to check how we were doing, and to offer help or advice. I'm happy he came into our lives,' she says.

Beaming with pride, Shakil chimes in. 'Raisa has a tough life. Her husband was sent to prison, and she had to take out a large loan to get him released. This was a few years ago, but she's still struggling to pay off this debt. Her husband hasn't been helpful in bringing in money. He drinks a lot and he's aggressive. He hits Raisa, and their teenage daughter.'

As Shakil tells us about Raisa's marital distress, I see her slump in her chair. She bows her head and dabs her eyes with her scarf. Shakil notices it too, and falls silent.

'It's hard,' says Raisa quietly. 'I don't care how my husband chooses to live his life, but I feel for my children. One time when he became violent, my daughter fled into the corridor to escape. But he ran after her and began hitting her in front of everyone else. No one dared intervene.' She is choking up. Tears are trickling down her cheeks.

'My daughter was so ashamed,' Raisa continues. 'She didn't want others to see her like that. Now, whenever her father starts hitting her, she just stays inside and endures it. The blows to her head have hurt her ears, she can no longer hear very well. It's a bad situation. But what can we do?'

I can feel my eyes welling up. I'm not alone. My colleagues look equally affected by Raisa's story. Although Shakil is familiar with Raisa's situation, he's also emotional.

'I try speaking to Raisa's husband,' he says, 'but there's a delicate balance to strike. I would like him to understand the hurt he's causing, but I don't want to trigger his violence even further. I can't address his aggression directly. I have to tread carefully.' He shakes his head in frustration. When he looks up again, though, the spark has returned to his eyes.

'What I can do, however, is talk with Raisa. I come here and listen to her concerns. I try to offer her hope and give practical advice whenever I can. About how she can pay off her loan, or where to get affordable treatment for her son.' Upon hearing the mention of his name, I feel the boy behind me stir once more.

'I'm really glad Shakil is here,' says Raisa. 'He may not be able to change the situation with my husband, but he listens. He lets me share my worries. He pays attention. It's unlike anyone else or any other organisation that has come into this community before. It makes me feel like I'm not crazy. He helps me see it might be possible for my daughter and my son to have a better future.'

Raisa is about to say more but is cut short by a neighbour poking her head through the door. She whispers something to Raisa and Shakil. 'Sorry, we need to go,' says Shakil. 'Raisa's husband is on his way home and it's not good if he finds out we're here.' We rise to our feet and are ushered out of the room in a hurry. I nod my thanks to Raisa, put my sandals on and walk back down the corridor.

It isn't until later in the day, back in the jarring comfort of my hotel room, that I realise the significance of the encounter with Shakil and Raisa. Shakil is part of a project I have been co-leading with colleagues in the UK and Bangladesh, trying to find a more respectful and dignified way to address issues of poverty.[2] In contrast to so many other anti-poverty interventions, we didn't want to come in with preconceived notions of the problems that are most pressing to community members, or standard solutions for how to solve them. By placing committed and compassionate community workers at the service of the area's residents and combining this with economic support, we're testing a radical new model for improving families' quality of life.

Shakil is one of 20 community mobilisers working with neighbourhood residents like Raisa to understand and find solutions to their most urgent needs. They take time to sit down with the residents, understand their concerns and work together to find ways to address them. For some, this means developing new initiatives to generate income, or find alternative jobs for their children so they no longer have to work with toxic chemicals or dangerous equipment. For others, like Raisa, domestic abuse, debt and medical expenses are at the top of the list of issues to resolve.

Working with families and individuals using this more open-ended and organic approach to problem-solving takes time. It comes with many unknowns. Plans need to be shaped and reshaped along the way. Trust, in oneself and one another, is key. But as I lie on my bed reflecting on the day's events, it dawns on me that Shakil displayed the most important aspect of all, the thing that makes his work and that of his fellow team members so powerful. Empathy.

The rise and rise of empathy

The phenomenon of empathy has occupied minds and been the subject of study and debate for hundreds of years. As far back as the eighteenth century, philosophers argued that humans have an ability to recognise and share someone else's thoughts and emotions. In 1739, in his book *A Treatise of Human Nature*, philosopher David Hume wrote that 'the minds of men are mirrors to one another'.[3] Two decades later, in *The Theory of Moral Sentiments*, Adam Smith – best known for his foundational influences on economic theory – suggested that we all have an innate capacity to take perspective, imagine what others are experiencing and share those feelings.

Psychologists and neuroscientists took up the baton in the twentieth century, extending the exploration of empathy's social and emotional implications. In fact, it was a psychologist – Edward Titchener – who translated the German '*Einfühlung*', or 'feeling into', and introduced the word 'empathy' to the English language in 1909.[4] Scientific understanding quickly advanced, with psychologists studying the role of empathy in our emotional development and our relationships with others. More recently, neuroscientists have started investigating what happens in our brains and nervous systems when we experience empathy.

But empathy's influences can be traced back to well before reason and science sought to grapple with it. Many religious traditions are predicated on values central to our current understanding of empathy. Think about the notion of compassion and kindness in Buddhism, the principle of non-violence – *ahimsa* – in Hinduism, or the Golden Rule that cuts across religions, suggesting we should treat others as we would like to be treated ourselves.

Despite this long and rich history, the concept of empathy was the preserve of clergy, scholarly thinkers and scientists for most of that time. While empathy may have been core to many spiritual teachings and practices for generations past, considerations about its relevance and use in everyday life didn't extend to the common person. How this has changed.

Today, empathy is everywhere. We all recognise and speak of it as a crucial aspect of human connection and social interaction. The word has become an integral part of popular parlance. When I look up how many times 'empathy' has been used as a search term in Google, I'm not surprised to be presented with a diagram displaying a large upward trend. The frequency with which it was entered in the search engine increased fourfold in the last two decades.[5] A quick browse of the shelves in my local bookshop equally reveals the wide appeal of empathy. The word appears on the covers of books that promise everything from boosting leadership skills and providing parenting advice to offering psychological insight and self-help support.

Empathy has also made its way onto the political stage. Often avoided for its connotations of being wishy-washy, or because it might be construed as a weakness or vulnerability, empathy is increasingly considered a desirable characteristic. When Jacinda Ardern was New Zealand's prime minister between 2017 and 2023, she had no qualms about advocating the positives of empathetic qualities in a leader. She suggested that it was a trait politicians needed more of, not less. 'We need our leaders to be able to empathise with the circumstances of others; to empathise with the next generation that we're making decisions on behalf of. And if we focus only on being seen to be the strongest, most powerful person in the room, then I think we lose what we're meant to be here for.'[6]

Empathy may have taken a long and winding road to where we are today, but now that it's here, it's here to stay. With its important role in everyday life scientifically tested and its moral, social and psychological merits widely recognised, it appeals to all corners of society. Whether you're a manager aiming to lead your team to higher ground, a nurse seeking to deliver the best care to your patients or a conscientious citizen trying to do good by your friends and family, empathy has become an indispensable attribute. Regardless of who we are, empathy has become integral to the way we think about how to connect and relate to others – both individually and the world at large.

Human mirrors

'That way, that way!' yells my two-and-a-half-year-old nephew Vigo at his younger brother, pointing to the opposite end of the room. It's to no avail. Daan stays the course and – with some speed – shoves his baby walker up against the bookshelf. He's stuck, and frustration quickly builds.

Vigo doesn't hesitate to get up from where he's playing with his toy cars, and runs over to Daan to free him from his awkward position. 'Like this, there,' he says as he gently coaxes his brother backwards and then sideways. Daan pulls the walker away from the shelf and starts pushing it to the right. Free from obstacles, he squeals with delight, and off he goes.

Many definitions of empathy go something like this: empathy is our ability to identify what someone else is thinking or feeling, and to respond to their thoughts and feelings with an appropriate emotion and action.[7]

Children illustrate this beautifully. The ability to empathise roughly develops in our second and third years of life, constituting a significant marker in our capacity to relate with and respond to others. Those first ventures into empathetic behaviour also make for endearing scenes. Whether we're parents or not, no doubt we'll all have observed a toddler taking a friend's hand to offer reassurance when they're scared of doing something new, or reaching out to their mum or dad when they see sadness in their parents' eyes.

Vigo's ability to put himself in his little brother's shoes is referred to as 'cognitive empathy'. It's the ability to take perspective and to imagine what someone else might be feeling.[8] When Vigo watched Daan get stuck, he had a clear understanding of what his sibling wanted to achieve, and of what was needed to help him on his way again. In the same vein, the comfort-offering toddler will have recognised their friend's fear, and holding their hand might just be the encouragement they need.

Now imagine that little Daan hadn't pushed his sturdy wooden walker up against a shelf. Instead, he rushed it towards his mum and crashed it into her ankle. Hard.

Did you flinch when you read this? Picturing the scene in your head, did you silently exclaim 'Ouch!'? There's every chance you will have done.

This mirroring or 'catching' of emotions is called 'affective empathy'.[9] When you see or even imagine someone else in pain, you yourself experience pain.[10] It's a type of emotional contagion, with the other person's feelings rubbing off on you. Common examples of this include your face lighting up with a smile as you witness someone else's joy. Or, in the case of negative experiences, becoming sad when you see your friend cry, or getting scared when watching someone else in fear.

In a ground-breaking experiment, neuroscientists from the UK recruited 16 couples to test how we process someone else's suffering.[11] The female partners were put in MRI head scanners before being administered painful electric shocks to their hands. The scans showed that all areas of the brain associated with pain lit up as they underwent the shocks. Still in the scanners, they were then told that their loved ones, who were in the same room, had had the same shocks administered. Despite the absence of anything physical happening to them, many of the pain-sensitive areas of the women's brains were activated. They didn't simply imagine their partners' pain; they felt it. The experiment provided proof that 'I feel your pain' isn't just a figure of speech.

But empathy doesn't stop at being able to understand or feel with the other person. It's also about action. After all, what's the point of being empathetic if it doesn't motivate change? Especially when it comes to injustice and suffering.

In his book *Zero Degrees of Empathy*, empathy scientist Simon Baron-Cohen uses the example of witnessing a fellow traveller struggle with a heavy suitcase. You might cognitively recognise their predicament and affectively feel their frustration, but if your only response is to continue watching them fight with their luggage, it's not empathy at all.[12] Shakil, by contrast, gained an understanding of Raisa's concerns, felt her pain and sought options to alleviate her suffering. Empathy encapsulates taking perspective, sharing in someone else's feelings and – in the case of negative emotions – acting to lessen their pain.

Empathy's ability to acknowledge others' misfortune and incentivise us to address it gives it the power to be truly transformative. What's more, empathy doesn't merely motivate us to reach out to those around us, but can inspire us to reshape the societies we live in. For this reason, philosopher Roman Krznaric sees it as nothing less than a radical power, arguing that it's a 'collective force that can shift the contours of the social and political landscape'.[13] Empathy serves as a moral code, guiding our actions well beyond the realm of our private lives. It compels us to stand up against social injustice, demand change and contribute to a fairer world for all.

It's in our genes

A blue bucket hangs off the mesh wall inside a large cage. It's filled with 30 red and green tokens, 15 of each. Behind the bucket sits a chimpanzee, ready for the task he'll soon be asked to perform. Another chimp sits in the adjoining cage, looking at his neighbour and waiting to see what happens.

A member of the research team, dressed in black protective clothing, including gloves and visor, holds out their hand in front of the bucket. The chimp instinctively knows what to do. He grabs a red token and pushes it through the mesh towards the researcher. The researcher takes the token and places it on a table in view of both cages. Already on the table are two treats. The researcher picks up both treats, and gives one of them to the chimp who just handed them the token. The other treat is put away, out of sight. The chimp in the adjoining cage is left empty-handed. He looks a bit forlorn, as if robbed of something he's entitled to.

In the next round, the chimp picks a green token and hands it over. Again the token is placed on the table in front of both cages and the researcher picks up two treats. But this time both animals receive a treat. The chimps, especially the one without the bucket, appear much more content with this outcome.

Multiple repetitions of this task, performed by this chimp and others, show that they consistently prefer the green token to the red. There's no obvious advantage to this choice. The treat they receive is the same regardless of the colour of the token, nor do the partner chimps in adjoining cages attempt any bribery or other tactics to motivate selection of the green token. What is happening here, conclude the researchers, is chimpanzees displaying prosocial behaviour.[14] Or, put differently, empathy.[15]

We humans share almost 99 per cent of our genetic make-up with chimpanzees.[16] This means that research about chimps and other primates tells us a lot about the extent to which some of our behaviour is innate. Primatologist Frans de Waal has dedicated much of his career to studying exactly this, and his work has been highly influential in shaping how we understand primates' social behaviour and, by extension, our own.

Penny, an older female chimp, was the centre of attention in one of de Waal's studies.[17] Her age led to her being increasingly frail and she was having trouble moving around. De Waal and colleagues kept a close eye.

What they observed was not what they expected. Penny wasn't left on the fringes of the ape community. Instead, the researchers noticed there was no shortage of helping hands to assist her in going about her monkey business. Younger females turned out to be incredibly helpful. They would suck up water from the tap and bring it over to Penny, spitting it into her mouth so she didn't have to make her way to the water point herself. Or they would help her up on the climbing frame, pushing her from below, so she could participate in the grooming ritual.

The young chimps' gestures can be interpreted as simple acts of kindness, especially as Penny wasn't able to reciprocate due to her frailty. Across the many years of his research, de Waal has found that apes show immense care for their companions. Communities are built around principles of collaboration, reciprocity and fairness rather than competition or aggression. Given humans' close genetic resemblance to primates, it has led him to conclude that we're a much more caring and collaborative species than we're often made to believe.

Psychological scientist Jamil Zaki would undoubtedly agree. In his book *The War for Kindness*, he rates the claim that evolution favours empathy as one that is extremely well documented and evidenced.[18] Empathy has evolved through our ancestors. We survive by building bonds and working together, not through warfare and aggression. It's in our genes. In her TEDx talk, psychiatry scholar Helen Riess summarises this very aptly. 'We all are here more because of mutual aid and cooperation than because of survival of the fittest. If we were only wired for survival of the fittest, we'd be wired to dominate others and to only look out for ourselves, but that's not how we're made.'[19]

Empathy deficit

If empathy is part of who we are, and given the popularity that the discourse around it currently enjoys, why do we see such little evidence of it? If the ability to understand the world from another's point of view and our desire to respond to someone else's needs is innate, how is it possible that we're living through a time of intense inequality and animosity? Empathy's promise and popularity stands in stark contrast to the reality of the world around us.

The diagnosis that we're suffering an empathy deficit isn't new. When Barack Obama was on the campaign trail in 2008 to become the next president of the US, he attributed a wide range of social concerns to a prevailing lack of empathy. Issues he identified at the time – unemployment, homelessness, child poverty – are arguably even more urgent now. Yet as I write this in the lead-up to the 2024 elections, Americans' willingness to take perspective and meaningfully engage with those on different steps of the socioeconomic ladder or at opposite ends of the political spectrum seems lower than ever.

The US isn't alone in this. Societies across the world experience deep divisions. According to a global survey on societal trust, more than half of respondents said their countries are more divided now than they were in the past. Argentina holds the dubious top position of being most divided, and those divisions being most entrenched. Other severely polarised countries include Colombia, South Africa, Spain and Sweden, with Brazil, France, the UK, Japan and others at risk of similar division.

Even in my home country, the Netherlands, widely perceived as tolerant, open-minded and progressive, widening gaps in socioeconomic opportunities have left their mark.

Reflecting on her political departure following the 2023 elections, former finance minister Sigrid Kaag voiced her disappointment at how political and social debates had hardened. 'I never expected, in a country like the Netherlands, that demonisation and dehumanisation are everyday realities in our politics.'[20]

A study with college students in the US provides further evidence for societies' hardening. Analysis of students' willingness to see someone else's point of view or listen to their arguments showed that empathy levels almost halved between 1979 and 2009.[21] Even more worrying is that large numbers of people think it won't be possible to see past their differences.[22]

So why does this happen? What causes this 'empathy erosion', as Baron-Cohen puts it?[23]

One explanation is a malfunction of the brain's empathy circuit. Such cross-wiring leads to someone simply being unable to feel with other people, or to imagine their experiences. It's what allows psychopaths to commit acts of cruelty, or narcissists to prioritise their own needs at the expense of others. But this is a lazy explanation. It attributes lack of empathy to a freak of nature, and one that conveniently places the responsibility outside ourselves. Most importantly, such physiological defects are very rare indeed. The vast majority of us have ample capacity to empathise. A few exceptions to the rule can't explain the collective lack of empathy underpinning the world's socioeconomic divisions.

There are two much more plausible reasons for the empathy paradox.

The first is ignorance. Those with higher disposable income simply don't know how much harder it is to make ends meet on a tight budget. If you're fortunate enough never to have to worry about how to pay next month's rent or choose between buying food and turning up the heating, how would you know what it's like? Without direct experience, trying to gain an understanding of the experience of poverty takes effort. If you have a comfortable life, seeing how living on little creates hurdles and puts up barriers requires being observant and paying attention. The world operates differently for those with and those without money. Yet if you have money, that's easy to ignore.

The second explanation for our disengagement is that we have far too much on our plates. To avoid the distress of feeling another person's suffering, many of us opt to distance ourselves from the pain experienced by others. When asked about the reasons for the decline in empathy among the US college students she studied, social psychologist Sara Konrath suggests it's not because young people have become less kind. Instead, she argues, the current generation of young people have more concerns of their own. Pressures on and expectations from, in this case, students have gone up tremendously in the past few decades. It's their need to focus on themselves that crowds out their ability to empathise with others.[24]

But it's not just college students who have had pressures and expectations piled on them in recent decades. Looking at job opportunities, earnings and home ownership, American millennials across all walks of life are worse off than the generations before them.[25] Secure employment with proper benefits is a thing of the past for most. More recently, the cost of living crisis has meant great anxiety about higher bills and being able to afford the rent or mortgage. And if you're a middle-ager caring for young children or elderly relatives or both, lack of affordable care services brings further costs and pressures. The resultant stress reduces headspace, including for empathy.

Back to Jamil Zaki, who describes the process underpinning how much empathy we feel as a tug-of-war. On one end of the rope there are forces pulling you into the pro-empathy corner. Think about the warm feelings when you're connecting with others, whether it be friends or strangers. Or the positive vibe that comes from 'doing the right thing'. Helping an older person cross a busy road or picking up the sock that slipped off a baby's foot without their parents noticing. These actions make us look good to others and help us feel good about ourselves.

At the other end of the rope, forces pull you towards the 'I couldn't care less' corner. These are the things that weigh on your mind or soul and compete for your head and heart space. It could be something as mundane as trying to work out what to cook for dinner, especially when there are fussy eaters joining the kitchen table. But it might also be something all-consuming, such as worrying about a friend's cancer treatment or experiencing burnout due to a stressful job or caring for an ill parent.

Failing to empathise isn't due to our inability to feel with others, or to lack of care. Instead, it's often the result of concerns and stress demanding so much of our attention that it leaves us sapped of energy and short of bandwidth that we might wish to dedicate to others. Empathy comes at a cost, demanding time and energy. If such costs outweigh the benefits of empathy, people will avoid it.[26] Most of us live busy, fast-paced and stressful lives in which preoccupation, overwhelm and worry become all-consuming. They pull us into a corner where introspection and selfishness trump consideration of others. Someone else's hardship and pain might be staring us in the face, but instead of tapping into our innate compassion, we turn the other way.

Dark side of empathy

Imagine yourself in a football stadium. It's full and rowdy. You're in the stand of the club you've been supporting since you were little, among fans who share the same passion as you do. The atmosphere is tense, heavy with expectation from two teams that are considered each other's greatest rival. The game is on a knife edge, both teams are giving it all they've got. The ball moves from one end of the field to the other in rapid succession.

Then, a kick. The ball flies through the air. It moves towards the upper left corner of the goal. The goalie jumps up, reaches across, touches the ball with their fingertips, but … GOAL!! A roar erupts. Everyone around you is yelling at the top of their lungs. So are you, jumping up and down as you celebrate. You can feel yourself getting hoarser every second. It was the striker of your team who scored, and you couldn't be happier.

But looking across to the other side of the stadium, you see sad faces. Expressions filled with disillusionment and frustration. You understand what it feels like, of course you do. In all those years supporting the club, you've been there yourself as well. But instead of feeling empathy, you take pleasure in your rivals' misery. You delight in their loss. It's what the Germans call 'Schadenfreude', and in Dutch it's referred to as 'leedvermaak'.

This very intuitive example was scientifically tested.[27] Male fans of two local football teams were recruited for an experiment during which they had to endure and witness electric shocks being administered to fans of their own team and fans of the rival team. As expected, research participants were uncomfortable watching a fellow fan from their own team suffering pain. They felt with them. But the opposite happened when seeing a fan from the rival team endure a shock, especially if the observer already had a negative perception of them. Seeing someone from the 'outgroup' wince with pain didn't elicit emphatic feelings; instead it gave a degree of pleasure.

This is the dark side of empathy. Football fanhood is an example of a type of tribalism that cuts across all lines of difference. From the music we like and the cars we drive to more socially pertinent ones such as class, race and political affiliation, difference is a key reason for empathy breakdown.[28] It underpins some of the massive schisms in our societies today, not least because politicians tap into our fears and anxieties by playing up difference rather than trying to overcome it.

When Russia invaded Ukraine in early 2022, the world looked on in shock. Within weeks, millions of Ukrainians had fled the war and sought refuge all over Europe. There was outrage at the aggressor and compassion for its victims. Ukraine hadn't done anything to provoke this attack, and its people were innocent.

But it was more than the Ukrainians' innocence that evoked such an empathetic response to the flow of refugees. A French journalist reportedly said, 'We're not talking here about Syrians fleeing the bombing of the Syrian regime backed by Putin; we're talking about Europeans leaving in cars that look like ours to save their lives.'[29] Similar observations were broadcast on other news channels, pointing out that these refugees were 'European people with blue eyes and blonde hair being killed'.[30]

There was widespread outrage at this biased, or racist, reporting on the war.[31] It laid bare the West's hypocrisy in its attitude and response to migrants. It shone a spotlight on the double standards that are applied when considering which refugee is deserving of our sympathy and help and which isn't.

The fact that we find it easier to put ourselves in the shoes of those who look like us and to feel compelled to help them, as thousands of Europeans have done by welcoming Ukrainians into their homes, is the flipside of empathy. We are far more likely to feel warmly towards those similar to us, or members of our 'ingroup' – like Ukrainians escaping Russian bombs. Yet, speaking as a white Westerner, we find it much more difficult, or actively choose not to, consider the situation of others who are in the 'outgroup' – such as Syrians fleeing war or Palestinians under siege in Gaza.

It's this flipside that also underlies lack of empathy for people in poverty. People in poverty are labelled as lazy, feckless and irresponsible. A few years ago, I asked readers of my blog Poverty Unpacked about words used in their country and language to describe people experiencing poverty or receiving income support.[32] There was no shortage of response. While some terminology highlights the severity of hardship, most serves to label, typecast and dehumanise.

In the UK, terms such as 'scroungers' or 'benefit broods' are commonplace to suggest that low-income individuals live off state support or have more children to gain access to further benefits. In German, the literal translation of '*sozial schwach*' is 'socially weak'. Despite its neutral appearance, it tends to be used in a derogatory way to suggest that those in poverty carry the blame. In the Philippines, '*palamunin*' describes someone unable to provide for themselves, relying on the support of others. In Pakistan, the Urdu terms '*muft khor*' and '*kaam chor*' serve to refer to freeloaders or those shirking from work.

Regardless of context and language, there is a common denominator to the pictures painted of people in poverty. Those struggling to make ends meet are projected as somehow less hard-working, less persistent and less deserving. They are weak and inept, and lack the moral compass of their well-off peers. In short: there's them, and there's us. And empathy for one of them tends to be in far shorter supply than it is for one of us.

Why do we think this way? Why do these stereotypes persist? Even if we feel a niggle of doubt that these prejudices may not be reflective of the truth, why do we hold onto them for dear life?

The field of psychology offers helpful insights, pointing us to one error and two biases.

First, there's something called 'fundamental attribution error'. This is the process by which we assume that misfortune in others' lives is the result of their own character or behaviour, while we attribute the same misfortune in our own lives to factors outside our control. Unemployment, debt or eviction. If it happens to them, it's their fault. If it happens to us, we're not to blame. When researchers in South Africa asked low-income mothers receiving child benefits about their predicament, they spoke about the difficulties of getting a job. But when they were asked about other mothers in the community also receiving income support, they commented on their neighbours' laziness and unwillingness to work.[33] It's the ultimate double standard. Thinking in terms of 'us versus them' comes naturally, even if 'they' are arguably very similar to 'us'.

Second, we're all inclined to submit to confirmation bias. Once a seed has been planted in our minds, our brains latch on to any information available to nurture and grow that seed. It's what my husband, Bart, calls the Daewoo effect.

In the late 1990s, his mother was on the lookout for a new car. She had her sights set on a Daewoo Matiz. A small hatchback, the model was presented as a cheap and reliable option, especially for those travelling short distances. Bart's family live in a part of the Netherlands where traffic is relatively quiet. It doesn't even have a motorway. But his mum was adamant that her car of choice was everywhere. She kept seeing them – on roads, in car parks, on driveways. She saw them more often than any other car.

It's unlikely there were many Daewoo Matizs out there. They certainly didn't outnumber any other makes and models at the time, not even in other parts of the country. Yet confirmation bias made Bart's mum take note of the few she did see and ignore the cars of a different make. It served as evidence for the popularity, and therefore desirability, of the car she so keenly preferred.

People aren't cars, of course. But the principle is the same. If we hold a certain belief about something or someone, we take notice of the things that confirm this belief. Our attention automatically pulls in that direction. Once we've developed the idea that poor people are poor of their own accord, we take note of information that confirms this idea. At the same time, we develop a blind spot for any intel that discounts our thinking. We overlook the fact that people in poverty take responsibility and work hard to swim against the tide. Instead, we hold onto the notion that poor people are somehow defective and to blame for their misfortune. This stops empathy in its tracks.

Third, we humans are prone to unconscious bias. Our attitudes about others are based on deep-seated assumptions of who they are or what they do, and we make judgements accordingly. Sex, race, ethnicity and socioeconomic status are some of the common markers that shape our opinion of someone and make us treat them in certain ways, even without knowing anything else about them.

It was a well-known, simple yet powerful riddle that I heard on the radio a few years back that impressed on me just how easy it is to succumb to unconscious bias. Indulge me as I put it to you.

A father and his son go out fishing on a nearby river. They get caught in a current and their boat capsizes. They both go under. Ambulances arrive and bodies are hauled out of the water. Sadly, the father doesn't survive the accident. The son is alive but needs urgent medical care, Yet when he's rushed into hospital, the doctor on duty looks at him and says, 'I can't operate on him, he's my son.'

If your first reaction was anything like mine, it would have been something along the lines of 'Huh, how's that possible?' Is it a trick question, did the father not die after all? Or maybe the doctor mistook the boy's identity?

Of course, the answer is much more straightforward than that: the doctor is the boy's mother.

Even for a self-proclaimed feminist resisting prejudice that withholds women from choosing the life and career paths they aspire to, the solution of this simple puzzle didn't immediately come to me. Instead, I tapped into persistent gendered stereotypes of what doctors look like and who occupies medical professions.

The point about unconscious bias is that we're unaware of these gut reactions and split-second responses. Even if, at a conscious level, we don't subscribe to those judgements. We might not agree with or deliberately submit to prejudice about people in poverty. Yet with stereotypes, tropes and negative narratives omnipresent and pervasive, we are inclined to latch onto them regardless. Unconscious bias undermines empathy without us realising it.

Engaging empathy

Fundamentally, we care. This chapter's whistlestop tour of empathy shows that, like our primate companions, we are all handed the genetic gift to put ourselves in the shoes of those around us, and to see the world through their eyes. A long history of religious and philosophical thought has placed empathy at the core of our moral and ethical values, compelling us to act in ways beneficial to others as much as ourselves. Modern science tells us that our ability to share each other's feelings isn't a mere figment of our imagination but part of how we are wired. Empathy's attributes can make it a powerful force for good.

That said, empathy doesn't come easy. Stress and over-whelm experienced by so many of us make it hard to allocate headspace or emotional bandwidth to others. Encouraged and reinforced by ubiquitous negative discourse about those on the lower end of the socioeconomic ladder, empathy's dark side means it's tempting to give in to the divisive forces of tribalism and succumb to considering people in poverty as 'them' rather than one of 'us'. Our inclination to denounce our own failures but make others own theirs, combined with our brains' natural tendencies to seek and see confirmation of negative stereotypes about low-income families further tests our capacity to empathise. As much as empathy is part of our DNA, engaging it requires effort and commitment. Empathy is crucial for the fight against poverty, but for it to be part of the solution, we need to tap into its positive properties and actively overcome the forces that work against it.

So, then, how? How to build and engage our empathy skills so we can turn the tables on poverty? To embark on and contribute to a journey towards a more equal world in which everyone can thrive? And to begin to fix what's so incredibly broken?

For us to come to grips with this daunting task, we can break it down into the three Rs outlined in the introduction: relate, realise and respond. They help us move through the stages of stepping outside of our own bubble into someone else's world, of interrogating and owning up to uncomfortable truths about what doesn't work and why, and of being proactive in challenging the status quo. Together, the three Rs transform empathy from a fuzzy concept into a practical tool for changing the needle on poverty.

If we're serious about alleviating hardship, the first step is for us to face up to the issue and *relate* to it. We need to see and grapple with the size, shape and experience of it. Poverty is often described as an invisible problem. Those who experience it tend to do everything in their power to hide their predicament. Those who don't know what it's like to live on little put great effort into looking away and ignoring the issue. So before we can even begin to think about addressing poverty, we need to be aware of what's going on.

This first R of empathy requires us to slow down. To start working our empathy muscle, we need to stand still, look around and take notice. To be curious. At a time when so many things demand our attention and energy, this may not be an easy feat. With social media algorithms trapping us into echo chambers of views and opinions that we are already familiar with or that we simply like hearing, it can be even harder to stay open to and remain aware of what goes on for others in distant social circles or less privileged positions. Empathy calls on us to go beyond the easy route. Instead, take a closer look. Read. Listen. Place judgements to one side. Keep an open mind.

Crucial for relating to the issue of poverty is perspective-taking. Stepping into someone else's shoes and considering how they experience life on little. In other words, we need to move beyond imagining how we ourselves might feel or be affected in a certain situation and take account of the other person's unique circumstances and how they shape their feelings and needs. This extends common understandings of how to practise compassion. Religion's Golden Rule is a prime example. In the Bible's New Testament, for example, the Gospel of Matthew (7:12) tells us to 'do to others what you would have them do to you'. While the rule calls for respect for and consideration of fellow humans, it does so from our own perspective. Yet empathy demands we move beyond this and cross the bridge into someone else's reality.

Once we have come to see the problem and relate to it, the second step is to *realise* why poverty persists and how it's perpetuated. We need to direct our attention to questions such as:

Why do societies' current socioeconomic configurations work against people in poverty? How is it that many policies only make matters worse? And how do insights about how poverty affects mind and behaviour play into individualisation of the problem, fallacious ideas about self-help and harmful rhetoric about self-reliance? Realising how poverty can persist in a world of unprecedented wealth means opening our eyes to how the rich are rewarded for the money they already have and the poor are punished for the cash they currently lack.

A vital but challenging component of realising how poverty is produced and perpetuated is for us to look in the mirror and examine our own role in propagating or silently acquiescing to others' disadvantage. Too often, the problem of poverty is placed with those who experience it, thereby conveniently removing those with deeper pockets from the picture and absolving them from the responsibility to take action towards addressing this injustice. However, as we'll see in this book, poverty is a collective crisis, not an individual shortcoming.

This second R of empathy requires each of us to be honest with ourselves about who holds responsibility. Doing so calls on us to move beyond the fundamental attribution error and overcome our tendencies towards confirmation and unconscious bias. Applying this to the issue of poverty, can we accept that others' misfortune isn't a result of their lack of character or effort? Can we admit that our own affluence is as much, or possibly more, a result of privilege as it is of our individual actions? Crucially, are we willing to see and acknowledge that the prosperity we might enjoy is cultivated on the back of disadvantage suffered by those on lower ranks of the socioeconomic ladder? Coming to terms with the fact that we are all pieces in the jigsaw puzzle of how wealth is generated and distributed is fundamental to realising how and why poverty is reproduced.

Finally, we need to *respond*. Empathy is only half-baked if relating to others' experiences of hardship and realising why they persist isn't followed by action. Change happens when intolerance of the status quo pushes us to do things differently. Actions can be big or small, involve large audiences or minor crowds, and play out in the public domain or the privacy of your own home. The point is that we push back against the structures, dynamics and, crucially, our own behaviours that – unwittingly or otherwise – feed into the cycle of poverty. How we choose to talk about welfare recipients, where we decide to spend our money, and how we opt to use our vote are seemingly small yet significant steps in changing the narrative and shifting the ways in which poverty is perceived and addressed.

From a definitional point of view, the notion that empathy encapsulates action isn't shared by everyone. Some argue that empathy stops at feeling someone else's experience; that it doesn't necessarily compel action. It's for this reason that Dutch lived-experience poverty expert Vanessa Umboh is in favour of the term 'compassion' rather than 'empathy'.[34] To tackle poverty, she notes, our ability to relate to and feel people's pain needs to translate into action to alleviate their suffering.

She's right, of course.

Not wanting to get bogged down by definitional squabbles, I consider desire and effort to make things better a crucial component of empathy. Response – the third R – is indispensable, entailing a consideration of what we – individually and as part of a collective – can do to change things. So that we adopt an approach that crosses divides and create a society in which everyone can feel secure, prosper and thrive.

The choice of the word 'response' here is deliberate. Reacting out of impulse might only serve to trigger the dark side of empathy, feed tribalism and entrench difference. Engaging our empathy in a positive and constructive manner demands action that is based on careful consideration.

With these three Rs in mind, let's begin. Join me on the journey to *relate* to the issue of poverty, *realise* its implications and our role in perpetuating it, and *respond* to it.

Tapping into universal experiences of stress, shame and aspiration, building on scientific evidence and drawing on my work from across the globe, Chapters 2 to 7 help us relate to the energy-sapping and soul-destroying impact of the struggle to make ends meet while at the same time helping us realise that however valuable such psychological insights might be, they also risk individualising the problem of poverty even further. Stories from those with first-hand experience elucidate the counterproductive nature of many policies seeking to tackle poverty, and highlight the harm caused by pejorative and punitive treatment propped up by seemingly benign self-help and self-reliance narratives.

Chapter 8 provides suggestions for changing tack, for a response to poverty that is more dignified and empathetic and for reshaping society so it is more equitable and respectful of everyone's contributions. Chapter 9 offers ideas for you to get involved, and to take action in the best way possible.

Empathy and its positive power is ready and waiting for us to tap into. All we have to do is engage it.

2

COGNITIVE COSTS AND POVERTY PREMIUMS

I'm sitting behind my desk at home, trying to focus on work, when my phone buzzes.

The local supermarket has a few slots available, reads the text message from my friend. *Better be quick!*

I log on to the shop's website and navigate my way to the page for home deliveries. I click on the link for next week's schedule. No openings. I check the week after. Nothing. Same thing the week after that. It's only been a few minutes since my friend alerted me, but any slots that might have been available are already gone.

It's May 2020. The world has come to a standstill. Within the space of a few weeks, the previously unknown COVID-19 virus is now ruling our lives. News reports are dominated by people falling seriously ill and gasping for air in intensive care units that are crumbling under the weight of this unprecedented health emergency.

Without cure or vaccination, the best way to stay safe is to avoid infection. As a result, life as we know it has been shut down. Planes are grounded, schools closed, stores boarded up and curfews imposed. Presidents and prime ministers are urging people to stay at home. Previously the stuff of dystopian novels or sci-fi movies, the word 'lockdown' has become part of everyday vernacular. We have become the cast in our own real-life version of the movie *Contagion*.

A kidney transplant recipient, my husband is clinically vulnerable. We've been told in no uncertain terms to be extra vigilant and to reduce his contact with the outside world to an absolute minimum. As his partner, I'm to do the same. So with supermarket trips now off limits, even with all precautions in place, we've started ordering our shopping online and getting supplies delivered to our doorstep.

It turns out we're not alone. After the first lockdown was announced, consumer behaviour changed almost overnight. The market for online grocery shopping exploded. Millions of Brits are now trying to avoid the supermarket queues, and slots for home delivery or collection of pre-ordered shopping are like gold dust.

Securing a delivery slot turns into a daily preoccupation. As much as my friend and I try to keep each other updated about newly added times, success isn't guaranteed. Take today: any new availability has evaporated as soon as I'm made aware of it. Determined to beat the odds, I develop a habit of logging on to the various supermarkets' websites multiple times a day. I try to spot a pattern as to when new slots are released, but there doesn't seem to be any rhyme or reason.

Sometimes they appear in the morning, other times mid afternoon or late evening. It's a guessing game.

We're now about six weeks into this pandemic, and my capacity to concentrate is starting to suffer. It's not just the energy taken up by managing our groceries. Concerns about COVID's health risks, worries about when I might be able to see my family in the Netherlands again, and a continuous state of anxiety brought on by the uncertainty surrounding everyday life occupy a lot of my headspace, crowding out other, more constructive thoughts. My sleep becomes ragged. Emails take longer to type, work longer to complete. I spend more and more time staring out of the window, becoming increasingly familiar with my neighbours' daily routines.

Talking to others, I quickly learn it's not just me. Family, friends, colleagues – many in my direct environment are experiencing the same. We talk about ways to cope, like going outside and getting fresh air when we can. But it does little to take the edge off. Worry and concern lead to a curious mix of constantly feeling on tenterhooks while at the same time being weighed down by thick fog that makes it hard to concentrate and pay attention.

And I'm someone speaking from a position of privilege. I have stable employment and can work from home, and I don't have children to home-school or care for at the same time. I can only imagine what it must be like for workers on the front line of this emergency, or those who lost their jobs due to the pandemic. The UK government has just started implementing its furlough scheme, temporarily paying workers if employers struggle to do so because of business closures and collapsed demand. It's protecting millions of jobs, giving income security to many. But those already in financially precarious conditions, such as gig workers and employees on zero-hour contracts, are excluded.[1] As stressful as the situation might be, I have many blessings to count.

I pick up my phone to thank my friend for alerting me but add that unfortunately it was to no avail. Still processing my frustration at the missed supermarket slot, I make a mental note of when to log back in. Maybe availability will open up later this evening. I sigh at the thought. For now, I need to get back to work. This online sojourn has taken another 20 minutes out of my day. What was I doing again?

Back behind my laptop, I notice a chat message at the bottom of my screen.

Hey, are you there?

My colleague has been trying to reach me. I must have missed the notification.

We're supposed to have a meeting right now. You didn't forget, did you?

Thinking straight is harder in hardship

Indulge me for a moment and conjure up an image of a snow globe. One of those colourful, toy-like home decor accessories, especially popular as Christmas ornaments. Shake them and white flakes whirl around little figurines, creating a dreamy fairy-tale scene. It gives these otherwise mostly tacky items a magic quality that draws people in, adults and children alike.

The whole thing looks simple enough. But there's a pre-condition for this magic to work. The globe needs to hold the right proportion of flakes to fluid. Too few flakes and it looks dull and boring. Too many and there's no space for them to float and dance.

Our brains work much the same. Fill them with thoughts, ideas and memories and you end up with a rich and stimulating inner life. However, balance is key. Too few preoccupations and you might start questioning the purpose of life. Too many and you're likely to get overwhelmed. To lose sight of everything that's going on and find it difficult to prioritise.

This is exactly what happened for many of us as COVID-19 took hold, when we had to adapt to a new way of living almost overnight. How likely am I to catch the virus when going out? How dangerous is it to fall ill? How do I manage work and care for my children? What will happen if I lose my job? Our brainy snow globes got flooded with additional flakes, clogging up the tiny space within them. We suffered what some dubbed 'pandemic brain',[2] a state of overwhelm and stress that made it incredibly hard to remain clear-headed and think straight.

Our ability to pay attention, consider the pros and cons of various options and take well-considered decisions is also referred to as our cognitive bandwidth. That bandwidth, or headspace, is limited. It's a scarce resource. The more we demand from our mind, the less able it is to do these things well. The more flakes, the less space for each of them to flutter and shine.

Multitasking is a perfect example of overcrowding our brains. Some of us might think we're good at doing multiple things at the same time, but experience tends to paint a different picture. Who hasn't forgotten their keys when they're busy talking on the phone on their way out of the house? Or sent a text message to the wrong person because they were watching TV while typing it?

While living through the pandemic placed a severe strain on my headspace, it was temporary. Once vaccinations were widely available, infection rates dropped and it was possible to travel again, the stress and anxiety dissipated. It took the best part of two years, but ultimately the fog lifted, and it became easier to maintain focus and concentration.

Now imagine that this state of distress isn't temporary. It's permanent. This is where poverty enters the equation.

Living on little takes up a lot of headspace. All the time. Days are spent worrying about the same questions over and over again, often without any obvious solutions. How much money is in my account? How much is coming in before the end of the week? What payments are pending, or bills outstanding? If I buy this, can I still afford this month's rent? Never mind what happens when the car breaks down or the washing machine suddenly dies.

Stress is constant. Worries are always front and centre. Anxiety becomes a permanent companion. The strain all this places on the brain constitutes the cognitive cost of poverty. Or, as behavioural scientists Sendhil Mullainathan and Eldar

Shafir call it, a 'bandwidth tax'.[3] If your income is low, you're constantly having to keep track of incomings and outgoings. There's little room for error, and mistakes can have dire consequences. It requires top-notch accountancy skills, which have to be applied alongside everything else that's going on in life. While those more affluent may outsource the complexities of money management, if you're poor you have to do it all yourself.

To illustrate what this entails, let me transport you to the small town of Lawrenceville in the US state of New Jersey. It's 2010, and a team of researchers venture out to the local mall to ask unsuspecting shoppers to take part in an experiment.[4] In return for a small sum of money as a token of appreciation, they'll have to do some cognitive tests and divulge their income levels. Just over 100 shoppers agree to take part.

Before taking the tests, participants are presented with four scenarios. They each represent a different financial shock, and the participants are asked what this shock would mean for them. For example, one scenario suggests their employer needs to make budget cuts and reduce wages. The participants are asked how they would manage this drop in earnings, and what changes would be required to make ends meet. Another scenario involves their refrigerator breaking down and needing replacement. There are two financing options: paying the full amount instantly without any extra charge or opting for 12 monthly payments, which allows for spreading the cost but incurs additional interest. Which to choose?

As an additional twist, each of these scenarios has two versions. An 'easy' version, meaning that financial consequences are relatively small, and a 'hard' version, involving more severe economic implications. In the wage-cut scenario, the easy condition assumes a drop in earnings of only 5 per cent. The hard condition entails a reduction of 15 per cent. In the refrigerator scenario, the one-off full cost in the easy version is $399. This compares to $999 in the hard condition.

Participants are randomly assigned to either the easy or the hard version of these scenarios. After having viewed their version of the scenario, and while still mulling over the financial implications, they must then perform two different activities to test their cognitive functioning.

First is the so-called Raven's test. Participants are shown a sequence of patterns on a computer screen. One shape is missing, and they have to choose from a range of alternatives to fill the gap. It's a much-used test to assess the capacity for logical thinking and problem-solving.

Next is an exercise to examine cognitive control. A heart or flower appears on screen at random, and participants must press different buttons depending on which item appears and which side of the screen it appears on. It may seem easy enough, but the activity's counter-intuitive aspect tends to catch people out, especially if they're thinking about something else at the same time.

All this testing with shoppers in small-town America confirms the psychological toll of poverty. Both richer and poorer shoppers did relatively well in the Raven's test when confronted with the scenarios' easy versions. However, results plummeted for shoppers with lower incomes when presented with the more costly scenarios. Even if cash-driven dilemmas are hypothetical, thinking about them makes it much harder to get our brains to apply themselves to a relatively simple cognitive task. When our budgets are smaller, financial woes weigh on our minds, especially when their consequences can be far-reaching.

The same was true for the test of cognitive control. It made no difference to richer research participants whether the scenarios' financial implications were trivial or severe; the accuracy and speed with which they responded to the flowers and hearts appearing on their screen was the same. Yet for those having little to live on, being confronted with hypothetical situations that triggered large monetary concerns resulted in them being far less able to concentrate and solve problems.

The mental tax of poverty isn't exclusive to living in richer countries such as the US. The same researchers also explored this issue in India, in the southern state of Tamil Nadu, exploiting seasonal fluctuations in the earnings farmers made from their harvests to assess the impact of low income on mental capacity.[5]

Seasonality plays a big role in farmers' lives, especially in poorer countries. Many rely on their own produce for consumption, and food supplies from previous harvests tend to run low just before the new harvest comes round. If farmers grow crops for cash, any earnings from last season's produce are also likely to have dried up just before the upcoming harvest. By contrast, post-harvest is a time of plenty. There's lots of fresh food to be eaten and produce to be sold.

The researchers visited a few hundred farmers before and after harvest time. As sugarcane farmers, they grow the crop for cash. The annual sale of produce represents the primary source of income. Financial pressures are considerably larger pre-harvest than they are post-harvest. Farmers are more likely to take out loans, pawn valuable items and face difficulties in paying regular expenses.

As with the shoppers in New Jersey, the research team asked the farmers in Tamil Nadu to take part in various tests to assess their cognitive capacity. This time, however, research participants weren't presented with hypothetical scenarios to trigger financial concern. Instead, tests were administered before and after harvest, making use of real-life differences in financial pressures to understand their impact on cognitive functioning.

Despite being in a different country and a very different context, findings were the same: struggling to make ends meet brings immense mental strain. Farmers performed less well on tests pre-harvest compared to post-harvest. Further analysis ruled out the role of other mediating factors, such as farmers needing to work extra hard and feeling physically exhausted or eating less before harvest time. In Tamil Nadu too, economic scarcity brings a cognitive tax. Thinking straight is more difficult in hardship.

When our minds are overloaded, it undermines our overall cognitive functioning. We become scatterbrained. This dynamic holds true for everyone, rich or poor. There are many things that can weigh on our minds, from everyday stressors such as how to get to work on time during rush hour to more severe concerns about ill health or care for elderly relatives, or coping with unusual events such as

COVID-19. They lead to us becoming less able to keep our concentration and perform tasks effectively. Financial insecurity, however, causes a level of perennial and subliminal stress that acts as a constant heavy weight, regardless of whatever else is going on. It crowds out headspace and reduces bandwidth in ways that those more affluent don't have to contend with.

Balancing today's gains against tomorrow's losses

It's 7.30 in the morning when I walk into the breakfast room. It's quiet. None of my colleagues are here yet. I grab a coffee and sit down at the table we've been enjoying our morning meals at since we arrived a few days ago. It's amazing how quickly habits develop.

The sun has only just risen high enough for its rays to peek through the palm trees on the resort's patio, but it already feels hot and humid. I'm in Lumbini, in the Terai plains of southern Nepal. The area is notorious for its sticky climate, making it a hotbed for diseases such as malaria. The city's more favourable claim to fame is that it's the birthplace of Siddhartha Gautama, more commonly known as the Buddha. With the majority of visitors to Nepal heading straight into the Himalayas, the government is keen to promote Lumbini as a place of interest. It's for this reason that my colleagues and I found ourselves on a small plane on a short but somewhat treacherous flight from Kathmandu to the nearby town of Siddharthanagar earlier that week.

Here, in a hotel in the country's new tourist destination of Lumbini, we were requested to train government staff on issues of poverty and welfare.

Day three of our course is about to get under way, and participants are starting to trickle into the restaurant. After two busy days having run various sessions, today is an easy one for me. No presentations or facilitation, simply supporting my colleagues as and when necessary. Delivering training is one of the most rewarding things to do, but it's also draining. It feels like a performance, having to be on your toes and fully concentrated throughout.

I'm about to check the time when one of my colleagues appears in the corner of my eye.

'Morning,' I say cheerfully. 'Did you have a good night?'

'Urghh,' he responds before making a beeline for the jar of instant coffee.

'Not good then?' I enquire as he sits down and places a cup of steaming near-black liquid in front of him. Dark circles frame his eyes.

'Oh, you know,' he sighs. 'I didn't manage to prepare today's slides before coming out here, so I had to do them all last night. It took me much longer than I thought it would. I think I got about two hours' sleep.'

'Gosh, that's not a lot at all. Will you be okay today?'

'I'll have to be. There's just always too much to do. There's never time to think about any of these things in advance.'

He yawns before downing his coffee.

'On the upside,' he says, 'I have incredible focus when it's down to the wire like this. Things become very clear in my head. I don't mean to brag or anything, but this morning's presentation is perfect.'

I roll my eyes at this announcement. Preparing a perfect presentation from scratch the night before, with only two hours to spare? Is that even possible?

Turns out it is. The slides are bright and clear, the messaging is on point and there are even some jokes thrown into the mix. The course participants love it.

My colleague benefited from the so-called 'focus dividend'.[6] When our headspace gets squeezed, we are forced to zoom in on what's in front of us. Right here, right now. This can work to our advantage. We direct our scarce brainpower towards the problem at hand. We don't let distractions get the better of us. Faced with a deadline, we become more careful with our time. We apply all our cognitive capacity to completing the task that needs doing, neglect unnecessary distractions and are more productive as a result.

But this is only half the story.

As much as there's a benefit to channelling our attention to the most urgent thing in front of us, there's also a cost. For my colleague to concentrate on crafting his training session, he had to turn off his email and switch off his phone. There was to be no distraction. What if his partner had been trying to reach him? They would have been ignored. And what about colleagues and students expecting a response to their emails? They would have to wait.

The flipside of focusing our full attention on one urgent task is that many other things get neglected. They move from our central line of focus into the periphery. Who hasn't forgotten a birthday because they were so caught up in work? Driven home to an empty fridge because they forgot to pop into the shop? Or failed to pay a bill on time because they were preoccupied with packing for a holiday?

While the narrowing of our headspace can lead to the benefit of concentration, as it did for my colleague, it can also result in singular focus with detrimental consequences, also referred to as 'tunnel vision', in which the mind automatically veers towards one way of doing things to achieve a certain objective, no longer open to other – better – alternatives. Yet this has implications, sometimes severe. It's the collateral damage of our mind hunkering down, of pushing away anything that may interfere with what's in our central line of vision.

Tunnel vision is an important reason why poor people stand accused of making bad decisions. To see why, let's transport ourselves to New Zealand, and consider Laura's story.[7]

A mother of two, Laura is trying to cope with the high costs associated with young children. To help her afford birthday gifts and other expensive necessities for her kids, like winter clothes, she started making use of so-called buy-now-pay-later (BNPL) schemes. Visit any large online retailer and you'll find them. You browse the collection, adding items to your virtual shopping basket as you go along, and when you're ready to check out, you're given a choice: get the entire amount charged to your card immediately, or delay payment by spreading it across regular instalments, often over a relatively short period of time.[8]

It's an attractive proposition, having your purchases delivered to your doorstep the next day but only having to lose money over it in the weeks or months to come. No surprise then that although BNPL hasn't been around for very long, it has boomed. The rise in online shopping coupled with the recent squeeze on household budgets has drawn many buyers in. In 2023, one in four New Zealanders held at least one BNPL account.[9] Unlike credit cards or regular loans, there are no credit or affordability checks when using BNPL in New Zealand, making it especially appealing to those on low incomes who would be unlikely to pass such checks.

At first, Laura only used BNPL to buy stuff she needed and couldn't otherwise afford. But things soon spiralled out of control. Instead of paying for small purchases immediately, she opted to delay those as well. It gave her a kick. She became addicted to being able to buy something at the click of a button yet only having to worry about the financial implications in the future. She racked up large debts, worsening her financial situation. What seemed like the most attractive option at the time turned into a living nightmare.

Weighing up the short-term benefits of financial decisions against their long-term costs is something few of us engage in for fun. It can also be difficult trying to figure out the actual cost of paying back a loan over a longer period of time. If money isn't in short supply, the need to consider those trade-offs is less urgent, and the consequences of choosing worse options less severe. However, when living on little, choices that solve short-term problems but may create challenges in future are more likely, and their implications more harmful.

When living in poverty, scarce attention is allocated to the here and now, making it more difficult to focus on problems that might arise tomorrow and beyond. Tunnel vision takes over, undermining the ability to consider and weigh up different options against each other. These insights into how financial insecurity affect the brain and can explain choices that may not be in a person's best interest are relatively new, and have been dubbed 'the psychology of poverty'.[10] The bandwidth tax of poverty plays into economic decisions that offer a quick fix but may have detrimental long-term consequences, or sticking to habits that are familiar but not necessarily preferred from a financial point of view. It can cause a feedback loop and perpetuate or reinforce poverty.

More than meets the eye

But is that all there is to it? Does the cognitive strain of being cash-strapped mean that people in poverty are destined to take financial decisions that will make things worse rather than better? Or is there more to say?

Take Hamid and Khadeja,[11] a young couple living in a densely populated and low-income area in Dhaka, the Bangladesh capital we visited in the previous chapter. Despite living in poverty, they're no strangers to stretching their cash as far as it can go. The couple have a multitude of savings accounts, loans and outstanding credit. Neither Hamid nor Khadeja can read or write, so they have to keep track of all this in their heads. They don't do this because they enjoy managing money; in fact, they'd rather not have to deal with any of this. They engage with all manner of banks, lenders and credit providers because they see no other choice. This type of financial diversification is their best bet at keeping safe the little money they earn.

Given their sophisticated financial strategising, it seems paradoxical that the couple are actually losing money. In particular, it's a microfinance loan that's weighing on their resources. Khadeja took one out so she could buy gold. The precious metal serves as an insurance policy in case Hamid is no longer able to support her, for whatever reason. Not only is such a purchase a wise forward-looking decision, it's also a progressive one in a society where women still have relatively little independence, financial or otherwise.

Khadeja is repaying her loan through small weekly instalments over a one-year period. As with any loan, she pays interest on top. However, given the fact that she's unlikely to need the gold before the year is up, it would have been cheaper for her to simply save the money herself. Not only that, without interest payments she would have managed to accumulate the required amount more quickly.

Khadeja may be illiterate and innumerate, but she's not stupid. She knows she's losing money by having taken out a loan. Her decision wasn't based on stress-induced short-term thinking either. Rather, she is aware that it will be difficult to put aside the required amount regularly enough to get to a point where she can buy the gold. More pressing needs might come up, and Khadeja knows she'll be tempted to take the cash that she put aside and use it for immediate problem-solving. She isn't going for the more expensive option because she hasn't properly balanced the immediate gains against future losses. She's choosing to lose money in the short term precisely because this option will serve her better in the long run.

People in poverty everywhere adopt intricate financial strategies to provide inflow of cash when needed or to act as a buffer in case something goes wrong. Notwithstanding the cognitive constraints imposed by the stress of poverty, management of elaborate webs of loans, credit and savings is core to the everyday effort of making ends meet. And first impressions may deceive. Seemingly unwise decisions turn out to be clever tactics.

I witnessed this in my own work in Bangladesh. Poor families who received a cash transfer commonly used their newly obtained funds to pay off loans. Not to get rid of debt entirely, but to shift from less desirable to preferable creditors. This could mean getting away from a loan shark demanding exorbitant interest rates. But it could also mean replacing loans held with relatives or friends with finance from more formal sources, such as a bank or microfinance institution. This may not be cheaper from a monetary point of view, but it does come without social strings attached. While we as outsiders may judge such decisions as poor financial management, they are the result of intricate cost–benefit analyses that weigh up a whole host of advantages and disadvantages. Money is not all that counts; higher interest rates may be cash well spent if it means ridding oneself of the scrutiny that comes with money borrowed from family members.

Consumption patterns of low-income families in Tanzania offer another pertinent example of financial decisions that are smarter than they seem. Having collected data from nearly 1,500 families, a group of researchers noticed that many of them shopped for non-perishable items in small quantities only.[12] It posed a puzzle. Buying in bulk, even if quantities are only slightly larger, can lead to considerable savings. The researchers estimated that bulk buying would allow families to afford 33 per cent more fuel, 50 per cent more cooking bananas, 24 per cent more cooking oil, 46 per cent more onions and 18 per cent more dried sardines at the same cost as making small-quantity purchases. These are substantial amounts. So why weren't families making more of their hard-earned money?

When the researchers dug deeper into their data, they found two reasons for this seemingly irrational spending behaviour.

First, buying only a few items at a time is a strategy to prevent over-consumption, especially of so-called 'temptation goods'. For many Tanzanians, sugar, rice, cooking oil, soap, cigarettes and sweet bananas fall into this category. Families displayed a preference for buying these in small quantities. Despite being aware this was more expensive than buying in bulk, they also knew that if they stocked up on items they were partial to, they would be using more of them than strictly necessary. Buying small amounts may cost more in the short term, but the way in which it forces rationing ultimately proves this strategy to be the more cost-effective one.

The second reason for buying little but often is to avoid the need to share. Returning home with large quantities of food and other goodies can be met with the expectation to spread the wealth. Family members, friends and neighbours might come knocking. The researchers call it 'social taxation', with those having more experiencing pressure to let others in on their good fortune. 'If I buy five kilograms of sugar, everyone will take their tea at my house' is how a member of one family who participated in the study explained it.

While Tanzanians' decisions to purchase less at relatively higher prices didn't seem sensible at first, it turns out their choices are incredibly clever. Buying small as a strategy to stop oneself from consuming too much and to prevent others from tucking in can be more advantageous than shopping large at a discount.

Much like Khadeja and the cash transfer recipients in Dhaka, there's more than meets the eye when it comes to how low-income families handle their money. Despite the stress of tight budgets, people in poverty tend to manage their finances with great ingenuity. While the 'psychology of poverty' helps to understand how living on little squeezes headspace and impedes cognitive bandwidth, it shouldn't serve as an excuse to dismiss poor people's financial choices as unwise, rash or reckless. Relating to the experience of financial decision-making tells us it's not as simple as that.

Poverty is expensive

'Aren't these on offer?'

I'm in the queue at a low-cost supermarket, placing my shopping on the belt as quickly as I can. The cashier has just finished scanning multiple packets of sausages, blocks of cheese and boxes of washing powder, and the belt is moving swiftly along. It seems like the customer in front of me is stocking up, trying to make best use of this week's offers.

'I'm sorry, sir, discounts are only available through the app,' says the cashier with a mixture of apology and impatience. 'Simply download and register on your phone.'

The man looks at the cashier in disbelief and shakes his head. 'I can't afford a smartphone. Why do you think I shop here in the first place?'

He has a point. Yet paradoxically, when you have little to spend, life becomes more expensive. There's a cost to budgets being tight or being unable to afford middle-class lifestyles. It's known as the 'poverty premium'.

The inability to buy in bulk and the money that's lost as a result is perhaps the most common way in which the poverty premium manifests itself. While Tanzanian families opted to purchase small quantities as a clever way to avoid over-consumption or having to share their scarce resources, for most buying a little at a time isn't the preferred choice. It's the lack of liquidity that prevents them from buying big. Purchasing the super-sized box of your favourite tea means you pay as little as possible for your cuppa, yet the higher price might leave you with too little to spend on other essentials.

For the same reason, multi-offer deals, especially on expensive products, are attractive but often out of reach. And the list goes on. Being on a tight budget prevents people from collecting points on loyalty schemes or saving up for discounts or freebies. Living in a low-income area tends to push up premiums for car or home insurance. Expensive pay-day loan providers prey on people who struggle to make their funds stretch until the end of the month. And then there are the higher prices low-income families are charged for their utilities.

Roughly four million households in the UK use prepayment meters to pay for their gas and electricity. Instead of getting billed for energy use monthly based on past usage, customers top up their accounts before turning on their appliances. Prepayment meters tend to be used by low-income customers, allowing them to top up in small amounts rather than having to face large sums every month. Fair enough, it seems.

However, the practice is far from fair. In addition to paying for effective usage of kilowatt hours of electricity and gas, bills also include so-called standing charges – the cost of being connected. They are a flat fee incurred every day, regardless of whether any energy is used. These charges are also paid through prepayment meters, and if there's no more credit on your meter, they'll simply accumulate. Even if you're trying to save on energy bills, for example by turning off the gas because you don't need the heating during the summer months, fees will still add up. And next time you top up, any amount that's added will go towards paying outstanding charges first. This might leave you with little credit to actually heat your home, and a need to top up again very soon.

The very idea of having to pay upfront for bare essentials such as a warm house, cold fridge and hot stove is problematic to begin with. Research by Citizens Advice shows that in 2022, 3.2 million UK households were cut off from their energy supply because they had run out of credit.[13] That's one person every 10 seconds having their rooms go dark or their much-needed food defrost in the freezer. This is uncomfortable at best and debilitating at worst.

Gemma's story is emblematic. She suffers from arthritis,[14] and the pain can sometimes be so agonising that she's unable to get out of bed. Her health condition forced her to give up work a few years earlier. With two children to care for, life is tough enough as it is. However, high energy prices made things even worse. Paying for her electricity and gas using a prepayment meter, Gemma is constantly having to weigh up use of one appliance against another. Cold leads to extreme pain, so staying warm is vital for her to remain mobile. But having the heating on full blast leaves no electricity for the washing machine, tumble dryer or dishwasher. Yet using the radiators to dry laundry will reduce the heat coming off them, and Gemma's back doesn't hold up long enough for her to do the washing-up in the sink.

It's a catch-22, which has meant that despite her chronic illness, Gemma has been without gas for up to two and a half weeks at a time. Her meter is almost constantly showing she's on emergency reserve. There have been occasions she and her children have spent time out of the house to avoid it running on empty, knowing that the next pay cheque is still weeks away.

Cold homes aren't without consequences. Health scientists have warned against the risks of going without warmth. A cold home can increase the risk of respiratory diseases like asthma or bronchitis. It can also lead to heart disease or exacerbate existing health issues such as diabetes.[15] Health effects are especially detrimental for children, as a cold environment might impair their biological development,[16] leading to problems in later life. No wonder some people have called it a public health and humanitarian crisis.[17]

Once you start looking for it, the poverty premium is everywhere. The campaign group Fair By Design and researchers from the University of Bristol estimate that almost all low-income households in the UK experience at least one type of cost incurred because they have a tight budget.[18] This doesn't just squeeze family budgets, they say; it also harms the economy. The money spent on additional fees, charges or premiums could instead be spent in local economies. Without the poverty premium, as much as £4.5 million could flow back to businesses and communities in the average local constituency.[19] With more than 600 constituencies across the UK, that amounts to a mind-boggling £2.8 billion lost to excess costs incurred by people who have least to spend.

And remember those BNPL schemes from earlier? It's not just financial stress standing in the way of rejecting a quick accumulation of debt. The way in which these schemes are set up makes them more attractive to those with lower budgets, but then penalises them if they can't keep up. In fact, as long as repayments are made on time, such schemes can help to spread cost and be a smart financial strategy. Middle-class shoppers with healthy budgets are well served by this type of credit. But if your income is small and you're struggling to make ends meet as it is, BNPL doesn't just suck you into a cycle of debt, as happened to Laura in New Zealand; it also slaps on considerable interest and late payment fees.

Although originally marketed at more affluent customers of fashion or luxury items, ease of access coupled with the sting of rising living costs has meant BNPL is increasingly used to buy basics. Many low-income families have no other option but to rely on the schemes to afford essentials such as food and groceries. This is true not just in New Zealand, but also elsewhere, such as the UK[20] and the US.[21] BNPL gives those who would be refused conventional loans – commonly those on lower incomes – access to cheap debt. It could be argued that this is a good thing. Access to credit is no longer the prerogative of the better-off, but is also open to those who most need it. Yet there are risks, and they can be considerable.

BNPL providers, and the retailers using them, want to hook you in. The more you buy, the more your credit ceiling is increased, regardless of whether you're actually able to afford any of the purchases. One study found that almost one third of BNPL users made purchases outside their budget.[22] As Laura found out, this opens the door to unaffordable debt. Outstanding payments accumulate with record speed. And as BNPL repayment periods are short, due dates come around very quickly. Late payments can incur high fees, making it even more difficult to repay the original debt. What's more, it's easy to have BNPL accounts with different providers at the same time. This type of loan 'stacking'[23] can lead debt to rack up unchecked. Once entering this vicious cycle of indebtedness, it's very hard to get out. Meanwhile, BNPL providers are cashing in.

We have seen how poor people are often accused of making poor decisions. But if we make the effort to relate to the common experience of stress and overload and realise how people in poverty cope with the constant onslaught on their mental capacity in the face of limited economic opportunities and predatory financial products, it becomes apparent that they often make the best decisions available to them.

Psychological insights provide important explanations for why poverty makes it harder to think straight. But while poverty may limit headspace for weighing up financial options, it's not all in the head. Living on little doesn't only impede the ability to make choices that optimise today's gains against tomorrow's costs; it also severely limits those options. Having less to spend results in paying higher prices for food, essentials and basic services than those who have larger budgets. Being strapped for cash requires sophisticated money management strategies to achieve the best possible outcome.

Perversely, it is those whose headspace is squeezed by lack of financial resources who need their cognitive capacity the most to make limited funds stretch as far as possible. Dismissing poor people's spending patterns as ill-considered and unwise simply because those with higher budgets don't understand them does a great disservice to people in poverty and the efforts to reduce it. Adopting an empathy lens allows us to see the cognitive costs and poverty premiums inherent to living on little, the tough choices they provoke and the ingenious ways people in poverty navigate them.

3

———

CAUGHT IN THE
WEB OF SHAME

'Good morning, everyone, let's get started, shall we?'

My course-mates and I pull ourselves away from our morning chat and find a seat. We are in one of the cosier classrooms in the university building, right at the top under the eaves. I have to duck to pull back my chair and sit down. Tables have been arranged in a horseshoe layout, so we can all face each other and make eye contact. The perfect setting for today's session. We're about to learn how to facilitate focus group discussions.

After a quick round of introductions, our teacher, Judy, dives straight into the main topic of the day.

'So, what makes a good facilitator?'

We're all eager to make best use of this opportunity to gain key skills for undertaking our research as postgraduate students, and responses come in thick and fast.

'The ability to listen!'

'Not being afraid to intervene!'

'Giving everybody a chance to speak!'

Judy nods her head in agreement. She's clearly pleased with her active audience this morning.

'Now imagine you are facilitating a group discussion. What are your biggest fears?'

There is a sudden shift of energy in the room. Instead of answers being shouted out, I hear bums shuffling on seats. Despite the room's clever set-up, we all manage to avoid eye contact. Judy doesn't seem too bothered. She probably expected this to happen; she must have run this workshop dozens of times before.

While most of us are busy inspecting our table or gazing intently at the wall opposite, the girl next to me is brave enough to share her anxiety.

'I'm worried about one person dominating the conversation, and then not knowing how to stop them. What do I do without offending anyone?'

I hear some murmuring around the room. She's not the only one to worry about this. Overseeing a conversation so that everyone feels comfortable and can contribute to the discussion is daunting at best, and outright scary at worst.

Now the silence has been broken, others chime in.

'I'm concerned about mispronouncing people's names. That would make me look really silly.'

'I worry that participants will get bored. What if they simply get up and leave the room? That would be a nightmare!'

Again Judy nods her approval. 'These are all valid concerns, and you will certainly encounter them at some point or another. But there are ways to reduce the risk of them happening and to deal with them when they do, so not to worry,' she reassures us. 'Are there any other things that bother you?'

More staring at tables and walls ensues. Judy looks around the room and waits patiently.

A classmate opposite me looks up hesitantly and says quietly, 'This might be silly, but … I'm concerned about blushing. It sometimes happens when I speak in public, and it really bothers me. I feel so embarrassed.'

Immediately I feel a flash of heat rising all the way from my feet through my legs and stomach in the direction of my head. I can sense my cheeks warming up and can almost see them changing colour. 'No, no, no!' my inner voice shouts. 'Can we PLEASE not have this conversation!' But the comment has piqued Judy's interest, and we *are* having this conversation.

'How fascinating,' I hear her say. 'Does anybody else share this concern?'

My heart sinks, and I slouch in my chair, hoping to disappear under the table, or even better, vanish into thin air. Yes, I share this concern. In fact, to me, the risk of blushing is the single most terrifying thing about speaking in a group. I hate the feeling of my cheeks heating up, slowly turning from lobster pink to a blazing tomato red.

It's not just the feeling that makes me reel. Over the years, I've had my fair share of comments in response to my spontaneous change of colour. One particularly memorable occasion occurred when, after I'd been teaching a group of mid-career professionals in a medium-sized lecture hall, a male member of the audience came up to me suggesting that maybe in future I should consider wearing make-up to conceal my blush. The irony of this comment was lost on me at the time, as was the misogyny underpinning it.

Sharing this anecdote would probably delight Judy, but I really don't want to talk about it. Not in a group setting, and certainly not with a face by now so hot you could probably fry an egg on it. But as Judy looks around the room, there is nowhere to hide.

'Oh, I see we have another blusher!' she squeals when her gaze lands on me.

I cringe as all eyes turn towards me. I can feel my whole face burning. There are a few silent sniggers and some uncomfortable smiles. I notice someone releasing a quiet sigh, no doubt expressing relief that it's me and not them being singled out.

'There's nothing to be worried about when blushing,' Judy says. 'It doesn't hurt. Nothing actually happens, does it?'

It's beginning to dawn on me that she doesn't have the faintest idea about blushing. Sadly, it doesn't stop her from trying to prove her point.

'To demonstrate to the blushers in this room that there's nothing to be afraid of, I want us to try a little experiment. Everyone, point your finger at Keetie and repeat after me: "Look, you're blushing!"'

I see a few puzzled faces, but any confusion is short-lived. Before I know it, I'm looking at 15 index fingers as their owners simultaneously call out an involuntary bodily reaction that I hate with every fibre of my being and try my utmost to disguise.

'Let's try that again,' encourages Judy, 'just to make sure it hits home.' The fingers remain up in the air while there is another round of 'Look, you're blushing!'

I sink deeper into my chair, but there is nowhere to go. I feel like running out of the room, but that's not really an option. Instead, I just sit there, hoping Judy will soon change the subject and this will all come to an end.

After three rounds of unnecessarily pointing out the obvious, Judy seems happy with the outcome of the exercise. 'See, nothing happened. There is nothing to be afraid of,' she concludes contentedly. All I can think is that my worst nightmare has just become reality, and it was every bit as bad as I always knew it was going to be.

'With this experience, you should feel confident to speak publicly and facilitate group discussions without letting the colour of your cheeks worry you! Now, let's discuss what excites you about being a facilitator, shall we?'

A wave of relief washes over me. The ordeal is finally over. But the rest of the workshop is a blur. I'm paralysed. Or at least it feels like that. The tentacles of shame are tugging at every part of my body. I have never felt so humiliated in my entire life.

Down the shame spiral

I'm pleased to say I'm no longer afflicted by the fear of blushing when having to speak in public. Over the years (and many sleepless nights in advance of staff meetings or speaking events), I have learned that the colour of my cheeks isn't what defines me or determines how others perceive me. For the most part, anyway. Nevertheless, despite more than two decades having passed since this experience, I'm still able to recount every minute of it. Transporting myself back to that room, I can feel my body tensing up and the feelings of shame bubbling to the surface.

That's because shame is powerful. It touches the very core of our being. It makes us think negatively about our self – about who we are. In one of the most popular TED talks of all time, self-proclaimed 'shame researcher' Brené Brown speaks of shame as the gremlin that says 'Uh uh. You're not good enough.'[1] When confronted with humiliating situations on a repeated basis, we can start to doubt ourselves, and to think about who we are in very self-deprecating ways. Talking to ourselves in the mirror, shame makes us say things like 'you're a failure' or 'you're worthless'.

Worse still, shame is everywhere. We all experience it. Reading about my humiliating experience may have brought back memories of your own. Maybe it took you as far back as primary school, when you weren't invited to the birthday party of the most popular kid in class. Or perhaps it made you relive more recent incidents, like when you went out for a drink with colleagues and accidentally said something that made everyone laugh at your expense.

The event itself may be small, possibly insignificant to others, but the feeling it dislodges can be huge. A funny look, quiet mumble or sneaky snigger is all it takes to feel out of place. We are often able to get up, brush ourselves off and move on. We may feel embarrassed, but we can shake it off. Other times, however, we can be thrown off balance entirely. We feel so negatively judged and so strongly disconnected that we get dragged down a spiral of self-blame. This is shame. It knocks us off course, harms our self-confidence and undermines our self-esteem. It happens a lot, certainly more than we like to admit.

If the threat of shame is a possibility for everyone, it is a certainty for those living on little. The emotions I felt in that classroom all those years ago were intense and deeply unpleasant, but ultimately they resulted from a relatively inconsequential situation. In that respect, Judy had a point when she said nothing actually happens when blushing. This couldn't be further from the truth for the experience of poverty and the relentless stream of humiliation and shame it brings.

The fact that financial hardship is a fertile breeding ground for shame has long been recognised. As far back as 1776, Adam Smith, the economist we met in Chapter 1, wrote about how day labourers appearing in public without wearing a linen shirt – the dress *du jour* at the time – would bring scorn and shame upon themselves.[2] More recently, Amartya Sen, winner of the Nobel Prize for Economics in 1998 for his ground-breaking work on poverty, referred to shame as constituting the 'absolute core' of deprivation. A lack of resources means being unable to act in accordance with prevailing social norms. It causes ridicule and rejection, and at its extreme, social ostracisation.

Put yourself in Stephanie's shoes. Living in Lancaster and separated from her husband,[3] Stephanie, together with her young daughter, Isla, moved in with her mother. Sadly, her mother was diagnosed with terminal cancer, and Stephanie fell on hard times caring for her and trying to get life back on track. Things were looking better for a while, but then misfortunes started piling up: an accident at work, debilitating injuries, her daughter falling ill and a lack of supply teaching work pushed Stephanie into unprecedented financial insecurity.

She ended up having to sell her house and everything else of value. As the funds in her bank account dwindled, having her card declined while shopping became a frequent occurrence. She started visiting food banks for basic supplies for herself and Isla. Taking out payday loans with high interest rates sent her into a spiral of debt. Eviction notices began arriving through the letter box.

Events like these can have a devastating effect. In addition to the constant worry about how to make ends meet, shame lurks around every corner. The stares of other shoppers when finding yourself unable to pay for your groceries. Passers-by looking away as you're waiting to receive your parcel at the food bank. The constant deluge of negative stereotyping on television and at newspaper stands, with headlines screaming 'benefits cheats' and 'scroungers'. Wherever you go, there's always someone ready to accuse you of stealing taxpayers' money.

In the face of such a torrent of abuse, internalisation seems the only possible outcome. Indeed, Stephanie started blaming herself. She felt her daughter would be better off without her. The combination of ill health, family breakdown and job insecurity – so often part of what pushes people into financial hardship – coupled with incessant negative typecasting about recipients of welfare, sent her into a vicious cycle of shame and self-hatred. To find a way to stop the negative thoughts spinning out of control, Stephanie began harming herself. But the cutting only offered momentary respite, with feelings of failure and defeat all the stronger afterwards.

Shame, and its pernicious effects, is a common denominator in the experience of poverty. A recent report by the Joseph Rowntree Foundation, an anti-poverty organisation in the UK, found shame to be a recurrent theme in conversations about living in hardship, and that it can be just as devastating and debilitating as material deprivation.[4] Shame eats away at self-esteem, denies people their dignity and makes them feel worthless.

The social and psychological costs of living in hardship aren't limited to rich countries either. From Stephanie having her card declined at the supermarket till to a young girl in Uganda attending a wedding ceremony in a second-hand dress and parents in Guinea-Bissau witnessing their children having to ask their neighbours for food, poverty is a universally shameful experience.[5] The world over, living on little is traumatic and painful.

Feeling worthless all the time

The first country to abolish slavery, and independent since 1804, Haiti is one of the poorest countries in the world. Post-colonial abuse of power, political turmoil, economic mismanagement and natural disasters[6] are reasons why more than half of the country's population struggle to get by. Despite sharing the same natural beauty and abundance of sunshine as neighbouring Dominican Republic – a popular holiday destination – the only tourists who visit Haiti are those who leave the confines of their cruise ship for an afternoon of sunbathing on an enclosed stretch of beach.

Meanwhile, most Haitians hardly get to enjoy the pleasures of their own country. The basic necessities required to live a healthy life are only available to a minority. Half the population has to make do without clean drinking water, two out of three people don't have access to proper toilets, and almost no one is able to cook food in a way that doesn't put them at risk of burning themselves or inhaling toxic fumes.[7] Children often carry the brunt of such deep deprivation. In Haiti, one in five children are severely malnourished. One in 12 do not reach the age of five.[8]

Local organisation Fondasyon Kole Zepòl (Fonkoze) has long been working to improve the lives of poor people in Haiti. Founded in 1994 by a group of community activists, the organisation's aim was to democratise the economy by providing financial services to those most marginalised and excluded. This meant a focus on women living in rural areas. Fonkoze originally concentrated on providing small loans to those who were too poor to qualify for financial services from banks or other organisations. But their membership fees for getting access to such loans, however small, proved prohibitive for those with little to no income. A different approach was required, and a new intervention was born: the Chemen

Lavi Miyò (CLM) programme, or 'path to a better life' in Haitian Creole.

The programme reaches out to highly disadvantaged women – often with young children – and provides them with a combination of cash, assets, skills training and coaching. The goal is to set in motion a positive cycle that allows women to continue improving their situation even after the programme comes to an end after 18 months. They receive financial support monthly, along with livestock they can breed to earn money, such as a goat or pig. The programme also trains them in setting up small businesses, advises on how to maintain good health, and provides building materials to upgrade their homes. Case managers regularly visit the women in their homes to check on their progress and offer additional support.

Fonkoze has been running this programme since the early 2000s, having made many adaptations and improvements along the way. Nevertheless, question marks regarding its impact remained. One big unknown was how the CLM programme affects the children of participating women. I was asked to find out.

Together with my Haitian colleagues, I designed a study to examine the intervention's impact on the participants' offspring. Literature on child development told us that maternal mental health is vital for children to grow up in safe, healthy and stimulating homes;[9] hence we made sure to include questions about the women's emotional state of mind. After a few days of working together in Fonkoze's field office, we set off to test whether our questionnaire would work.

The programme was scheduled to be implemented in a number of different communities, some of which were located in the country's Central Plateau, about two hours away from the capital, Port-au-Prince (on a good day, without traffic), via a road that wound along limestone quarries up to the green and lush plateau. On a previous visit, we had to abandon our 4x4 and tackle the last steep and muddy incline to the most remote villages on foot. For the purposes of this trip, however, we chose to go to a more easily accessible area, driving along the banks of the Artibonite river with rolling hills in the background.

Having arrived at our destination, we asked around to see if anyone was willing to work with us. A few women kindly volunteered to help us with our test. We split up into two teams, each with one interviewer and one observer. It's vital for one person to concentrate on asking questions and another on how questions are received and understood. I paired up with my colleague Ed Philippe, and Soimène – one of the women who had volunteered – invited us to come into her yard and sit down in front of her house.

As we were settling in, Soimène told us she was 35 years old and living with her younger brother and her six young children. The compound was empty apart from a few mango peelings and some very scrawny chickens. Catching a glimpse of the kitchen area, I could tell that no fire had been lit or food cooked in the last day or so. Her two youngest children were roaming around looking hungry and undernourished. Soimène herself was friendly but appeared tired and weary.

She listened intently to the questions we asked her and answered carefully, albeit with hesitation. Although I don't speak Haitian Creole and had to rely on limited translation as Ed focused on conducting the interview, Soimène's body language and facial expressions provided much valuable information. Hunched over and slightly slumping, she appeared to want to make herself as small as possible. But when Ed started asking about how she felt about her life and about herself, he hit a nerve.

'Do you think you have any good qualities?' he asked. I noticed a tenseness shoot up Soimène's small frame. She had made little eye contact throughout the conversation, but now her eyes were fully fixed on the floor in front of her. Barely audible, she softly but adamantly declared that she did not have any of these attributes. 'I don't have much to be proud of,' she whispered. Ed and I both nodded, neither of us sure how to respond to her admission.

After a solemn silence, Ed continued the conversation. Soimène shifted in her seat, beginning to feel more comfortable about speaking. The emotional impact of her material deprivation was palpable. 'I feel worthless most of the time,' she confided. 'I don't think I'm any good at all.'

Hope that Soimène's situation might be an exception was soon quashed when the other team members told me they had received similar responses. When we returned to the office, CLM programme staff expressed no surprise at our findings. Having worked with women like Soimène for many years, they knew all too well how deep poverty went hand-in-hand with feelings of shame and mental health struggles.

The data proved the programme staff right.[10] Soimène's responses were mirrored by most of the 750 women we interviewed. Three out of four women suggested they were no good at all. More than 60 per cent said they felt worthless some or most of the time. One in three women confided they felt hopeless all or most of the time. One woman explained, 'When you can't meet his needs you feel ashamed for both you and your child'; and another, 'I sit down to think about how other people take care of their children, and I'm unable to do that. Sometimes I want to kill myself.'

The struggle to make ends meet takes a severe toll on mental health. Although this is nothing new to those who live this reality every day, the wider world has paid little attention to the psychosocial side of getting by on tight budgets. Efforts have mostly focused on establishing the income threshold below which someone qualifies as poor, with limited consideration of the devastating effects on mental well-being or other aspects of emotional life. Conversations about poverty are dominated by stories of material deprivation or lack of money, but rarely do we relate to its devastating psychological effects.

Yet poverty is nothing short of a mental health crisis. Among the women we interviewed in Haiti, we found that one in three suffered from severe mental health issues. In the UK, the poorest fifth of the population are twice as likely to be at risk of developing mental health problems as those on an average income. Half of adults with a debt problem also have a common mental health condition.[11] An article in *Science* magazine, one of the most reputable academic journals, highlights the causal relationship between poverty and mental illness.[12] Global evidence shows that sudden drops in income, volatile earnings and poor housing conditions cause anxiety, stress and shame, sucking people into a spiral of psychological distress.

This causal relationship goes two ways. Not only does poverty undermine mental health, psychological ill-being also plays into poverty. The first relationship is referred to as social causation, asserting that poverty contributes to poor mental health. The reverse relationship is known as social drift. Stress, anxiety or depression make it harder to be proactive or take up opportunities, thereby trapping people in a situation of disadvantage.

With issues of mental health commonly overlooked and ignored, this leaves people in poverty at a double disadvantage: not only are they more likely to experience mental distress, but psychological ill-being also makes it more difficult to improve socioeconomic circumstance. Like the bandwidth tax discussed in the previous chapter, financial hardship places constraints on the brain's cognitive capacities at a time when they're needed the most. It leads to a mutually reinforcing negative cycle, sucking low-income individuals into a loop that's near impossible to escape.

Withdrawal and avoidance

I meet Lee on a sunny spring Saturday afternoon in Milton Keynes, a so-called 'new town' in central England. He's standing just outside the entrance of the city's futuristic-looking shopping centre, holding up copies of *The Big Issue*, a magazine that offers rough sleepers or those with no fixed home an opportunity to make some income. *Big Issue* vendors are a well-known sight in UK cities and towns, sporting their bright red gilets and wide smiles to attract attention from prospective buyers.

As so often happens in England, Lee and I have a little chat about the weather. We comment how lovely it is at this time of year. Lee thinks the sunshine has boosted sales. The sun's positive effect on people's mood means shoppers are less likely to ignore him and more inclined to buy his magazine. By the time I arrived, he had sold almost all his stock. Selling out is a welcome break for Lee. He's currently living in a hostel and saving up to see his daughter. She lives a few hours north and the journey there requires an expensive train ticket. 'And then there's the £12 it costs me to travel here from Cambridge,' he adds.

The price of the round-trip ticket represents roughly half his profit after selling all the magazines. I ask why he goes to the trouble and expense of coming to Milton Keynes. Wouldn't it be easier and cheaper to sell the magazine in Cambridge? 'No way, I can't be seen selling it round where I live. Most of my friends don't know I lost my home, and I don't want them to find out by seeing me on the streets.' Lee is also applying for jobs, and worried that potential employers might recognise him and be prejudiced.

Even though selling *The Big Issue* in Cambridge would enable Lee to buy his train ticket more quickly and see his daughter sooner, these benefits don't weigh up against the shame of exposing his situation to those around him. He doesn't want anyone who knows him to see him as a homeless person. Rather than prioritising what makes most sense financially, he opts for dignity instead. It's not limited headspace or tunnel vision influencing this decision; it's shame.

The inability to live up to expectations – one's own or those imposed by others – can set in motion a spiral of self-criticism and judgement. What's more, shame leads us to take action that isn't necessarily in our best interest. Triggered by the oldest parts of the human brain, it tells us to either flee or fight. It happens instinctively and subconsciously, similar to when experiencing a physical attack.[13] Common strategies for dealing with these strong emotions can include blaming others, or sometimes becoming aggressive. Most often they cause sufferers to withdraw from everyday life. For those already struggling to make ends meet, this coping mechanism entrenches their hardship even further.[14]

The situation of farmers in India shows just how shame reinforces the poverty trap.[15] Repeated crop failures and drops in produce prices have made financial crisis part of everyday life. Defaulting on debt repayments, particularly when having borrowed money from relatives or friends, and being harassed in public by aggressive moneylenders are just two situations that elicit deep humiliation. Lack of clean clothing and the inability to participate in social events in accordance with social mores are also frequent triggers for shame.

Some farmers manage to withstand these attacks on their mental well-being. They adopt positive strategies, such as finding other sources of income – growing different crops, starting a small business or learning new skills. Intra-family solidarity and family identity – the 'we-self' – also acts as a buffer against internalising financial hardship as an individual failure.

Nevertheless, many farmers do blame themselves and adopt destructive behaviours to take the pressure off. Some resort to excessive alcohol consumption, with intoxication allowing for an escape from anxiety and negative feelings. In other cases, suicide is seen as the only way out. In fact, suicide rates among farmers in India rose at an alarming rate in the early 2000s, with increased financial strain and cycles of indebtedness identified as one of the leading causes.[16]

Thousands of miles to the west of India, new mothers and mothers-to-be in Gabon, a country in Central Africa, are also no strangers to poverty-induced shame, with far-reaching consequences.

At the turn of the century, fewer than one in five infants in Gabon had received all recommended immunisations for easily preventable illnesses such as diphtheria and typhoid.[17] Vaccinations for children in Gabon are free, and health officials had long been wondering why uptake was so slow. The answer: avoidance.

Research found that pejorative and debasing treatment at health facilities proved a key reason for mothers to drop out of the vaccination programme. Health care staff are more likely to treat women in a derogatory manner when babies look scruffy or underfed. Antenatal treatment and getting newborns immunised comes with disapproving tut-tutting, rolling of eyes or judgemental finger-pointing. If mothers had missed previous rounds of inoculation, they were told off for not taking care of their children properly. In the words of a 30-year-old mother of five children, 'If you arrive at the mother and child care clinic and the baby is not in a good condition, the nurses inevitably confront you because of the baby. That makes you feel ashamed. You cannot bring a baby like that.' Forgoing health care for their infants was the only way for women to prevent the humiliation they would inevitably face.

Poverty-induced shame is a common issue in low take-up of health services across the world. Having to see a doctor in dirty clothing or showing signs of low income gives rise to a sense of failure, which is only exacerbated if treated in a judgemental or disparaging manner. Being asked to explain again and again why your children aren't well-nourished while going hungry yourself and being judged as a bad parent to boot is like rubbing salt in an open wound. No wonder some choose to miss out on health care altogether, even though it's free. The cost of losing one's dignity is far higher.

Can shame be good?

Despite shame's negative effects, it has long been used to promote socially desirable behaviour. It can serve as an incentive to stay in step, and to conform to social norms and values. Some argue that shame is more effective for regulating behaviour than rules or punitive action ever will be. In referring to public humiliation of perpetrators of sexual assault following the #MeToo movement, historian Rutger Bregman suggests that the prospect of being publicly outed will reduce the risk of such assaults happening in future.[18] Others maintain that shame serves to hold government and large corporations accountable for their actions. In her book *Is Shame Necessary?*, environmental scientist Jennifer Jacquet argues that it can be an effective tool to tackle large collective problems such as climate change and environmental degradation.[19]

Yet directing shame at people in poverty as a tactic to change their situation comes with considerable risk.

Picture this. You live in a house without the luxury of its own bathroom. There's not even a toilet. Whenever you have to relieve yourself, you're resigned to finding a quiet spot behind some bushes in a field or in the corner of a dark alleyway. When you're done, there is nowhere to wash your hands, let alone soap to get rid of the germs. If you think this is bad, imagine how instead of your excrement being transported away out of sight through an underground sewage system, you watch it float through the local stream for everyone to see.

This is everyday reality for millions around the world. In many poorer countries, inadequate hygiene is one of the leading causes of illness and death.[20] Almost one in ten of the world's population practises open defecation.[21] Simply put, about 850 million people pee and poo in fields, bushes or open water.[22]

Cue the Community-Led Total Sanitation (CLTS) initiative. This development programme was first implemented in Bangladesh in 1999, representing a radical departure from top-down and expensive interventions that focused on building high-standard latrines, which would then not be used or fall into disrepair. Instead of providing the sanitary 'hardware', CLTS supports local communities to conduct their own analysis of open defecation and what is needed to become 'open defecation free'.[23]

Public humiliation is central to the CLTS approach. The approach deliberately uses shame as an incentive for behaviour change. During the 'walk of shame' – as it is called in Zambia – community groups walk through their villages and are encouraged to spend as much time as possible standing around in places where people defecate in the open. As you can imagine, the look and smell are immensely uncomfortable, and it is highly humiliating knowing that some of the excrement is yours.

This so-called 'triggering process' is continued by bringing faeces back into the village to showcase how it contaminates food, with attendees watching how flies move between poop and food. It brings the health risks of open defecation up close and personal. The community then forms a sanitation committee responsible for developing plans and taking action to eliminate open defecation.

One of the main activities of such committees is to check whether community members do indeed abstain from open defecation. This kind of 'poop policing' can involve calling out individuals on where they empty their bowels, sometimes by putting up lists of those who break the rules. There have even been examples of photos of people relieving themselves out in the open displayed on communal noticeboards.

This paparazzi-style of policing is not encouraged or condoned by CLTS. Still, the fact that some communities adopt this way of working is a reflection of the risks when opening the door to public shaming as a tool for changing behaviour. Those working on CLTS have pointed to the distinction between good and bad shame, with bad shame (such as distributing photos of those 'caught in the act') to be firmly avoided. Good shame, they argue, allows individuals to reflect on their practices, reach a level of self-realisation and take responsibility for avoiding open defecation.[24] Strong facilitation is key to ensuring that the approach triggers good shame as opposed to bad shame.

This argument doesn't convince everyone. Researchers from the University of Wollongong in Australia looked at CLTS in Cambodia[25] and concluded that the programme's use of shame is problematic. It does not have adequate mechanisms in place to avoid bad shame, in addition, the use of shame can antagonise local communities and stop them from engaging with efforts to improve sanitation in the first place.[26] This represents the worst of both worlds: people are subjected to shame and there isn't even anything to show for it. As a result, in Cambodia, local CLTS facilitators actually reduced the reliance on shame as they considered it inappropriate and offensive.

An additional reason for why shame is unlikely to promote positive outcomes is that it tends to reinforce existing social inequalities. Poorer families are least able to avoid open defecation or comply with requirements put in place by sanitation committees, such as building latrines. Singling out such families and subjecting them to public humiliation only adds to their vulnerability and leaves them ostracised. In Bangladesh, CLTS was successful in changing social norms about sanitation in wealthier segments of the community, rendering open defecation unacceptable among those who were able to afford alternatives. The flipside of this success was poorer families, who were unable to use anything else but open spaces, being humiliated and socially rejected.[27]

What we learn from this unappetising example is just how unappealing shame is as a tactic for promoting positive change, especially for those already at the margins of society. Shame may drive people towards desired behaviour, yet the consequences are unethical at best and entirely counterproductive at worst.

Stigma as a conduit for shame

We cannot discuss shame without also discussing stigma. Shame and stigma are inextricably intertwined in the experiences of social exclusion, discrimination and dehumanisation. While shame is about internalised beliefs of worthlessness, we can think of stigma as the mechanism through which feelings of shame are shaped. Consider the sanitation example above: stigma is the process of publicly humiliating people, and shame is the actual emotion it triggers.

Back in the 1960s, sociologist Erving Goffman[28] wrote one of the most widely used texts on stigma. He theorised that stigma follows a personal characteristic that deviates from what is accepted as 'normal' and somehow makes individuals less human. Having a physical disability, a learning difficulty or a skin condition are just a few examples of signs that suggest someone is 'different'. Responses can be subtle, such as avoiding eye contact; or overt, such as ostracising people or downright humiliating them. Think of refusal to shake hands with someone who is HIV-positive, or jokes about those struggling with obesity.

Despite its continued influence on how we think about stigma, Goffman's theory is too limited. It focuses on the individual, and the extent to which they are able to live up to social expectations. It does not, however, pay attention to the wider political and societal powers that produce stigma. After all, who decides what is socially acceptable?

Financial hardship may be widespread, but it certainly isn't socially acceptable. It is shrouded in popular myths that those who experience it are somehow deficient, lazy or inept. These ideas do not fall from the sky; they represent carefully crafted narratives that are reproduced by those with voice and power. Popular media, politicians and big business are keen to feed the idea that deprivation is due to lack of effort, as opposed to a shortage of well-paid jobs and affordable public services. Lack of money is framed as a personal fault and down to individual deficiency, rather than grounded in society's economic, social and political structures. And it leads to some pretty horrific forms of stigmatisation.

No example illustrates this more clearly than the practice of 'lunch shaming' in the US. I first came across this a few years ago when starting my research into linkages between poverty and shame, and I simply could not believe what I read. Lunch shaming consists of physically marking children by stamping their arms when there are insufficient funds in their school lunch accounts. The policy is justified by the argument that emails, letters or other forms of communication with parents are ineffective.[29] Instead, branding children with temporary tattoos saying 'lunch' or 'lunch money' is impossible to ignore and compels parents to pay up.

This practice of deliberately objectifying and dehumanising children started popping up after the Healthy Hunger-Free Kids Act was passed in 2010. The act's main purpose is to combat childhood obesity by setting nutrition standards for school meals. It also requires school districts to have clear policies on how they address school meal debt, making sure that adequate funding is available to provide quality school meals. However, no clear guidelines were given as to how schools should go about doing this, and the practice of lunch shaming rose to prominence.[30]

At one point, more than three quarters of all school districts employed some form of physically marking children for school meal debt. There has been considerable pushback against it, and 2019 saw the introduction of the No Shame at School Act, which seeks to ban the stigmatisation and shaming of children over school meal debt. Nevertheless, the fact that a policy that subjects children to a practice not unlike the penal tattooing of prisoners and slaves as far back as Ancient Greek times is so widely implemented in this day and age really baffled me.

I was naïve.

According to sociologist Imogen Tyler, stigma is never accidental or unintentional.[31] Instead, it's an exercise of power that is meticulously planned and carefully orchestrated. It greases the cogs in the machinery of inequality, used by governments to maintain social hierarchies and push back anyone who challenges the status quo. Asking how it is possible that so many people in the UK were willing to accept a decade of crippling austerity after the financial crisis in 2008, Tyler found that the deliberate use of stigma ensured the wider public would not only accept austerity but come to see it as the only way forward. The UK government actively shaped and pushed the message that rolling back the welfare state would both balance the books and counter the moral depletion in society. Shaming and blaming tactics were expressly used to rationalise policies that undermined the lives of those already struggling. Pitting the 'honest taxpayer' against the 'dependent welfare claimant' was key to the success of the austerity project, making dire poverty and widespread hardship acceptable in one of the richest countries in the world.

Journalist Mary O'Hara drew similar conclusions when I interviewed her for my podcast.[32] Stigma has always been used as a tool for maintaining the status quo in favour of those in power, she explained, and against those who do not fit their main narrative. 'You can go back in history in almost every country, and the power structures in the countries tend to exist because … a culture suggests that those people who aren't further up the hierarchy must be somehow ineffective or defective as individuals.' The rise of neoliberalism after the Second World War 'turbocharged' this narrative. Wealth creation was attributed to hard work and talent, while those living on little were considered in charge of, and therefore demonised for, their own misfortune.

One might argue that stigma associated with financial hardship is more likely to emerge in contexts with low prevalence of poverty. In richer countries where poor people present a minority, it is easier to think of 'them' versus 'us'. But poverty-related stigma can be found across the globe, including in places where deprivation is more common. When I interviewed Diana Skelton from anti-poverty organisation ATD Fourth World, she said, 'When you're in poverty … you grow up always hearing your family, your parents, your ancestors spoken about like they're less than nothing. And it really shapes how you see your own future and how you relate to people.'[33] It doesn't matter whether making ends meet is a struggle for a few or a daily reality for many, stigma is a common denominator.

Tapping into our own experiences of shame and humiliation can help us relate to poverty's pernicious effects on mental health. A deeper consideration of the wider structures that have to be navigated and manoeuvred when living on little helps us realise that it isn't financial insecurity alone that causes poverty's mental health crisis. It's the interaction between deprivation and hardship and nasty narratives, deriding discourse and punitive policies that pushes people into a cycle of shame and self-blame.

Engendered through everyday interactions and enacted through policies with stigma as part of its fabric inequality, those experiencing financial hardship are left to internalise failure and worthlessness. Poverty is both a cause and a consequence of mental illness. With policies aiming to reduce poverty often devoid of empathy, they contribute to rather than break this vicious cycle. As long as we fail to see the shame and stigma of the struggle to make ends meet, efforts to tackle hardship and improve the lives of Stephanie, Soimène, Lee and so many others will come to little.

4

ASPIRING TO
BRIGHTER FUTURES

'What's your dream? What would you like to do when you're older?'

I wait for my Ethiopian colleague to translate the question. Abrehet nods before looking me straight in the eye to deliver her answer. I might not understand the words, but her body speaks volumes.

'She wants to be an engineer,' says my colleague. Abrehet is still looking at me, her eyes steely with determination.

I'm in Tigray, Ethiopia's most northern state. Home to magnificent centuries-old churches carved into cliffs and escarpment edges, some only accessible by climbing across sheer rock faces, the region is steeped in history. Legend has it that the Queen of Sheba was from here – a source of great pride for Ethiopians. No wonder Tigray is considered the cradle of Ethiopian civilisation. Sadly, the region and its people have seen more than their fair share of conflict and crises. In the mid 1980s, the area was the epicentre of one of the worst famines in recent history, a catastrophe that motivated Bob Geldof to organise the famed Live Aid benefit concerts in July 1985.

'Why an engineer? Why not something else?' I ask. My colleague translates again.

'There's so much poverty in my village. It can't be reached by car. We need people to construct roads.'

I see what she means. Nestled at the top of Africa's Great Rift Valley, Tigray's mountainous and rugged terrain isn't easy to navigate. Much of our journey here was spent moving heavy rocks out of the way of our car so we could traverse the hilly landscape. It made for an adventurous trip, but obviously that's not what anyone is looking for. For the residents of this remote community, it's detrimental to their economic opportunities and social development. For children like Abrehet, it's yet another barrier to them realising their dreams.

I'm in Tigray to learn about what those dreams are, and how children and their families try to make them happen. Sitting in front of her small, square brick house, I ask Abrehet if she can tell us more about her plans. She speaks with passion and resolve. She may only be 16 years old, but she has thought this through very carefully.

Abrehet says she likes studying. She's currently in secondary school, with national exams just around the corner. After passing those, she wants to continue her studies at a vocational college in a nearby town. She knows her chosen path won't be without challenges. She tells us that ever since her parents split up and her mother left the house, she's had to do all the tasks that are usually left to women. Cooking, fetching water, washing, looking after the chickens and rearing the goats roaming their little compound. In fact, she was sweeping the floor when we approached her house. All these tasks take precious time away from studying, especially as Abrehet has no siblings.

'My life is good and bad. It's good because I go to school. It's bad because when I return from school, I have to work hard at home.'

She confides that her relationship with her father is tense. I'm not surprised. We spoke with him before sitting down with Abrehet. He told us he's not keen on her going to vocational school. Once the exams are over, he would like her to work at home, on the farm. It's the path taken by many other children in this community. If she were to go to vocational school, there wouldn't be anyone to help him out, never mind the practical difficulties and cost of pursuing education in another town.

But staying at home isn't what Abrehet wants. Neither does she wish to follow in the footsteps of so many other young women in her village, who travel to Saudi Arabia to work as domestic servants. We've heard stories of girls earning good money while living with wealthy Saudis and sending home cash on a regular basis. No wonder this is an attractive option for so many. But there are risks too, with girls as young as 13 relying on smugglers to make the perilous journey across deserts and through war-torn Yemen.[1] Rape and torture are the rule rather than the exception, and many of the girls are treated horribly when do they finally make it to their destination.

Abrehet has no desire to go down this path and put herself at risk of abuse by working as a maid in a far-off land. She has her own imagined future. Her aspiration is to contribute to the development of her community. To create opportunities for her own future. To make a difference to her family, friends and neighbours. It won't be easy, but she is ready for the challenge.

Window of aspirations

What vision did you have for yourself growing up? To be a teacher, lawyer or firefighter? To become a doctor, a carpenter or an actor, maybe?

The things we dream of and aim for aren't plucked from thin air. The future we imagine for ourselves is based on our personal experiences and what we see around us. Think back to your own childhood dreams. Chances are you modelled your ambition on what you were exposed to. Jobs held by uncles, aunts and neighbours. Occupations portrayed in books, stories or history classes. Glamorous careers broadcast on television and in movies. They hold up illustrations of what is possible, an idea of what may lie ahead.

The range of examples we tap into for moulding our aims for the future is what some scholars have referred to as the aspirations window,[2] or our cognitive window.[3] When I interviewed economist Katrina Kosec for my podcast, she described it as 'the people and experiences that are at our fingertips'.[4] It's those individuals and their achievements from which we draw inspiration. They constitute our frame of reference, and form the go-to set of options that shape our ambitions.

The aspirational shifts and turns during my own childhood give an indication of just how socially determined our ambitions are. Inspired by the role models I was exposed to, either in real life or through media and television, visions of my future self veered from being a desk-bound office manager to working as a lab-based biologist and being admired as a catwalk-strutting model.

My goals in life were framed against the backdrop of a wide scope of educational and occupational prospects open to me as a middle-class teenager, and an active push by the Dutch government to increase women's participation in the labour market. More than 30 years on, I still recall the slogan from the public awareness campaign: *'Een slimme meid is op haar toekomst voorbereid'*, which roughly translates into the more clunky 'A clever girl is prepared to take on her own future'. No doubt this boost for women to become economically independent, combined with many more opportunities available to me than to the generations of women before me, helped me to push back against prevailing societal understandings of what success looked like for a young woman.

Around the same time, thousands of miles east of the Dutch town where I grew up, the power of female representation in raising aspirations among women and girls became evident on a much larger scale.

In the 1990s in West Bengal, a state in eastern India, only 6 per cent of villages had a female councillor.[5] In 1998, a gender quota was introduced, stipulating that one third of local village councils had to have a female chief councillor. As a result, some councils suddenly had female leaders. Other villages, however, retained their male leaders. Researchers from Northwestern University in the US exploited this natural experiment to investigate whether the rapid rise in female leadership had an impact on girls' aspirations.[6]

The academic team interviewed thousands of young people and their parents, in both villages with the old male leadership models and those led by female councillors. Findings showed that in villages with female councillors, girls' aspirations were considerably higher. Girls were more likely to hold ambitions beyond being a housewife. They rejected the suggestion that their parents-in-law should decide their occupation. And they wanted jobs that required an education. It didn't stop there. Parents also held greater ambitions for their daughters compared to villages with the traditional male leadership. Mothers especially wanted their daughters to have a greater say in their own destiny.

From a scientific point of view, these findings aren't necessarily surprising. Psychologists have long studied our human tendency to observe and model our behaviour on that of others. In the 1960s, psychologist Albert Bandura developed his influential 'social learning theory'. It cemented the understanding that context is crucial in shaping our view of the world and how we act within it. What we see happening around us – where we live, who we interact with, what role models we are exposed to – shapes what we aim for in the future. It provides a framing of what we consider possible to achieve in our own lives, and thereby acts as a calibrator for our imagined futures. In the same way as my younger self was influenced by an awareness campaign portraying young women taking up careers as health professionals or officers in the armed services, girls in West Bengal were inspired by the women leading their village councils.

The flipside of this story is that if we grow up with limited exposure to socioeconomic achievement and opportunity, our aspirations window will be smaller. Our position on the income distribution scale as well as many other factors that play into our wealth profile – like gender, class, race and caste, to name a few – make a big difference in terms of the examples of success that are available to us, and in turn to the futures we imagine for ourselves. Richer people have a much wider range of possibilities and a larger network for them to tap into, and are therefore more likely to have a broader set of objectives for their lives. As they watch others' achievements, they also feel more affirmed in the capacity to reach their own goals. For the rich, success is the norm, and this sets the standard for their own lives.

For the poor, the picture looks very different.

'If you don't see yourself out there, it's hard to believe you can belong.'

Mahsuda Snaith, a British Bangladeshi child, was born and raised by her single mum on a social housing council estate in Leicester.[7] She knew from a young age what she wanted to do in life. 'I decided when I was eight years old that I'd be a writer. That's the type of child I was.' But when she went to secondary school in a more affluent area of town, she quickly learned that there were different views of children who grew up on council estates. 'There was a different expectation of what you would do with your life.' Becoming a writer no longer seemed like a suitable option. Becoming a hairdresser or shopkeeper might be more appropriate. 'I was suddenly aware my experience wasn't reflected.'

Not seeing people like herself represented in the literary world and unable to shake the expectation that she should get a 'proper job'. Mahsuda found work as a primary school teacher. 'I was miserable. I wasn't doing the thing that I absolutely loved doing.' It wasn't until quite a few years later that she decided to listen to her 'inner child' and pursue her dream. She is now an award-winning author.

Mahsuda bucked the trend. So did Abrehet, with her impassioned vision and plan to work as an engineer for the betterment of her community.

Imagining a future that defies societal expectation and challenges the norm and holding on to that vision from childhood into adulthood is unusual. The environment that we grow up in is vital for shaping our orientation towards the future. If we're raised in a family where no one has gone to college, live in an area without schools or are confronted with the suggestion that certain career choices are unavailable to us, we're less likely to consider this a possibility for ourselves. As a director of the OECD intergovernmental organisation put it: 'You can't be what you can't see.'[8]

Seeing beyond life's limitations

According to the *Cambridge Dictionary*, an aspiration is 'something that you hope to achieve'.[9] Aspirations are our aims, goals and objectives in life. They are the difference between where we currently stand and where we want to go. They give us meaning and purpose; they motivate and drive us.

We hold aspirations across many domains of our lives. Like Abrehet, we may have the ambition to pursue education and learn a certain skill. We might strive to earn lots of money, or establish a level of financial security that allows the enjoyment of life's pleasures and offers a comfortable cushion in case anything goes awry. We could be driven by a desire to have many friends, be socially connected and cultivate meaningful relationships. It might be all those things combined. Whether it's in the realm of education, pursuing a career, obtaining wealth or fostering our social lives, aspirations are about growth and development.

A vital component of aspirations is the belief that we ourselves have the power to make change happen. Aspirations aren't about mere wishful thinking. Instead, they carry a sense of optimism that moves us to behave in ways that help us achieve our goals.[10] As the dictionary definition points out, hope is an inextricable part of aspiration. Yet there's a difference between hoping you'll win the lottery and hoping your new business will do well and earn you good money. In the former case, success is left to chance. In the latter, personal action is key to converting hope into an actual outcome. It's for that reason that aspirations inspire future-oriented behaviour, a willingness to move forward.

Feeling that our own behaviour can influence where we get to in life doesn't necessarily mean that we expect our dreams to become reality. Ambitions may be within reach, or they might be outside the realm of what is possible.[11] Dreaming big without becoming bogged down by the likelihood of such aspirations becoming reality can be especially powerful for children. Growing up to train and find a job as a teacher or police officer is a realistic aim for a fair share of the population. Making it as an astronaut, successful singer or competitive athlete is the privilege of a select few. But even if dreams for the future aren't necessarily tenable, they can still positively influence children's outlook on life.

About a decade ago, I ran a research project on child poverty. Instead of relying on statistics, we wanted to know how children themselves felt about their lives and what their expectations were for the future. It was as part of this work that Abrehet told me about her engineering aspirations.

In addition to Ethiopia, the research also took me to Burundi and Vietnam. In all three countries the research teams asked children about their dreams. What did they want to be when they grew up? Without fail, regardless of where we were, little boys would tell us they wanted to be famous footballers. At the time, Robin van Persie and Ronaldo were frequently mentioned role models. The desire to become a high-flying football player is an optimistic but unattainable dream for thousands of children around the world. Even more so for those playing footie in the dirt far away from where they might be scouted. Yet in remote villages where expensive generators and makeshift solar panels are the only sources of electricity, football manages to inspire young generations no less.

It's the motivating quality of aspirations that has led scientists to ask whether holding ambition for the future can also help to improve one's life in the present. If being aspirational puts a spring in our step and makes us allocate time and effort to realising our aims, can it also make us more successful? What is the actual power of aspirations?

Cue Phiona. Ten years old, she lives with her mother and younger siblings in Katwe, a slum in Uganda's capital, Kampala. She spends most of her days doing household chores and looking after her baby brother. There's no money for her to go to school, and the only way to find distraction from her daily tasks is to roam the narrow alleyways of her neighbourhood. She dreams of a better life, but her sister tells her she shouldn't bother. It will only leave her disappointed.

One morning during another of her neighbourhood wanders, Phiona's attention is drawn to a ramshackle building squished between Katwe's many shacks and makeshift houses. She hears excited voices. Children are chattering and laughing. Curious, she steps onto the concrete plinth and peeks through the wooden slats. Squinting to get a better view, she watches how boxes of strangely shaped white and black ornaments are upturned over tables with equally odd-looking black and white chequered boards.

Phiona's curious peeks don't go unnoticed. 'Young girl, come inside,' calls a man from within. This, he tells her, is chess. Would she like to play? She is directed towards one of the wobbly tables and sits down. It's the start of a new world opening up.

Phiona turns out to be a quick learner. Before long, she is beating the other children in her neighbourhood. Despite never having set foot in a classroom, she enters school tournaments. Opponents give her a tough time for being from a poor area, but her talent shines through regardless. Her coach tells her she could become the best in Uganda. And she does. Driven by passion and perseverance, she learns how to read and write, gets into a top school, and goes on to compete in international competitions. Her success in the game comes with monetary reward. Becoming a chess champion brings her what she always dreamed of: an escape from the life of hardship for her and her family.

Some of you might recognise Phiona's story as the plotline of *Queen of Katwe*. Released in 2016, it's a film that aims to inspire and lift the spirits. Aspirations are at the heart of the narrative. The trailer opens with a quote from Ellen Johnson Sirleaf, former president of Liberia: 'The size of your dreams must always exceed your current capacity to achieve them.' When Phiona is unsure about her chosen path, coach Robert tells her, 'You belong where you believe you belong.' The moral of the story is: dream big, believe in yourself, and everything is possible.

Queen of Katwe is an inspirational movie indeed, not least because it's based on real events. The message is simple but compelling: growing up in hardship doesn't mean you're destined for a life on the fringes. Change is possible. It's the perfect story to ignite the spark of aspiration, especially among teenage girls like Phiona. If she can beat the odds, so can they.

It's this line of reasoning that inspired researchers from the University of Oxford to set up an experiment to put the power of aspirations to the test.[12] Could Phiona serve as a role model for young boys and girls, instil a positive attitude and inspire them to study harder and improve their performance in school?

The research team went to Kampala, including the Katwe neighbourhood, and recruited 1,500 secondary school students for their study. They then divided them into two groups. One group was shown *Queen of Katwe*. Children in the other group watched *Miss Peregrine's Home for Peculiar Children*, a fantasy film about a children's home in the UK. The researchers timed the showings carefully, making sure the children were exposed to either Phiona's inspirational story or a largely unrelatable imaginary tale only a few weeks ahead of sitting their national exams. Once the results were in, they compared students' performances.

The findings didn't disappoint. Students who had watched *Queen of Katwe* did noticeably better than their peers. They scored higher on their maths tests than those who had watched the other movie. They were also less likely to fail their exams compared to pupils who had been shown the fantasy movie. Watching *Queen of Katwe* even improved the chances of getting a place at a public university. Many of these impacts were largest for girls. The study's findings led the researchers to conclude that movie role models can be one way of improving educational attainment for secondary school students.

Around the world, including in richer countries like the UK, young people do better when they aspire to a brighter future. This is especially true for schooling. If children in their early years of schooling think they will continue their education, they are significantly more likely to do so. Test scores are higher, even after accounting for family background and other factors.[13] In the US, it was found that educational ambitions translate into higher chances of graduating from high school, and higher incomes in adulthood.[14]

The idea that anything is possible, that you can live your dream regardless of background or upbringing, is a powerful motivator. But how do aspirations work their magic? Drawing on Katrina Kosec's words once more: 'Individuals with high aspirations, we should think of them as holding beliefs and preferences that are minimising restrictive features of their environment and really focusing on possibilities. Keeping their eyes on the prize, so to speak, thinking about what they would like to obtain.'[15]

Kosec also draws this conclusion from her own work in rural Pakistan. She found that families who had set clear goals for themselves and were committed to achieving them were more financially secure. They were more savvy in identifying savings opportunities that rewarded them with higher interest rates. Aspirational families were also more likely to branch out into multiple income-generating opportunities.[16] As most money-making activities are informal and unpredictable, this type of income diversification is a smart strategy to improve economic health. Aspirations can help direct energy and attention to behaviour that can help to achieve goals, including escaping economic hardship and promoting social mobility.

A logical extension of this line of thinking is that helping individuals to be more ambitious can inspire them to take positive action and achieve more in life. If it's lack of ambition that feeds into a cycle of aiming too low, could a push towards thinking out of the box and raising expectations make a difference?

It's certainly a popular idea. Policymakers and politicians increasingly latch on to aspirations as a panacea to reduce poverty and tackle inequality. In the UK, successive prime ministers from across the political divide have pointed to the need to raise young people's aspirations to promote social mobility. In 2007, Gordon Brown said, 'The greater failure is not the child who doesn't reach the stars, but the child who has no stars that they feel they are reaching for.'[17] Six years later, David Cameron commented that 'You've got to get out there and find people, win them over, get them to raise aspirations, get them to think they can get all the way to the top.'[18]

The world over, we see initiatives that aim to raise aspirations, many of which are targeted at young people. And with some success. In Italy, a tutoring and career counselling programme helped to raise educational aspirations among teenage immigrants and led to them doing better in school.[19] Comparable programmes in places like Portugal and the United States had very similar effects: combinations of academic tutoring and mentoring that focused on aspects of self-confidence and motivation reduced dropout and increased the likelihood that students would choose to stay in education after completing secondary school, including opting for more demanding courses.

Interventions that increase exposure to role models can also boost aspirations and, in turn, improve outcomes. Watching Phiona become a chess champion in *Queen of Katwe* helped girls in Kampala's slum areas to do better in school. A similar experiment with farmers in Ethiopia, who were shown inspirational videos of villagers setting goals and achieving them through careful planning and hard work, also found increased aspirations. This in turn led to higher savings and investment in children's education.[20]

All these examples try to achieve a shift in mindset, also sometimes referred to as the 'mental model'. They bring new possibilities into view, coupled with the belief that one's own actions can transform possibility into reality: 'If they can do, so can I.' Focus shifts from planning for today and tomorrow to strategising for the future. Having a positive outlook increases the likelihood that life will unfold itself in bigger and better ways, turning a negative cycle between low aspirations and muted outcomes into a positively reinforcing one.

The curse of frustrated aspirations

For all the promise that aspirations hold, their potential also has clear limits.

As much as having a positive outlook on life can drive positive action, it can't take away the structural barriers that prevent dreams from becoming reality. Income, gender, race, class – they are decisive factors in how far individuals can reach for the stars. In the UK, men and women from ethnic minority, and often disadvantaged, backgrounds have fewer chances to move up the social ladder, despite doing much better in education compared to their white British peers.[21] In Ethiopia, India, Peru and Vietnam, aspirations help children beat the odds if they go hand-in-hand with positive family or community environments that support them in their endeavours.[22]

Enthusiasm about the power of aspirations risks a blindness to the reality that even if disadvantaged youngsters or low-income adults imagine alternative futures for themselves, they are unlikely to achieve them due to barriers beyond their control. Young girls might feel inspired watching *Queen of Katwe*, but if the quality of education they receive is low, or lack of electricity in their home stops them from studying at night, their maths scores won't improve. Abrehet in Ethiopia has enthusiastic plans to become an engineer, but without funds to pay for her travel and accommodation to allow her to go to school away from home, she won't achieve her goal no matter how hard she tries.

Not only does an overemphasis on increasing aspirations place undue responsibility on the individual for improving their situation, it also risks being counterproductive. Too big a divide between our situation at present and where we desire to be in future stifles efforts rather than encouraging them. Unless we're very young and still able to dream big unencumbered – about starring in a Hollywood blockbuster or scoring a goal in the Premier League – if the space between what we want to achieve and the likelihood of getting there looks like it can never be overcome, we get discouraged. Set the bar too high and there's a backlash. Instead of striving for more, we get bogged down by the realisation that our future goals are unattainable. It can lead to what some economists have called 'frustrated aspirations'.[23]

The curse of frustrated aspirations might never have been as pertinent as it is for the Zoomers, or Generation Z. Those born between the mid to late 1990s and the early 2010s are faced with an enormous schism between the norms of a perfect life as portrayed by popular and social media and the reality of the job market and socioeconomic opportunities. Those economic and social realities stop people from striving for more. It's all well and good to dream big, but if reality only allows for tapping into a narrow range of possibilities, well, what's the point?

In 2021, I spoke to Thomas Rochow, another guest on my podcast.[24] As a researcher at the University of Glasgow, he had just spent several years analysing data about aspirations of young people in the UK. He looked at those who had been or were still in receipt of welfare at the time they were interviewed, and so would have been struggling to make ends meet. The findings of his research were rather depressing. He found that millennials didn't have many grand plans or ambitions for their future. They didn't talk about what job they wanted to do, what exciting things they wanted to spend their time on or outrageous goals they wished to achieve. Their hopes were much more muted. A decent job, secure housing, a reliable flow of income. These were the desires at the top of the list of aspirations for most British 20-somethings in the study.

Thomas reflected on some of the answers that the young people had provided in response to questions about what they wanted to achieve in the upcoming year. Jamie, a 21-year-old from London, for example, was working towards having a job, any job. That was the full extent of his ambition. Similarly, 25-year-old Maria from Bath expressed the hope 'to be working somewhere that is maybe not necessarily enjoyable but like just nice. Nothing bad happening, nothing overly stressful. Just to have a stable place to work and stable accommodation.'

These modest life goals are a result of the lack of opportunities in modern-day Britain, explained Thomas. Zero-hour contracts are now more rule than exception for many in the workforce. Wages from one job no longer suffice to pay the bills. Finding an affordable place to live is a tall order, never mind getting on the property ladder. Generations Y and Z have become 'generation rent'. It's not hard to see how the prospect of spending adult life toiling away to merely make ends meet grates with ambitious plans to break the mould.

The Prince's Trust – a charity for young people in the UK – reported that throughout the pandemic, half of 16-to-25-year-olds believed it was impossible to achieve their future goals. As many as one in three young people had lost hope in the future.[25] The way in which lack of opportunities feeds into low aspirations easily turns into a self-fulfilling prophecy. Aspirations are greater when we believe in our own capabilities, and when we believe that we have some control over our lives' trajectories. The more the opposite is proven, the more bogged down we become by the realities of life around us. Optimism is replaced by more pessimistic views of possibilities and opportunities.

Higher inequality inevitably adds fuel to the fire. After all, the larger the gap between the haves and have-nots, the more likely it is that life goals based on wealthier role models or examples of success will be unattainable for individuals at the lower end of the wealth distribution.

When I interviewed political scientist Cecilia Mo,[26] she explained that even if the standard of living for those on lower incomes rises, high inequality means the gap between them and the rich, with their coveted lifestyles, remains impossible to overcome. This leads to discontent and can drive self-defeating behaviour.

If we lose the sense of agency and the feeling that our actions help us to achieve a desired outcome – and especially an outcome for which we see no alternative – positivity shifts into negative emotions and action. Feelings of discouragement and demotivation may lead to disengagement, pulling us away from the positive behaviour that aspirations were supposed to inspire in the first place. This can also lead to risky strategies that leave people worse off, explained Cecilia, such as participating in lotteries or going to a casino to gamble. People are aware that the odds aren't in their favour and that they're at risk of losing a lot of money. But without a viable alternative route to achieve their goal, they're willing to take their chances. Often with devastating consequences.

Whose aspirations count?

'What makes a good job good?'

It's a question that Barack Obama asks in the 2023 Netflix documentary *Working: What We Do All Day*. Narrated by the former US President, it explores the role that work plays in our lives, and how portrayals and expectations of what constitutes gainful employment have changed over time.

American television series in the 1970s and early 80s often featured working-class families making light of their many trials and tribulations. Who doesn't know Al Bundy, the bread-winner and protagonist in the well-known sitcom *Married with Children*? Despite being a grumpy and somewhat miserable character, he works as a salesman in the local mall enticing customers to buy shoes. In the iconic series *Happy Days*, father Howard runs a hardware store, while in the classic 1970s show *All in the Family*, patriarch Archie is a World War II veteran working in the docks by day and driving a taxi by night.

These shows projected examples of families who had to work hard to keep their heads above water, with worries about money a recurrent theme, into millions of living rooms in the US and the world over on a weekly basis. They reflected a model of family life that many could relate to. They didn't merely paint a picture of the average American life in a humorous way. They also paid tribute to hard and honest graft, and to earning wages that could support the worker and their family. Working-class lives were not something to be sniffed at or looked down upon. They embodied modest but decent lives that one could aspire to.

This all changed in the mid 1980s and 90s. Gone were the blue-collar workers, and in came the lawyers, doctors and creative occupations. Jerry Seinfeld, main protagonist in the eponymous sitcom *Seinfeld*, is a stand-up comedian. In *Will & Grace*, Will is a high-flying lawyer and Grace an interior designer. More recently, we watched Carrie Bradshaw in *Sex and the City* fund her high-end fashion collection by working as a columnist and, later, best-selling author.

These more recent programmes were undoubtedly more progressive than their older counterparts in many important ways. Women were no longer a mere sidekick to their husbands but had meaningful lives and rich stories of their own. Family representations weren't confined to the nuclear model, with a heterosexual couple at the helm of their own offspring, but could be the coming-together of all manner of relationships.

At the same time, these more modern series also played into new tropes about desirable careers and ways to make a living. Capitalist and neoliberal ideals of making lots of money started taking over. Holding down a steady job as a plumber or factory worker was no longer a worthwhile aspiration. The trading floor of a stock exchange, a courthouse or a boardroom were the places you'd want to find yourself. If you weren't wearing a suit to work, you didn't count. And if you weren't earning big money, you were doing something wrong.

This societal change in what is deemed a desirable job or admirable career has inevitably shifted aspirations. We have come to idolise the rich and famous. At no other point in time did we find ourselves looking in on the lives of the insanely wealthy with the ease and frequency we do now. From Paris Hilton and Nicole Richie's ironically titled *The Simple Life* to *Keeping up with the Kardashians* and *Bling Empire*, these reality TV series feed a voyeuristic obsession with glitter and glamour, and a suggestion that money can buy happiness. It has led to a normalisation of being obscenely rich, and the notion that this way of life is what everyone should aspire to.

Not only does this societal shift in expectations raise the bar to such unrealistic levels that it leads to frustrated aspirations, it also leads to downplaying the value of a 'simple life'. Wanting to earn enough to raise a happy and healthy family is no longer something to be proud of. Making an honest income by learning a craft or trade or taking up a working-class occupation is devalued. Anything less than a college degree or university qualification tends to be sniffed at. Blue-collar jobs or manual labour – however skilful – garner less respect than climbing the ranks in an office environment.

Aspirations that are centred around owning a large home, driving a big car and having a flashy job have become the 'gold standard'. This leads to working-class youngsters, who may attach less value to obtaining the highest grades, being typecast as lacking in ambition. But as educational scholar Garth Stahl argues, it's not that these young people don't have ambition; they simply don't ascribe to the middle-class view of aspirations.[27] Instead of aiming for high-flying careers, their goal is to have an ordinary life free from greed with a decent job that puts food on the table. As Stahl put it, it's about earning an honest day's pay in return for an honest day's work.

Yet dominant middle-class narratives about enviable careers or life trajectories render working-class ambitions inferior.

Aspirations can be a life-changer. Imagining a future for yourself without being constrained by lack of positive examples or societal expectations while feeling a sense of control over achieving that future is a powerful motivator for any individual. Yet poverty and socioeconomic disadvantage limit the range of futures imaginable, acting as a brake on forward-looking behaviour. Raising aspirations through exposure to role models or alternative realities can help broaden the imagined window of opportunities and ignite a spark towards improving life outcomes.

At the same time, this focus on a lack of aspirations and how it holds people back overlooks structural obstacles impossible to overcome by wishing and working to achieve more. An emphasis on the failure to aspire and on promoting greater ambition as a way out of poverty places the burden of responsibility for socioeconomic improvement with individuals, and especially young people. It suggests that doing better in school and obtaining a well-paid job is within reach if only boys and girls were able to imagine that for themselves. The reality is often very different, with socioeconomic conditions scuppering efforts to make dreams come true.

Taking an empathetic perspective of the role of aspirations shows us they are a vital piece of the puzzle, yet it also makes us realise they are not a silver bullet for changing lives. Thinking about the ambitions we held for ourselves when we were little and how they changed as we grew older helps us relate to the motivating power of aspirations. At the same time, a critical consideration of how we came to hold those aspirations brings an understanding that the range of options is socially determined and that the ability to achieve the goals we set for ourselves is often outside of individual control.

Holding a more nuanced view is vital to avoid blaming individuals for having aspirations that may diverge from the norm, for being unable to achieve them due to forces outside their control, or for displaying undesirable behaviour when the gap between reality and what is desired is simply too large. It helps us see aspirations for what they are: a powerful personal motivator that everyone should have access to, but only a small cog in the poverty machinery.

5

THE OTHER SIDE
OF THE COIN

The immigration officer looks up and studies my face. Confident that it matches the photo in the passport in front of him, he grabs a heavy-looking stamp and confirms my departure from Rwanda with a loud bang. I'm relieved. Border proceedings always make me nervous.

The officer looks at me again and tilts his head to the right. A subtle gesture to point me in the direction of his Burundian colleague. As I make my way to the adjacent desk, my passport is already being subjected to its second inspection. This time the officer is mostly interested in the paperwork required to obtain a visa. After carefully considering the documentation, he slams down his own stamp and grants me access to his country.

I'm on my way to Burundi to work with Irish charity Concern Worldwide as part of a team to study their flagship anti-poverty programme. The organisation set up shop here in 1997 when Burundi was deep in civil war, estimated to have caused 300,000 deaths.[1] At present, this small landlocked country in Central Africa is one of the poorest in the world. Every two out of three Burundians live below the poverty line. Basic needs such as adequate nutrition and access to schools or hospitals are only enjoyed by a small minority of the population.[2]

These are not just numbers. Crossing the border into Burundi reveals a lush landscape with an abundance of natural riches. Peering out of the window, I see bundles of bananas dangling underneath large green leaves, sprawling trees laden with masses of appetising mangoes, and patches of strikingly bright and beautiful sunflowers. Yet most houses look sparse and unstable, built out of mud and thatch. Although we make our way into Burundi during the day, night-time drives in the pitch black reveal that electricity is scarce. Cars are a rare sight on roads that are primarily occupied by pedestrians and cyclists.

After an hour of driving through gently rolling countryside, we arrive in Kirundo, the capital of the eponymous region in the country's north. The charity's office is in a former governor's house located on top of a hill, with stunning vistas overlooking the town. The team has been expecting us, and we receive a warm welcome. We also meet our fellow researchers, who have driven up from the capital, Bujumbura, where they are based. After months of corresponding with each other via email, it's a pleasure to finally meet everyone in person.

Once introductions and pleasantries are out of the way, it's time to get down to business. The team leader explains that the programme we'll be studying has been under way for a few months. Focused on the extremely poor, it aims to establish activities that can boost income and create greater financial security. It also tries to improve the nutrition and health outcomes of those participating in the programme and their family members. To reach these objectives, participants receive a monthly stipend, a sizeable injection of cash, group training, and regular visits from so-called case managers.

Our trip to Kirundo is timely. In the preceding weeks, meetings were held in the participating communities to explain the programme and who has been selected to take part. The case managers introduced themselves to the families they'll be working with and handed participants mobile phones with which to receive their stipends. Payment of cash via mobile phones – basic sturdy ones rather than expensive, flimsy and electricity-hungry smartphones – has quite a few advantages. It's safer for the recipients, as they won't be carrying around or having to hide physical cash. The accounts set up to facilitate transactions also allow for access to other financial services, potentially widening further economic opportunities.

The programme staff are excitedly telling us about their work so far, and their passion and commitment is infectious. They have clearly put a lot of thought into developing an intervention that is fit for purpose, and are dedicated to making a real difference. Yet I'm sceptical, as are my fellow researchers. How much can a programme like this really achieve for people who have been struggling to make a living almost their entire lives? Especially when economic opportunities are so limited. It seems a tall order.

The next morning, we sit down with women participating in the programme. Huddled together in a shady spot under a large tree, we hear story after story of how the programme has improved their lives. 'Finally we can buy food for our families, purchase kitchen supplies and pay off outstanding debt. We have gone and bought new clothing for ourselves and our children!' And this, the women tell us excitedly, makes a huge difference. 'We can leave our homes with heads up high. Our neighbours are beginning to respect us.' They are now able to stand tall and mix in, rather than stand out and be avoided. Indeed, all the women look positively radiant in their brightly coloured wraps, proudly wearing their mobile phones in equally colourful pouches around their necks.

These positive experiences weren't a one-off. My initial pessimism was misplaced. As we continued to have many more conversations and collected data over several more years, we found that the programme led to significant improvements for the women and men taking part.[3] Eating three meals a day may be the norm for most of us, but it is an exception for the majority of Kirundo residents. The monthly stipends helped participants to feed themselves and their children on a more regular basis, and hunger decreased. The larger cash injections were used for business investments, leading to higher and more secure streams of income. Instead of working as day labourers cultivating crops on somebody else's land, participants started their own farms or trading enterprises.

The starkest impact, however, was on participants' perceptions of themselves and their outlook on life. The programme and the support it provided suddenly made its participants visible, in a good way. They were considered worthy members of their community. Finally they stood on a par with others, something they had not experienced before.

Money matters

Policymakers and politicians around the world have caught on to the power of giving cash to those who most need it, dubbed by some the 'quiet revolution'.[4] Cash payments have long been a widely used form of welfare in rich countries, but they are also increasingly used in poorer countries. The provision of regular income assistance to those in hardship has become a vital mechanism to alleviate poverty, reduce inequality and improve the targeted population's living standards and well-being.

The simple act of giving money to people in poverty now happens across the globe, from Africa to Asia and from Australia to Latin America. The last two decades saw an enormous expansion of this type of assistance. In 2015, 843 million people received income benefits, a tenfold increase since the turn of the century.[5] To put it into perspective, that means handing out cash to all residents of the US, Brazil and Nigeria combined.[6] This practice grew even further during the pandemic. Cash transfer schemes were widely used to support those unable to go to work or earn an income when lockdown restrictions were in place, reaching as many as 1.4 billion individuals across the world in 2020.[7]

Findings from studies conducted over the last two decades involving the recipients of such assistance are overwhelmingly positive. Fewer children go hungry, more people receive health care and economic autonomy is boosted.[8] In Zambia, cash transfers increased daily food intake on average by 215 calories, roughly 10 per cent of the recommended quantity.[9] This effect was even larger for the poorest beneficiaries. In Kenya, businesses in communities where cash transfers were paid to the poorest members saw their revenue go up by almost 50 per cent.[10]

When speaking to those with decision-making power about how budgets are allocated, I often get asked about cash transfers' negative effects. Don't they create dependency? Doesn't the money get wasted on drugs and alcohol? I recall a government official in Lesotho once telling me that he didn't believe child benefits were a good idea as they would only lead to poor women having more babies.

I'm sure some of this does happen. But concerns about such types of myopic behaviour taking place on a sizeable scale are unfounded.[11] There's no evidence to suggest that people systematically turn to government for handouts rather than work for their keep. Studies that have looked at how beneficiaries use their transfers find no significant increase in spending on 'temptation goods' such as alcohol or tobacco.[12] Transfers directed at families with young children don't lead to increased fertility. Instead of preventing economic activity, transfers encourage entrepreneurial action, improve living conditions and give children a better chance in life.

A secure flow of income isn't just about advancing one's economic situation. The positive effects on psychological well-being that I witnessed in Burundi are replicated across the board. Access to financial resources to meet basic needs and cope with unexpected expenses gives a sense of stability, thereby improving mental well-being. In Zimbabwe, women receiving monthly welfare support said that the scheme meant that 'they now see us as real people with worth'.[13] In Kenya, a female pensioner told researchers that, 'When I didn't have the pension money, I was looked down upon and not respected. But now that I receive the pension, I feel more loved, because people come and ask me for things.'[14] In our own research in northern Ethiopia, a male recipient of monthly cash transfers said, 'When I receive my money during the pay period, I feel confident. I communicate confidently with people who are better off.'[15]

Cash transfers can also instil hope and optimism for the future. Recipients can invest the income supplements in their own or their children's education, start a small business or improve their living conditions. Individuals and families feel better able to take control of their own lives, bringing a sense of empowerment. Economic security counteracts feelings of shame, alleviates depression and can even stop people from taking their own lives.

In my years of researching anti-poverty programmes, I have spoken to many beneficiaries of cash transfers and heard numerous stories of their powerful impact. The women in Burundi were filled with such optimism and positive energy when I spoke with them up in the hills of Kirundo. In

Ghana, a 15-year old girl told me she was grateful for the money her family received from the government because it allowed her to stay at home rather than be sent away to live with her auntie. In Bangladesh, I saw first-hand how cash stipends energised families as they were able to set up new businesses and re-enrol their children in school. But my meeting with Kondanani in Malawi was probably the most powerful encounter in bringing home the potential of cash transfers to instil hope.

I met Kondanani in 2011. I was in Malawi at the invitation of the United Nations' children's agency, UNICEF. The country had been implementing a cash transfer scheme for a few years and I was asked to study its impact. UNICEF was especially interested in how the scheme helped poor and vulnerable families with members affected by HIV or having lost someone to the virus. Malawi, along with many other countries in the southern Africa region, was badly affected by the HIV/AIDS crisis that started in the 1980s. More than one in ten of the country's children lost their parents.[16]

While many HIV/AIDS initiatives focused on tackling the psychological trauma and social isolation of children orphaned following the epidemic, there was also great need for financial support. Teenagers were suddenly left with the responsibility to care for younger siblings, finding themselves in charge of feeding multiple mouths. More often, however, children who had lost their parents were taken in by grandparents or family members already struggling to make ends meet. UNICEF wanted to know whether Malawi's cash transfer scheme was able to offer a vital economic lifeline.

It had been a long day when we finally made our way to meet Kondanani. We had already paid fascinating visits to a childcare centre and social welfare office, but I was looking forward to speaking with Kondanani about her experience of receiving the monthly government stipends.

Small-framed and frail-looking, she greeted us warmly before inviting us into her compound. Two young boys and a girl were playing in the area around her house, chasing each other in a game of tag. They were Kondanani's grandchildren. Carefully avoiding the beans that lay drying in the sun, I tiptoed my way to the small bench in front of the house.

Once we were all seated, my colleague from UNICEF initiated the conversation. She asked Kondanani about her grandchildren, and why they were staying with her. Kondanani explained that both her daughter and son-in-law had passed away a few years previously, and that there was no one to look after their children. They were still very young so couldn't be left on their own: 'I'm their grandmother, so of course I took them in.' But, she confided, fulfilling the role of mother all over again was hard, physically and financially. Money was tight, especially with the children growing older and costs rising.

We were only a few minutes into our conversation when we suddenly heard loud wailing. It appeared to come from one of the houses nearby. A young woman was howling at the top of her lungs, and others joined in. It was so visceral, it sent shivers down my spine. We were all startled, and at first we couldn't make out what was happening. But soon enough everyone recognised the emotion, regardless of whether we spoke the local language. What we heard was the unmistakable sound of grief.

'Their mother must have passed away,' explained Kondanani. Apparently she had been ill for some time. 'It will be me next,' Kondanani then declared, deadpan and with little emotion in her face. She presented it as a statement of fact.

I was taken aback. How to respond to such information? We had only just met Kondanani. My colleague, also visibly shocked but quicker to regain her composure, asked her to elaborate.

'I also have it.'

There was no need to probe any further; we all knew what that meant. Although Kondanani had received treatment, she hadn't been able to take her medication on a regular basis. She had slowly felt her health deteriorate and was now becoming weaker by the day.

'There's nothing that can be done. There is no hope for me. I will soon be gone.'

I nodded solemnly. It seemed Kondanani had witnessed what had happened to her neighbours often enough not to harbour any false expectations of a long life.

Given the trauma that was taking place a few metres from where we sat and the gravity of what Kondanani had just shared about her own life's prospects, I was somewhat surprised by what she said next.

'I may not be here much longer, but I do have hope for my grandchildren. The government cash will keep them alive. It will help them achieve their goals.'

Small amounts of cash provided to poor households such as those headed by Kondanani can make a big difference when income is scarce and putting food on the table is a daily struggle. They're not a silver bullet. Transfers were insufficient to prevent Kondanani's health from deteriorating and they won't provide for her grandchildren without additional resources. But what they do offer is a buffer against the hardship of poverty, a stepping stone towards better lives, and in this case, reassurance that Kondanani won't leave her loved ones empty-handed. It's much-needed solace in desperate times.

There is more to me than poverty

In addition to improving a family's financial situation and instilling optimism and hope, another way that cash makes people feel better about themselves and their ability to change their lives is how it allows them to affirm their identity.[17] Time and again, studies show that one of the first things people do when they receive their initial payment is to purchase a new set of clothes or get a haircut. Research also shows that these things transform people's perceptions of themselves as well as their standing within their communities. We saw this in Burundi, where Concern Worldwide's anti-poverty programme allowed women to buy bright and colourful wraps that they wore with much pride.

Regardless of where you go in the world, being able to maintain at least a basic level of personal care and dress is important for dignity and self-respect. This has nothing to do with how much money someone has saved in their bank account or stashed away under their mattress. Take yourself back to a situation when you needed a confidence boost: the first day in a new job, having to make a speech, or being introduced to your prospective parents-in-law. I bet that one of the ways you prepared yourself was by going out and buying a new shirt, upgrading your make-up selection, or picking up polish to revive that formal but tired-looking pair of shoes at the back of the wardrobe.

If this holds for you (and me), why would it be different for people who receive cash assistance? Investing in a fresh look is crucial for mustering up the confidence to set foot in the office where a job interview takes place, or in the bank to open an account. This is especially true when everything about these places shouts that they are reserved for people with money. In some cases, looking smart is a necessity to be allowed into buildings like that. It is not uncommon to hear stories of people being refused access to banks because of their appearance, thereby denying them their right to withdraw cash, for example.

And yet when people in poverty receive income support, spending cash on personal care or new clothes is often dismissed as frivolous and unnecessary. It's taken as evidence that such people squander the support they receive. The derogatory moniker 'welfare queen' in the US – made part of popular vocabulary by Ronald Reagan – is still widely used to refer to women ostensibly gaming the benefit system to live lavish lifestyles at the expense of hard-working taxpayers.[18] References to expensive clothing and glamorous looks are often part of this narrative.

The reality couldn't be more different. Apart from the hard truth that cases of welfare fraud – and especially the extent to which they allow for buying designer clothes or flashy outfits – are few and far between, spending money on one's appearance is often the opposite of luxury.

Scientific thinking backs this up. Remember Erving Goffman, the sociologist who wrote the popular book on stigma? In addition to theorising about what constitutes stigma, Goffman also considered how people avoid being stigmatised. Whether someone is subject to stigmatisation will in large part depend on whether those around them are aware of the characteristic that is looked down upon. This, in turn, will depend on how visible the characteristic is, or the potential for hiding it. For example, if stammering results in being laughed at, someone who suffers from a speech impediment might avoid speaking altogether, thereby avoiding being stigmatised.

Following the same logic, if living in poverty is looked down upon – and we know that it very often is – pejorative treatment is more likely to occur when signs of poverty are more obvious. Goffman refers to these visible signs as 'stigma symbols'. Dirty clothing, worn-out shoes and bad teeth are all snippets of information based on which others pass judgement. The larger the stigma associated with poverty, the higher the chances people will misuse this information and behave badly towards the person in front of them.

Now imagine economic support entering the picture. A small but meaningful injection of cash. What would you do?

Well, you're likely to do what millions of people in poverty do. You invest in so-called 'disidentifiers'. You might buy a new pair of trousers, get your shoes mended, or make an appointment with the beautician. You might even get the newest iPhone, if that's what prevents you from being labelled as living on little. Because there is no stronger trigger for stigmatisation and no surer pathway to shame than standing out from others in a negative way. It is therefore no surprise that spending money on things that help someone fit in is high on the priority list. Not just for people in poverty, but for everyone.

In her book *Hand to Mouth*, Linda Tirado provides a powerful account of the state of her teeth being the most obvious marker of her poverty. Low wages and insecure employment left Linda in a position of always having to stretch her money further than it could go, despite working multiple jobs at the same time. Needing to choose between paying the electricity bill and putting food on the table meant that seeing a dentist was out of reach, and her teeth bore the signs. When she was hit by a drunk driver, her jaw was heavily damaged and it set in motion a process of dental decay. Insurance payments were barely enough to get her a new car, let alone dental surgery. In the end, her teeth were discoloured and rotten to the extent that she had to get the front ones pulled. A denture plate prevented there being a glaring gap in her mouth, but it came off a few years later and there was no money to fix it.

The result of this inspired the title of her book. She wasn't just living hand to mouth in a proverbial sense; it had also become second nature for her to hide her mouth behind her hand. 'I watch the tooth-bleaching ads and cringe, because

I know exactly what I am being pegged as. Incapable. Uneducated. Oblivious.'[19] Linda only eats or speaks behind the protective screen of her hand. Smiling is no-go territory. And a seemingly innocuous act of intimacy between partners – kissing – is a minefield.

There's no question about it. Spending money on outward appearance is no luxury, and certainly no quandary. It is vital to maintaining a sense of identity and being able to go through life with dignity. When cash is short, income assistance meets many needs.

Nothing for nothing

Unfortunately, not all that glitters is gold. Welfare and other social support is not immune to negative stereotypes and toxic narratives about those in poverty. Instead of recognising the agony of poverty and trusting in people's motivation and hard work, policies seem predicated on the notion that people prefer to stay stuck or cycle in and out of hardship. Images of someone languishing on their couch while watching daytime TV or sitting with a beer in hand outside the local watering hole in the midday sun are persistent and get imprinted in the minds of those formulating policies. The fact that such imagery bears little relation to reality is irrelevant. Instead of offering constructive support, policies are often designed around the idea that their beneficiaries cannot be trusted and that they need to be coaxed or forced to do the 'right' thing. The myth that poverty is a failure of character finds its way into every nook and cranny of the support that is supposed to make life better.

Many programmes that provide income support come with strings attached. Applying for jobs, attending parenting classes or sending children to school can all serve as preconditions for support. Often in the name of making policies more effective, the mixing and matching of conditions and sanctions has become commonplace in social policies across the world. Despite their seemingly positive rationale, these conditions tie people's hands, forcing them to engage in activities in ways that are often time-consuming and impractical. Not to mention the level of pejorative treatment that participants may be subjected to along the way.

We don't have to look far to see how the imposition of conditions and sanctions counters the positive effects of economic support. Over the past two decades, the UK's welfare system has become increasingly harsh. When someone loses their job and needs to receive benefits to bridge the employment gap, they are required to engage in full-time job seeking, training, or other work requirements. Non-compliance puts them at risk of losing their support. Yet despite all these stringent forms of 'activation', research shows that the most likely outcome is a sporadic stint of employment in short-term and low-paid work.[20] Instead of getting people into secure employment, the policy is more likely to loop them into a cycle of temporary low-wage jobs with low-level benefits plugging the gap.

This type of unforgiving response to missing meetings, applying for too few jobs or otherwise failing to meet the many requirements achieves the opposite of what is intended.

People feel discouraged rather than empowered. Psychological distress increases.[21] For some, this means being pushed into clinical depression. A more punitive welfare system has even been linked to an increase in prescriptions for antidepressants.[22] Most shockingly, increasingly stringent procedures to assess disability status and eligibility for incapacity benefits in the UK have been linked to as many as 600 suicides over a period of three years.[23]

The UK isn't alone in its shift towards more conditional forms of welfare provision. Welfare support in high-income countries has long placed emphasis on beneficiaries' own behaviour and responsibilities. This line of thinking suggests that giving 'something for nothing' only perpetuates the cycle of dependency and encourages 'living off the state'. External incentives are necessary to correct people's wayward actions and get them back on track. The temporary or indefinite withdrawal of benefits in cases of non-compliance is often part of the package.

Take Wendy, from Adelaide in Australia, who was in her mid fifties when she lost her job.[24] She had been in work for nearly 40 years, with qualifications in physics and chemistry. She even had a forklift licence. Wendy was made redundant when the factory that employed her closed down. Unbeknownst to her at the time, this marked the end of a career and the start of a life unravelled.

She immediately started applying for other jobs. But she kept receiving the same response to her applications: she was overqualified and too expensive. At the end of her tether, Wendy was enrolled in Jobactive, a government service that supported people to help them find employment. Her case-worker flagged the same problem as the companies Wendy had reached out to: her CV was too long. No one was going to employ her if they had to pay a wage commensurate with nearly four decades of work experience. And so the caseworker removed Wendy's work experience from her CV altogether. A career erased at the click of a button.

The requirements of Jobactive meant Wendy was then pushed into jobs for which she really didn't have the experience, or that were impossible for her to do due to her arthritis. She was forced to interview for a job in retail that specifically asked for at least five years' experience. Wendy had never worked in sales. But a no-show would result in getting her benefits cut, so she went anyway.

She kept fighting to get her qualifications back into the system, but to no avail. Then her caseworker was replaced by someone new, and instead of Wendy being forced to hide her qualifications, she was now challenged about why she didn't have any. How was it possible that in her entire life, she hadn't managed to complete a course or obtain a degree? In a Kafkaesque turn of events, Wendy was now threatened with her benefits being cut off not because she had too many qualifications, but because she was supposedly lying about not having any at all. It was a farcical, humiliating and deeply stressful time: 'You're treated like a child … in an infinite loop, constantly afraid they'll cut off your payments again and you'll fall behind on your bills.'[25]

So many complaints were made about the Jobactive scheme that an inquiry was held. The report that followed could not have been more scathing: 'Jobactive is not welfare to work, it is welfare to nowhere.' It concluded that 'the government's punitive and paternalistic approach to employment services has failed'.[26]

Experiences like Wendy's are increasingly common. Welfare cuts and years of austerity following the 2008 financial crisis have hollowed out assistance to people in need, especially in richer countries. Making such cuts palatable to the general public, and especially those who turn up at the ballot box at election time, is far easier if people in need are projected as lazy, dependent and unwilling to work. This in turn leads to policies assuming poor people are incapable of making sensible decisions and need to be pushed in the 'right direction'.

This line of thinking can be found around the world. In the last two decades, so-called conditional cash transfers have gained unprecedented popularity in the fight against poverty, primarily in Latin America. Like other benefit schemes, this type of transfer provides poor families with a regular income supplement. But to receive the cash, they must comply with conditions. Requirements commonly focus on children, ensuring they are enrolled in school, get immunised and have regular health check-ups. In some cases, caregivers are also asked to participate in parenting classes or other training. In Brazil alone, 14 million families benefited from the Bolsa Familia programme in 2020.[27] This accounts for almost one in every five families in the country.

The aim of conditional cash transfers is twofold. Their immediate goal is to alleviate hardship and deprivation.

But they also explicitly seek to break the intergenerational cycle of poverty. This is why behavioural requirements are especially geared towards improving the situation of children, the rationale being that investing in children now will ensure that they don't grow up to live in poverty like their parents.

And it works. Poverty goes down, school attendance goes up, children stay in school for longer, and there are a whole host of health and nutrition improvements.[28] There is some indication that it also leads to better skills and job opportunities as children grow into adults, although the research on this is still pretty sketchy.[29]

So, if these programmes help children in poverty, what's the problem?

Well, it's not actually clear whether these positive effects are due to the conditions attached to the cash, or whether it is simply the cash that does the trick. Researchers have been scratching their heads over the value added of conditionality over and above simply providing money. There are studies that show that cash transfers are more likely to keep children attending school[30] or health care[31] when conditions are attached. Other studies, however, show no difference at all.[32] Children are just as likely to be in class or go to get immunised when families receive the cash without any strings attached. There is no clear-cut case for conditionality on the grounds of it being more effective.

What makes conditional cash transfers problematic, then, is how they build on and reinforce a prevailing sense of 'us' versus 'them', with the design of programmes feeding into the narrative that people in poverty need to be coerced into action. With most behavioural requirements focused on the younger generation accessing basic services, there's an assumption that poor parents don't have their children's best interests at heart. The only way to motivate vulnerable caregivers to make the 'right' decision is by threatening to withhold payment of cash transfers.

Having directives attached to the receipt of funds is appreciated by some who receive them, with conditions affording them clear guidance and a nascent sense of entitlement.[33] They're not just taking 'something for nothing' but receiving cash in exchange for clearly spelled-out activities that are to the benefit of their children and the family as a whole. It allows them to distance themselves from negative stereotypes of welfare beneficiaries lazily feeding off the state.

Yet the reality for many is that complying with conditions is hard. Not for lack of graft or grit, but for reasons outside of individual control. In Jamaica, parents receiving conditional cash transfers find it difficult to send their children to school because the money they receive simply isn't enough to cover the costs associated with education.[34] Children go to school even when they're ill to avoid having benefits withdrawn. In Mexico, children of indigenous people living in remote areas with chronic underinvestment in infrastructure and basic services simply don't have access to a school that they are required to attend[35]. Families are punished twice: first they have to jump through many and sometimes impossible hoops to receive income support, and then their support is withdrawn when they are unable to abide by programme regulations.

In the case of conditional cash transfers, these negative effects are also extremely gendered. With women acting as primary caregivers the world over, meeting conditions designed to improve outcomes for children often falls on mothers' shoulders. Women bear the brunt of taking part in meetings, queuing up to collect money, and worrying about failing to meet requirements. In Peru, high up in the Andes mountains, it's not uncommon for female beneficiaries of the Juntós conditional cash transfer programme to walk three to four hours to their nearest health clinic for a required check-up, only to find it closed.[36] This adds to the already high demands on women's time, having to juggle paid work while running their household and caring for their children.

Another problematic aspect of conditions is that they reinforce power differentials, placing welfare recipients at the mercy of anyone who gets to sign off on compliance. Teachers, doctors and caseworkers may all be called upon to give their blessing. It can lead to anyone with sanctioning power asking recipients to do more than is officially required, such as attending additional meetings or keeping the bathroom neat and tidy. In her book *Unjust Conditions*, feminist researcher Tara Cookson refers to these as 'shadow conditions'.[37] Women comply because they're too scared of losing income support. Instead of empowering recipients to improve the lives of their children and themselves, programmes with compliance requirements lead to a sword hanging over beneficiaries' heads.

Assuming the worst

It's a grey and dreary Friday afternoon in the middle of January 2021. The Netherlands is in the grip of a second COVID-19 lockdown and its residents are urged to stay at home. But while streets around the country are eerily quiet, the inner court of the parliamentary buildings in The Hague – the Binnenhof – is bustling. Journalists and photographers are trying to get a glimpse of Prime Minister Mark Rutte. He is about to emerge from his office to announce his and the government's resignation to King Willem-Alexander. In true Dutch style, he will make the short journey to the royal palace by bike.[38]

These events conclude a tumultuous week following the publication of a scathing report about the country's childcare benefit scandal. Since 2012, more than 20,000 recipients of childcare benefits have been wrongly accused of fraud.[39] Almost half were forced to pay fines and return the support they had received, sometimes adding up to tens of thousands of euros.[40] By 2021, thousands of families had been left in ruins, devastating them economically and psychologically.

One of the seeds for this scandal was planted almost a decade earlier. In 2013, a Dutch documentary showed families in Bulgaria claiming childcare benefits by registering false addresses in the Netherlands.[41] Images of a man standing in front of his house in Bulgaria waving his Dutch debit cards and dubbing himself 'the village ATM' became the focal point of public and political outrage.

The story fuelled already persistent perceptions of widespread benefit fraud, with parties across the political spectrum calling for the 'bad apples' to be weeded out. The fact that the value of fraudulent claims constituted less than 1 per cent of all benefits was ignored. At the same time, the knowledge that many honest people would fall victim to the obsession to fight fraud at all costs was accepted by many politicians – including left-leaning ones – as an inevitable but necessary consequence.

Fast-forward to 2021. Layer upon layer of rules mixed with exceptions, exemptions and amendments had made it almost impossible for families to navigate the benefit system. Combined with a fairly brutal fraud detection system, this meant that honest mistakes, or even no mistakes at all, were flagged as fraud. Even worse, discrimination and racism became institutionalised practice, with claimants holding dual citizenship automatically flagged as potentially fraudulent. Over the years, thousands of families were pushed into debt, causing widespread hardship and misery.

Many families complained. The daily news regularly showed parents desperate at the nightmare situation they found themselves in. They knew they had done nothing wrong, yet no one believed them. Even children felt compelled to make their voices heard. In a letter to the ombudsman, one boy wrote: 'My parents argued a lot because there was no money and they needed to work more. I felt bad and alone. If something was up, I didn't want to say because I didn't want to give my parents more to worry about.'[42] But their griev-ances fell on deaf ears.

Finally, after years of filing court cases, campaigning and protesting, affected families were heard. Following the damning parliamentary report, the government admitted they were in the wrong. Despite repeated warnings and the many stories about how their approach to tackling fraud was unfair, reeked of racism and led to crippling financial strain and unmeasurable heartache, they had failed to push the brake and change gear. Close to 26,000 families were wrongly accused of cheating the system.[43] 'Mistakes were made at every level of the state, with the result that terrible injustice was done to thousands of parents,' said PM Rutte. Resignation was the government's mea culpa.

Of course, there should be systems to detect and counter benefit fraud, and these should be rigorous. However, not only does the pervasive assumption that welfare beneficiaries are out to trick the system and the obsession with rooting out the bad apples lead to inhumane and harmful practices, it also pays lip service to double standards. In 2016, the UK government faced questions over why there were ten times as many inspectors working to detect fraud with benefit payments than identifying and tackling tax evasion.[44] More than 3,000 staff within the Department for Work and Pensions were assigned to detect people on low incomes receiving support they didn't qualify for. At the same time, only 300 inspectors were working on cases of the very rich seeking to avoid paying taxes.

Like in the Netherlands, despite a persistent belief that benefit fraud is pervasive, it only accounts for a small proportion of the UK government's overall budget, estimated at less than 1 per cent.[45] The total amount of money lost from the government's coffers as a result of tax evasion or avoidance is much higher. Between 2009 and 2019, 23 times as many prosecutions took place for benefit fraud than for tax offences. Even so, the value of detected tax fraud was nine times that of benefit fraud.[46] People on lower incomes are held to greater scrutiny than those with their wealth stowed away in offshore accounts.

The rise of technology risks making matters worse. Governments hold vast amounts of data about each of us, and algorithms are taking over as main decision-makers about who is eligible for support or committing fraud. This push towards the digitisation of welfare against the backdrop of fundamental distrust of people in poverty gives reason for concern. Indeed, in the Netherlands, it was the use of algorithms that flagged dual passport holders or those with certain ethnic origins as more likely to commit fraud, and put them at greater risk of having benefits withdrawn. This misplaced use of technology forced the Dutch government to admit to racial profiling, and contributed to its decision to resign.

Beyond algorithms, the rigid enforcement of rules through web portals and automated telephone lines leaves those who are most in need without support. Hiding behind computer screens and protected from being directly challenged has made it easier for authorities to dismiss people in poverty. Under the guise of achieving greater efficiency, improving the quality of support and getting taxpayers a better deal, technology has facilitated an even more ruthless and inhumane system of assuming the worst. A missing signature on one of dozens of forms, a blurry picture or an outdated proof of residence can all lead to benefits being withdrawn, or an applicant being flagged a fraudster.

It leads to infuriating tales of claimants being accused of failing to comply, or of refusing to cooperate despite having sent the required documentation or having waited next to the phone in anticipation of an eligibility check. Understaffed call centres make it impossible to speak to someone to clarify or rectify issues. You only have to think about your own experiences of being stuck in a telephone queue at your bank, insurance company or internet provider to know how frustrating this is. Now consider what it is like if your life depends on getting to speak to a person at the other end of the line and having them hear your story.

Political scientist Virginia Eubanks has been at the forefront of studying and calling out the harm and suffering caused by the digitisation of the welfare state, especially in the US. In her book *Automating Inequality*, she tells the story of Omega Young. Fifty years old and diagnosed with terminal cancer, Omega lost her food and health care support because she failed to attend an appointment for re-certification of eligibility. She was hospitalised at the time of her appointment, and she had notified the authorities of why she was unable to attend. But to no avail. The automated system simply flagged her as a no-show and her benefits were discontinued. She lost all the support she received, including food stamps, and was no longer able to afford her much-needed medication. She appealed the decision, and won. But victory came too late: Omega died the day before her support was reinstated.

Closer to home, in the UK, the harrowing tale of Philippa Day highlights just how ruthless the increasingly impersonal benefit system can be. Only 27 years old, with a young son,

Philippa died from an insulin overdose after failing to get her disability benefits reinstated.[47] The amount she received was drastically reduced from £228 to £60 per week due to missing paperwork, pushing her deep into debt. Already struggling with her mental health, she became even more anxious and developed suicidal thoughts. When her request for a renewed capability assessment to be undertaken at home, rather than in the welfare office, was denied, she saw no other way out than to take her own life.

An inquest into Philippa's death concluded that the many failures in how her case was handled contributed to her suicide.[48] In a recording of one of the phone calls she made to benefits officials, she could be heard begging for her support to be reinstated. 'I've been waiting for six months now. I'm literally starving, I can't survive for much longer.' But instead of being met with empathy, her calls for help went unheard.

The provision of cash is a widely used mechanism for welfare support around the world, and for good reason. It improves living conditions, helps increase outcomes for children and can instil dignity and hope. However, the way payments are dispensed matters. The imposition of conditions, scrutiny over how money is spent, subjection to pejorative treatment and the opaque way in which technology decides who is deserving all render interventions ineffective at best and harmful at worst. Empathy is nowhere to be seen.

Considering welfare provision through the lens of empathy – by relating to how the availability of cash isn't just indispensable for meeting basic needs but also for envisaging a future, while at the same time realising that those with less are held to greater scrutiny – makes it evident that it's not about just giving money to the poor; it's also about how the cash is allocated and awarded. Instead of supporting those who most need it in the best way possible, benefit systems often create walls of bureaucracy, adding insult to injury. With people in poverty widely regarded as second-class citizens, policies that are supposed to help the poor turn into schemes that police and punish them.[49] They can push people to and sometimes over the edge of despair.

Cash can do a lot of good, but too often we fail to see the other side of the coin. Empathy is the foundation for acknowledging policies' shortcomings and building more dignified, respectful and ultimately effective welfare schemes.

6

A NUDGE IN THE
WRONG DIRECTION

'Argh, not again!' I think to myself as I'm picking through various piles in the wardrobe. I'm searching for my favourite pair of jeans, without success. A rummage through the laundry basket confirms my suspicions: the denims haven't been washed yet.

I dig up some more items of a similar colour and quickly load the washing machine. It's only a few more minutes before the working day starts and I'd better find an alternative pair of trousers before sitting myself down behind my desk and starting my online meeting. The person on the other end of the screen might not be able to see what I'm wearing below the waist, but I will know.

A laundry day, of the sort that I remember growing up, would certainly help me avoid this kind of mishap. I recall how, when I was little, Monday was washing day. After the lull of Sunday came the busyness of a new week, and once my dad had left for the office and my brother and I had got on our bikes to pedal to school, my mum would start the weekly slog that was the family's laundry.

Without fail, she'd spend the entire day sorting, washing, drying and ironing. The washing machine and dryer would be tumbling and turning from early morning, with light- and dark-coloured shirts, socks and towels neatly separated to avoid crisp white turning grubby grey. Countless trips would be made between the utility room and the garage. With the laundry basket hinged firmly onto her hip, my mum would transport heavy wet garments out there to dry and return with clean and creased apparel to mould them back into shape. T-shirts, trousers and jumpers would all be smoothed out on the large ironing board, with added steam for persistent crinkles. Even my dad's handkerchiefs wouldn't escape. And by the time I came home in the afternoon, the smelly sheets, stained shirts and dirty underwear were – as if by some sort of miracle – all clean and fragrant once more, neatly folded back into the cupboard or hung in the wardrobe. Just for the cycle to start all over again.

Now in charge of my own laundry, I know there's nothing miraculous about the transformation from dirty to clean, from smelly to scented. Instead, what it takes is time and effort.

Unable to dedicate a full day to the chore, I fit laundry into my schedule as and when I can. One load on a weekday evening, a few on Saturday and Sunday. Today's wash happens to occur on a Friday morning, a day and time born out of necessity rather than my choosing. Keen to spend as little time on the washing palaver as possible, ironing is a step in the process I cut out almost entirely. A good shake of wet washing and a firm folding of dry items seems to do the trick just as well, in my opinion. I'm not sure my mum would agree.

I make these complaints having it easy, washing-wise. It's just me and my husband, so the amount of laundry we accumulate is limited. Plus, he does his own share, I hasten to add. The washing machine is ours alone, which means I can fill it up and turn it on whenever I want to. The house is big enough to accommodate a drying rack, so that I can leave the laundry out to dry without it blocking my view of the TV or barricading the kitchen door. The relatively recent shift towards predominantly working from home has made it even easier to fit the washing in with my schedule.

And yet clothes go missing from my wardrobe for weeks on end, either languishing in the laundry basket or lying in wait in the spare room, ready to be folded away. Because, let's face it, laundry is a time suck: it's no fun, it can't be done quickly, and worst of all, it keeps repeating itself. The pleasure of having finally returned socks, shirts and sheets to where they belong is inevitably cut short by the sight of a growing pile of newly soiled counterparts.

Fortunately, any lingering sense of frustration at my washing mishap quickly dissipates when I start my meeting: another recording for my podcast.

'I would say that it was the first government programme ever set up specifically for families living in poverty that everybody wanted. It was enormously popular. People loved it.' On this markedly grey and dreary morning, Naomi

Eisenstadt speaks with striking clarity and intent. It's a joy to listen to her, not just because it will make my job of editing the forthcoming episode a lot easier, but mostly because what she has to say makes so much sense.

'The culture of Sure Start, although it was explicitly aimed at poor areas and at families living in poverty, was incredibly inclusive and open, and parents absolutely loved it.'

Sure Start was a ground-breaking government programme to help improve outcomes and life chances for children in low-income families. Having served as its first director in England, from 1999 to 2006, Naomi knows it like no other.

What made the policy so unique, she explains, is that instead of providing services separately, it brought them together. Delivered through local Sure Start centres, the programme offered a whole range of support, from childcare and toddler groups to welfare advice. It was an area-based initiative, meaning that everyone living in the catchment area was welcome and could make use of the service. Its open-door policy meant that centres were visible and welcoming spaces, serving as vital hubs for local communities.

While this open-access approach was crucial for getting people through the door, Naomi emphasises that more was needed to ensure it reached the most disadvantaged families.

'There was a huge amount of work that went into making sure that the people least likely to come forward would come forward.'

Outreach workers ensured families were aware of the support available. Long opening hours allowed parents to drop in when it suited them best. Empathetic staff offered a listening ear and provided constructive advice. These were all deliberate attempts at reducing barriers – practical or otherwise – to families taking up services for the benefit of their children. With success. Naomi describes how the programme led to improvements in the home-learning environment and reduced hospitalisations of children. It even led to some improvements in employment, with mothers who benefited from the service continuing to work for Sure Start themselves or becoming social workers.

Sadly, the last decade has seen the closure of many Sure Start centres, or, if they are still in place, a decimation of their services. Austerity and welfare cuts have led to them no longer being the welcoming and supportive spaces they were set up to be, with the open-access ethos replaced by a strategy of narrowly targeting 'troubled families'.

However, for family policy to work, Naomi points out, it should reduce pressure as much as increase capability. It's all well and good to provide advice, offer training and build skills, but if the pressures of poverty aren't addressed, it will make little difference.

'Do I think parents will read to their children if I tell them to read to their children? No, of course I don't. It's about recognising that a lot of the difficulties that people on a low income have are very practical. And unless you provide some practical support that reduces the pressures, it's unlikely they will have the headspace to think about how to parent their children.'

As Naomi is speaking, I can hear that the machine downstairs has started its spin cycle. It's slightly off-kilter, and I worry the microphone will pick up on the racket as it starts banging against the kitchen cabinets. But I shouldn't have worried, because no sooner have I had the thought than Naomi starts talking about washing machines, of all things.

While for me laundry is an unenjoyable task that I prefer to do without, it's a true headache for those on a low income. Not only does it take up valuable time; there are also electricity bills and maintenance costs to contend with. Washing machines are the perfect example of a small solution that can make a big difference.

'Do you want low-income parents to come to parenting classes? Install well-functioning washing machines. Would you like families to avail themselves of services and advice? Make them happen in a launderette.' For programmes to work, Naomi concludes, they need to make life easier, not harder. Reduce the pressure, and there's space for positive change.

As I thank Naomi for her insights, I hear beeping in the background. Right on cue. Better rescue those jeans before they get too crumpled and – God forbid – I need to get the iron out.

Automatic pilot

'Actions speak louder than words', so the saying goes. It suggests that what we do is somehow more truthful than what we say. That while it's easy to utter words we may not really mean, it's harder to conceal our true intentions when it comes to how we behave. This couldn't be further from the truth.

We all do things all the time that are out of sync with what we know to be right or desirable. Every day, good intentions fall by the wayside, replaced with less favourable but more comfortable or familiar alternatives. We drive rather than cycle or walk, even for short distances. We spend hours looking at our phones instead of having a meaningful conversation with a dear friend. We raise our voice even when we notice it hurts the person in front of us. We indulge in unhealthy foods. We smoke and drink. We make promises we don't keep.

Why do we behave in this way? It's not because we're stupid. We tend to know that what we do isn't in keeping with what we would like to do. It's a paradox: if we know the behaviours we display are in conflict with our intentions, plans or values, why do we engage in them? What drives us to do things that rationally or emotionally we don't really want?

It's our brains that are to blame, and their clever mechanism to help us get through life as efficiently and effectively as possible.

Most of what we do is an act of habit. In going about our everyday lives, we're guided by intuition and routine. Much of our behaviour is governed by subconscious processes rather than deliberate action. From the moment we step out of bed to the second we return to our place of rest, most of our behaviour takes place without giving it very much thought. That's because if we were to weigh up the pros and cons of each decision we take, our heads would explode.

Take the decision to brush your teeth. Most of us have integrated it into our daily morning and evening routines.

We cover our brush with paste and stick it into our mouth without giving it a second thought. Then there are multiple decisions in the act of brushing itself. How to hold your brush, or which teeth to brush first. Whether to brush your teeth only, or to include your gums and tongue as well. How long to brush for, and when to rinse. When you start considering all the minute steps involved, the modest and much-repeated act of cleaning our teeth isn't all that simple after all. But if I ask you to recall each of your tooth-brushing decisions, would you be able to give me a step-by-step account? Probably not.

Much like driving a car, we navigate our lives in automatic pilot mode. We don't consciously think about pushing the brake when needing to slow down, or flicking the indicator lever up or down before making a turn. It's the very fact that we don't need to dwell on these actions that allows us to drive in the first place. Driving safely requires us to make split-second decisions. Any delay in engaging the brake when making an emergency stop, for example, can have serious consequences. That's why drinking and driving are such a bad mix.

The fact that we rely on automated and habitual processes for navigating life is part of our evolutionary tale. In the early days, humans' survival rested on the ability to act fast in the face of danger. There was no time to think through the implications of various actions when eye-to-eye with a lion or other predator. Our old reptilian brain tells us to flee, fight or freeze. Decisions need to be made immediately; there's no time to ponder the possibilities.

Humans' hard-wired inclination to act before thinking is what psychologist and economics Nobel laureate Daniel Kahneman referred to as 'system 1' thinking. In his bestseller *Thinking, Fast and Slow*,[1] he argues that humans have two ways of thinking. System 1 is what comes up in your mind automatically. Connections that your brain makes in an instant, without effort. You have no control over this; it's involuntary, like pushing the brake when you see a pedestrian crossing the street, or pressing the right combination of numbers on a keypad when you make a payment. By contrast, 'system 2' is thinking that is effortful and deliberate. It's the kind of thinking that you control, that can do difficult computation, make tricky connections.

Automatic thought processes are by far the more dominant. We allocate most of our attention subconsciously, not consciously. It may not feel like that; if you're anything like me, it seems like our minds are constantly hard at work. But in fact, out of the thousands of actions we take from minute to minute and hour to hour every day, most are taken habitually. For us to function as human beings, we rely on routine: from breathing, walking and talking to more complex tasks such as cooking, cycling and driving. They may start off as effortful endeavours, but once repeated often enough, effort turns into habit. The task is absorbed in the automatic system. Kahneman also refers to this state as one of 'cognitive ease'. By contrast, deliberate decision-making, in the second system, requires 'cognitive strain', and we will avoid it if we can.

A psychology experiment involving jam – of all things – offers a pertinent example of how we avoid demanding too much effort from our brain if we can.[2] Researchers in the US dressed up as store employees and set up shop in a local supermarket to invite unsuspecting shoppers to try a new range of jam. The team alternated between having a small display with six flavours and a large display with 24 flavours. Customers who were presented with a larger choice were expected to buy more than those who had fewer flavours to choose from. After all, having more options means there's more to purchase.

In fact the opposite happened. Much to the researchers' surprise, shoppers bought more jam when they had less choice. Having more options didn't incentivise customers to spend more. Instead, all that choice stopped them in their tracks. While the smaller display presented a relatively easy choice that could have been made on impulse – 'I like ginger, let me try that one' – the larger selection of flavours required customers to engage. To take time and think about which of the 24 flavours they liked best. 'There's quince, various raspberry flavours, and I wonder what damson tastes like.' Suddenly, buying jam becomes an overwhelming task. Something to put your mind to, that involves cognitive strain. No wonder the shoppers decided to keep their money in their pockets.

Our ability to do things without actively thinking about them is vital for our functioning. If we had to think about every decision we make and every action we take, we wouldn't be able to cope. Our brains would get overloaded. We trust ourselves that once we finished cooking, we turned off the hob. That we blew out the candles before going to bed. Or made sure that we locked the door when leaving the house.

It's an efficient way for the brain to operate, and to go through life. Once you've repeated a certain task several times and have established a routine, it becomes a habit. The brain no longer allocates attention to the task; you do it without actively thinking about it.

As much as our automatic behaviours help us to get through many aspects of our lives efficiently and effectively, we are at a disadvantage when the easy route isn't the most beneficial one. If cognitive ease takes us down a path that doesn't serve us financially, physically or socially. Or, conversely, if the option that entails an element of cognitive strain is the one that helps us save money, be more active or live more healthily.

This is where people in poverty are caught between a rock and a hard place. As we saw in Chapter 2, the mental strain of living in poverty limits cognitive bandwidth. It taxes the brain and makes it more difficult to allocate attention to key decisions, such as where to get the best loan or which expenses to prioritise. Now combine this with the fact that we're all wired to go down well-trodden paths or choose the easy option, and it becomes clear that people in poverty are once more drawing the short straw. For those who can least afford to drop the ball, it's hardest to stay focused. What's more, while those with ample funds can use cash to help shake off the negative consequences of unwise decisions, those on tight budgets are pulled down even further. The way in which our brains are wired works to entrench poverty, not alleviate it.

Tricking the brain

Now for the good news. The knowledge that much of what we do is out of habit or motivated by impulse rather than the result of a deliberate decision-making process allows us to find ways to help us change our behaviour. To trick our brains so that we act in accordance with our intentions, and move towards achieving our ambitions. How? By making the desirable action the easy choice.

Are you one of those people pushing the snooze button on your alarm for half an hour before getting out of bed? Move the alarm clock or phone out of arm's length and you're up and out in an instant. Are you struggling to transform good intentions to get more exercise into making your way to the gym? Pack your gym bag the night before so it's ready and waiting for you before you leave the house in the morning. Do you, like me, find it hard to resist the call of a bag of crisps from behind the kitchen cupboard door whenever you're feeling peckish? Make sure not to throw one in the trolley during your next weekly shop. Most definitely don't go shopping when you're hungry.

These are all examples of small incentives that can lower the barrier for us to make more desirable choices. They constitute minor adjustments to how we go about our everyday business but can alter our behaviour in favourable and sometimes powerful ways. Behavioural scientist Paul Dolan goes as far as to argue that we can greatly enhance our happiness by employing tricks like these. If most of our decisions are made subconsciously, by extension this implies that if the behaviours that improve our well-being are made easier, we're naturally inclined to choose that option and thus increase our happiness.[3]

Tricks like these are also referred to as nudges. Exploiting the behavioural insight that our minds are wired to follow the path of least resistance, they constitute tweaks or changes that make it easier to opt for actions that are more beneficial or desirable. And their use extends well beyond the small techniques we adopt within the private sphere of our personal lives – like moving the alarm clock out of easy reach or placing a packed gym bag in a strategic position.

Nudges are everywhere, manipulating many of our every-day actions. Supermarkets get us to spend more by placing expensive items at eye height. Restaurants make us order larger portions by making them the default option. Train companies motivate us to travel outside of peak time by lowering ticket prices after the morning rush. Do we realise we're being manipulated in this way? Unless we're paying attention, probably not. Yet the impact of seemingly small prods can have large effects.

Take visits to the doctor or hospital. No-shows at medical appointments represent a huge cost to health services and make it more difficult for others to see a doctor when they need to. In England in 2021/22, as the COVID-19 pandemic was losing its intensity, 7.6 per cent of outpatient appointments were left unattended. This may not sound like a lot, but with more than 100 million of such appointments scheduled annually, this translates into 650,000 slots being lost every month. It turns out that something as simple as sending reminders – via letters, text messaging and phone calls – can reduce non-attendance by up to 80 per cent.[4]

It's no surprise then that behavioural interventions have grown incredibly popular. Governments have caught on to the power of tricking their populations' brains as a way of tackling sticky problems. Many countries now have their own behavioural policy units, devising schemes to incentivise us to act in ways that are in our own best interest or serve the greater good. From motivating us to slow down when approaching a dangerous bend in the road ahead to convincing us to wear masks at a time of global pandemic, behavioural experts will have had a say.

Prompts and prods

Saving money is one of those behaviours that we know is a wise thing to do but often proves hard to put into practice. Building a financial buffer serves a long-term purpose rather than an immediate benefit and can therefore be difficult to prioritise. More than that, while funds may be accumulated with the plan to invest in life-changing education or pay for a holiday to a bucket-list location, the reality is they are often used for unexpected and less glamorous expenses, such as a broken boiler or emergency dental treatment.

Nudges are widely employed to help overcome the difficulty of prioritising long-term financial health. Take pensions. Ever since I started working as an academic, first in the

Netherlands and then in the UK, I have been saving up for old age. In both countries, academic staff are automatically enrolled into the sector's pension scheme, with employees and employers both contributing to retirement savings. It means pension contributions are deducted from my salary before it reaches my bank account, an ultimate example of transforming a difficult choice into an easy option. Instead of being confronted with the choice of how to allocate my income on a monthly basis and having to prioritise long-term savings over short-term expenses 12 times a year, the need to dedicate headspace to this decision has been taken away from me entirely.

Paradoxically, mechanisms that support sound financial management, such as pension plans, are more available and far easier to access for those already relatively well off. In the case of workplace pension schemes, you need to be employed in a job that offers one. With most jobs in poorer countries being informal, this is an exception rather than a rule. But even in richer countries, decades of chipping away at labour rights and hollowing-out of pension plans means that saving for retirement through workplace pension schemes is increasingly a luxury for a minority of workers. Low-paid staff, those on zero-hour contracts and informal workers not only have to contend with uncertain and irregular pay in the present, but are also excluded from nudges that could help them be more financially resilient in future.

In an attempt to disrupt this pattern, the government in Tanzania, together with nonprofit organisation ideas42 and the World Bank, set out to test whether the use of nudges can also support families on a low income to save more. Roughly half of the country's population get by on less than $2.15 per day, a very small amount even for Tanzanian standards. The poorest families have to make do with even less money and face deprivation in many areas of their lives. On top of that, a lack of financial buffer makes them vulnerable to the economic fallout of unforeseen events that give rise to high expenses, whether it's large climate-related disasters such as floods or individual health problems.

This is where the Productive Social Safety Net Program[5] comes in. It's Tanzania's largest welfare scheme, boosting the incomes of the poorest families by offering regular benefits – cash in hand – while at the same time finding ways to make them more financially resilient. Savings are vital in building up this resilience, yet most families had little to no money set aside. When the team investigated what exactly stopped families from holding back cash for a rainy day or investing in equipment that could help them make money, recipients said that saving wasn't common practice in their communities, therefore they didn't consider it something they should be doing. They also struggled to make plans for how to make the cash stretch as far as possible, especially as they only received their transfers once every two months. This is a long period for anyone to think about their budget, let alone when every penny counts.

With this in mind, the team wondered whether a few subtle nudges could help. Might people in poverty benefit from the monetary management strategies that are available to those with more money to spare?

Various tweaks were introduced to how the Tanzanian welfare programme was implemented. Posters with illustrations of community members moving aside some of their cash and using it to buy chickens or invest in a market stall were put up in frequently visited public spaces. Welfare recipients were invited to take part in goal setting and planning exercises, thinking about what they would like to achieve and how they might manage their money to reach their objectives. And – the most tangible tweak of all – families were provided with pouches, small fabric bags with a zip on either end to create two separate compartments. Upon collection of their cash, they were then encouraged to split their transfer, placing some into the pocket labelled for consumption and some in the pocket intended for savings. It was thought that the combination of a positive nudge – deliberately allocating some of the money to immediate expenses and holding some of it back for another time – with the introduction of a small barrier – the use of the cash from the savings compartment requiring a turning-over of the pouch and opening another zip – would serve as a small but significant incentive.

An evaluation of these tweaks to the Productive Social Safety Net Program proved the team right. Findings showed that recipients who were exposed to the various nudges were far more likely to build up savings and to invest in activities that could help earn money in future than those who weren't. As ideas42's former managing director Saugato Datta explained to me, these tweaks are about putting up the scaffolding that supports people in poverty in managing their money to help them achieve the goals they set for themselves. He's keen to point out that it's not due to some sort of inherent character flaw that individuals experiencing poverty don't act in their own financial self-interest. It's the context that makes it difficult.

Interventions that focus on breaking some of the behavioural deadlocks that exacerbate a seemingly inescapable situation of deprivation and hardship have grown incredibly popular over the last few decades. Experiments trying to work out what kind of prod works best for different groups of people in different circumstances abound. A trial in Bolivia, Peru and the Philippines found that sending monthly reminders to low-income savings account holders helped them save more and reach their savings goals compared to clients who did not receive any prompts.[6] Other schemes seek to capitalise on the positive role of aspirations, as we saw in Chapter 4. In an experiment in Kenya, researchers found that rural women's participation in a workshop that asked them to articulate their aspirations and plans for achieving them led to improvements across a range of economic outcomes, from greater investment in agricultural inputs such as fertiliser and seed to an increase in livestock and savings.[7]

The promise of such humble interventions in tackling something so intractable and sticky as poverty has been widely applauded. This is probably best illustrated by Abhijit Banerjee, Esther Duflo and Michael Kremer winning the Nobel Prize for Economics in 2019 for their ground-breaking work in poverty reduction. They were awarded the prestigious prize in large part as a result of advancing the application of behavioural science to devise and test small-scale solutions that could provide answers to big poverty-related problems.

Interventions such as providing recipients of income support with a money pouch, reminding account holders of their savings targets and asking rural women to engage in planning their activities all ride the wave of nudge enthusiasm. Gentle prompts, relevant advice and positive examples serve as small but effective prods. They can help counteract our innate tendency to choose the easy option or take the familiar route and instead act more strategically in support of our financial health and economic well-being. This holds for those with more as well as little money, rich and poor. Simple, cheap, and bearing positive outcomes, nudges offer high return on investment. Or in plain terms: a big bang for your buck. What's not to like?

Double standards

Imagine this: you've just come off the train on the Underground and want to make your way up to ground level. As you follow the signs to the exit, you're presented with two choices: climbing a flight of stairs or stepping onto an escalator. You know the right thing to do – move your body and get some exercise – but the look of those stairs alone makes you sigh with effort. Like most people, you will opt for the escalator.

The next day, you follow the same routine. As usual, you get off the train, walk towards the exit, and are presented with the same two options: stairs or escalator. This morning, however, the steps of the stairs are adorned with brightly coloured footprints, as if someone walked up them with paint on the soles of their shoes.

There's every chance that you won't even notice these footprints, but your brain will. And despite there not being any change in the amount of effort required to head up the stairs compared to yesterday, or the fact that the newly painted footprints might have escaped your attention altogether, the likelihood of you opting for the stairs instead of the escalator has suddenly become a lot higher. The mere suggestion that someone walked up those stairs before you makes you change your mind and, crucially, your behaviour.

A common criticism is that nudges, and the way in which they guide us towards decisions we may not otherwise have taken, infringe on personal autonomy. Instead of us acting out of free will, Big Brother is pulling the levers. Founding fathers of nudge theory Richard Thaler and Cass Sunstein refute this criticism by pointing out that nudge interventions are those that gently coax people towards desirable behaviour. There shouldn't be any force, or penalties for individuals who don't take the desired action. Like those painted footprints, nudges are often imperceptible, and there is a choice not to follow them.

And as proponents of nudges are keen to point out, there is no such thing as pure free will anyway, or a world in which we choose our actions devoid of any external influences. All our choices are affected in some way or another by the environment in which we make them, whether we like it or not. Toilets need to be kitted out with a basin, restaurants require menus, and benefits must be paid in one way or another. Yet where the basin is located, what the menu looks like, or how benefits reach their recipients will influence whether we wash our hands, what we order, or how we manage our money. Nudges are simply a way of changing this environment, or the 'choice architecture', as Thaler and Sunstein put it, to direct us towards behaviour that is more desirable. From getting commuters on the Underground to be more physically active to incentivising cash transfer recipients in Tanzania to build up savings, small prompts can be effective at motivating us to do the right thing.

But here's the catch. Who decides what's right? And from whom do we expect what kind of behaviour?

Having others determine what's in our best interest and devise incentives to coax us towards this behaviour is inherently paternalistic. It assumes individuals don't know what's best for them, or if they do, don't act in accordance with their intentions. The science of the mind tells us there's truth in this. Habit and impulse govern our actions more than deliberate decision-making does, and this can result in behaviour that doesn't necessarily serve us – like stepping onto the escalator instead of walking the stairs. Still, taking the decision about desirable behaviour away from individuals themselves is a moral and ethical minefield.

Concerns are heightened when it comes to governments meddling with how we live our lives. There's a beautiful word in Dutch for the state interfering in our personal affairs: 'overheidsbetutteling'. Or, in less poetic terms, the nanny state. The Dutch tend to have a strong aversion to overheidsbetutteling. Plans aimed at changing behaviour are commonly met with resistance, with opponents invariably noting that the state shouldn't intervene in individual freedom and choice.

Whether it be proposals to prevent tempting displays of sweets and crisps at the till, or a ban on personal fireworks to reduce the number of casualties during New Year's celebrations, the common refrain is: 'We're very able to decide for ourselves, thank you very much.'

While there's great strength of feeling against motivating the average person to live a healthier or safer life – in the Netherlands and elsewhere – the opposite seems true when it comes to low-income individuals. Societies are obsessed with making sure that poor people are deserving of any support they receive, and use it in ways that taxpayers consider appropriate or desirable. This comes with a degree of entitlement in demanding behaviours from the poor that we wouldn't dare ask of those better off. Rich kids may snort cocaine all they want, but heaven forbid their poorer peers smoke a spliff. We don't want poor people wasting their money on alcohol and gambling, but no one bats an eyelid at the wealthy spending fortunes on lavish parties or losing thousands in a single poker game. And hard-working middle classes should all be able to take the pressure off by going for a pint or enjoying themselves at the races, shouldn't they?

About 10 years ago, I led a study to investigate the effects of welfare on the well-being of children in low-income families. One of the countries we looked at, South Africa, has a very well-established system to support those living in poverty. The largest welfare scheme, not just in the country but in the entire continent, is the Child Support Grant. Its reach is massive. In 2023, more than 13 million children received it.[8] With a child population of just over 20 million, it means that as many as two thirds of all South African under-18s are in receipt of financial support.

As is evident in the scheme's name, the Child Support Grant is explicitly targeted at children. The money is delivered to their primary caregiver, but they are to use it for their offspring's benefit. This isn't a formal stipulation; the use of the transfer isn't restricted, and the cash can be spent on anything. Yet there's no mistaking who this benefit should serve. When we asked mothers and grandmothers, who constitute the majority of recipients, about the purpose of the cash support, they were all very clear: it was to provide for the children in their care. The money is to be spent on food, school uniforms, bus fares and other expenditure that stands to benefit the youngsters.

Introduced in 1998, the grant has now been in place for more than 25 years. With this relatively long history and many of South Africa's children in receipt of support, it's no surprise that the scheme's purpose is well known. Arguably an important contributor to this is its name: Child Support Grant. It does what it says on the tin.

This might seem too obvious to reflect on, but labels can make a big difference. In the UK, the government provides cash transfer to older households with the objective of helping them stay warm throughout the winter. Research found that labelling those transfers 'Winter Fuel Payments' increased the likelihood of them being spent on household fuel by 38 per cent compared to the transfer having a neutral label.[9]

Labelling is a nudge of any policymaker's dream: low cost, high returns.

To recipients of the Child Support Grant, the equation looks a bit more complicated. Because the scheme is so widespread and it's so obvious what the money is supposed to be spent on, it comes with strong social control. People keep a close eye on their neighbours or parents with small children who are likely to receive the grant, looking out for whether they may have misappropriated the children's cash. If a caregiver is spotted wearing new clothes or having a drink in the local watering hole, gossip spreads quickly. 'What do your parents do with your money? They fix their hair? Buy alcohol, face creams?' This is how teachers confronted children with their suspicions about parents misusing welfare funds.

But, as caregivers taking part in our study pointed out, money can't be separated in such a simple manner. It might be strategic to spend money at the hairdresser to look well prepared for a job interview that can ultimately bring in more income. Or to purchase medication for an adult family member to avoid ill health, further medical bills and loss of income. Though these expenses may not immediately benefit the children, they will ultimately be in their best interest. While the scheme's official guidelines don't prevent caregivers from using the funds for these purposes, the strong notion that the entirety of the grant should be allocated towards children's direct needs – as encapsulated by its name – gives rise to undue social pressure.

And it's not just adults keeping caregivers in check. Children also leverage widely accepted social norms about the use of Child Support Grant money to make financial demands. Caregivers of teenagers find it difficult to withstand requests for expensive clothing or shoes from desirable brands. Adolescents will remind them that the funds they receive from the government are to be used on them. 'They tell us "Granny, you have our money",' explained one of the older women raising her grandchildren. Caregivers feel pressure to give in to such requests, even if their cost outweighs the monthly monetary support.

When it comes to deciding who should behave in what way, double standards are at play. The behaviour of those at the bottom of the socioeconomic ladder is scrutinised to a far greater extent than those with money to spare. Behavioural interventions for the 'common person' are pored over to find a comfortable equilibrium between the desire to improve outcomes while maintaining a degree of individual freedom. This is the very definition of 'libertarian paternalism', the concept underpinning nudge theory. Yet when it comes to the working class or people living on little, there's far less objection to steering them towards doing things differently.

Nudges for people in poverty are justified on the grounds of their diminished ability to make rational and smart decisions. From labelling their benefits to incentivise desired spending patterns, like in South Africa, and giving out money pouches to motivate savings, such as in Tanzania, to making the receipt of money conditional on sending children to school, as is the case for the conditional cash transfer programmes that we saw in Chapter 5, low-income individuals are pushed around much more than anyone else, and probably more than the average person would accept. While the use of behavioural tricks makes sense through the prism of psychology and behavioural science, it also risks playing into a two-tier system that guards the freedom of choice for the better-off but takes it away from those facing socioeconomic disadvantage.

'Support to the poor is paid for by us, the taxpayer. That's why we get to have a say in how they should behave,' is a common justification for double standards. Apart from demonstrating a staggering lack of solidarity, this retort also ignores the fact that middle-class lifestyles weigh on government coffers no less than those of the financially insecure. In fact, when it comes to the use of state funds to shift consumption behaviour, the better-off stand to benefit the most.

Take the example of subsidies to incentivise the move towards more sustainable products. In a bid to halt the deepening of the climate crisis and reduce our carbon footprint, many countries offer compensation or rebate if customers adopt more environmentally sustainable choices. In a bid to convince you to ditch your petrol car and drive an electric vehicle instead, to install solar panels on your roof, or to replace your boiler with an expensive heat pump, governments offer hefty payments and generous tax exemptions.

A quick search of schemes available across Europe in early 2024 gives an indication of just how much cash is available for those wishing to make their homes more eco friendly. In the UK,[10] installation of electric vehicle charge points is funded up to 75 per cent of the cost. In Germany,[11] households are exempt from paying VAT when installing solar panels. In the Netherlands,[12] there's a minimum subsidy of €500 when installing a heat pump, rising to more than €10,000 for the most expensive options.

These incentives are undoubtedly worthwhile investments to stop further depletion of the planet's resources and
promote a shift towards more sustainable lifestyles. But they
are also incredibly regressive. It's those already affluent enough
to own the house they live in and with ample money to spare
to invest in carbon-saving apparatus who stand to benefit
from potentially thousands in government support. For some,
this support is vital in overcoming the financial barrier that
prevented them from making hefty climate-friendly modifica-
tions. For others, the monetary incentive is a welcome but not
strictly necessary bonus.

Compare this to how the poor are advised to be more
energy-savvy. Instead of being handed enough money to
properly heat their homes, they're encouraged to place tin foil
behind their radiators to reflect warmth back into the room
and stuff gaps underneath doors or around window frames
to avoid draughts. If complaints about substandard housing
conditions don't lead to eviction, tenants are ignored or gas-
lighted, and forced to suffer the consequences.

The tragic case of two-year-old Awaab Ishak from Rochdale
in the UK is a case in point. Despite his parents having made
complaint after complaint to their landlord about mould
covering the walls in their flat, nothing was done to address
it. Instead, they were told the mould was a result of their
lifestyle and bathing habits. Living in these dangerously damp
conditions proved fatal for Awaab. He died from a respiratory
condition in 2020.[13]

While homeowners get to take advantage of financially
attractive nudges to create comfort and save on future energy

costs, low-income renters are blamed for structural defects in their place of residence and left to put up with the subsequent misery. This double standard isn't just about money, however. It signifies something much more fundamental: namely the glaring gap between the unquestionable trust we place in people with money to do the right thing, and the deep distrust we hold of those without cash to spare to act out of good intentions.

Spikes and barriers

As I walked towards the entrance of Milton Keynes train station, I couldn't help but think something had changed. It somehow looked different from usual, but I couldn't put my finger on it. When I returned a few days later, the penny dropped. Instead of the spaces left and right of the entrance being wide open, they were now home to massive square steel containers. They must have been at least a metre and a half in width, length and height and were filled to the top with soil, suggesting they would serve to liven up the place with plants and flowers.

At first, I was delighted. Despite Milton Keynes being incredibly green, its station square lived up to the city's reputation of being a concrete jungle. There's nothing like greenery to make a space more welcoming, and the thought of an urban garden was very appealing. But walking past those containers, and there must have been at least five of them on either side of the entrance, I was struck by what they had replaced.

Gone were the mattresses, blankets and shopping bags filled with clothes and other personal belongings. With the station's facade being a fairly sheltered spot, it was an attractive location for those sleeping rough. Over the years, during my weekly commute to Brighton, I had observed how the number of men and women taking up residence in front of the station had grown. At the height of the homelessness crisis in 2017, mirroring nationwide trends, an estimated one in 110 people in Milton Keynes were sleeping rough.[14] With small encampments set up in underpasses across the centre, it led to the new town being dubbed 'tent city'.[15] A few years later, with only centimetres between the giant containers, there was no more space for people without a home to seek refuge under the station entrance's overhang.

The (re)design of public spaces in ways that make them less attractive for sleeping or loitering is often deliberate rather than coincidental. There's even a term for this: hostile architecture. The obstruction of sheltered spots, installation of spikes on building's ledges, or segmentation of long benches into single seats are all intentional efforts to deter people from having a rest or idling for too long. Instead of offering gentle prompts towards positive action, as nudges tend to do, this type of urban design exists to disincentivise undesirable behaviour. Rather than trying to invite people in by making their lives easier – such as giving access to washing machines, as we saw earlier – the aim is to push individuals away by creating inhospitable and harsh spaces.

To be fair to Milton Keynes, apart from the giant containers in front of its train station – remarkably replete with plants most of the time – there is actually little hostile architecture to be found in the city. This doesn't appear to be a coincidence. On the whole, the city's response to the rise in the number of rough sleepers seems to have been positive rather than punitive.

Instead of trying to tackle homelessness by making the provision of tents a civil offence,[16] or using so-called public spaces protection orders to criminalise rough sleeping,[17] the council, homelessness organisations, the police and charities joined forces to seek a more dignified solution. A night shelter was established to offer a safe and warm night's sleep for those without a permanent home, including those no longer able to bed down in front of the station. In the same building, a one-stop shop of statutory and voluntary services offers support for a more sustainable solution to homelessness. The number of rough sleepers has come down considerably since the peak of the crisis, with many having been supported into accommodation. Those still out there are visited by outreach workers, not to confiscate their belongings or force them to move on but instead to help them with their complex needs in the best way possible.

This approach echoes the sentiment expressed by Naomi Eisenstadt at the beginning of this chapter. Any intervention aimed at reducing poverty requires easing the pressure on those who experience it. This is in line with the logic of nudges: make things easier, and behaviour – of anyone, poor or rich – will follow suit. Apply subtle prompts and gentle prods, and decisions previously considered too difficult or cumbersome become the obvious choice.

For people in poverty, however, nudges often constitute the opposite. Instead of creating conditions that invite them in, barriers are put in place to push them away. Hostile architecture isn't limited to design of public spaces. Similar tactics are deployed when it comes to public services.

Providing support to the poor and the poor only is a perennial puzzle for those in charge of welfare interventions. How to identify and allocate benefits for those eligible for and notably deserving of support is a difficult task, especially in contexts with little information about earnings or assets. For this reason, many schemes across lower-income countries don't rely on income data. Instead, they use other indicators to assess whether a family or its members are poor, such as the type of house they live in, how many cows they have, or what they eat for dinner.

As simple as it may seem to collect and use this information to consider who is poor, the reality proves more difficult. People may not want to share the true number of livestock they have, over- or underestimate the assets they own, or simply don't recall how many meals they ate last week. And even if data collection wasn't a problem, so-called proxy indicators to assess who is poor are often inaccurate, with individuals in need commonly excluded from support.

One mechanism to get around this problem is self-targeting. Instead of someone else assessing and concluding whether someone is poor enough to claim support, the decision is left to individuals themselves. It goes like this: make access to benefits as unattractive, hard and undignified as possible and only the neediest will come forward. Increase the burden and reduce the reward to such an extent that anyone with another option will pass on the opportunity.

If this sounds outrageous, it isn't. Public works schemes are especially notorious for adopting the logic of self-targeting. From India to Rwanda, programmes offer employment to millions of their poorest residents, who often see them as a last resort to put food on the table. Wages are low, typically below market rates, and much of the employment on offer is piecemeal. The work is hard, tedious or pointless, and sometimes all three at the same time. While many schemes focus on creating valuable infrastructure, by building roads, digging irrigation streams or terracing steep hillsides, such projects may not always be on offer. Speaking to public works participants in Ethiopia, I heard how they were asked to dig trenches only to fill them back up and start digging again. Pointless from a productivity point of view, but effective in ensuring that only the poorest put themselves forward to receive welfare support.

Nudges cut both ways. They can offer a soft push or subtle prompt towards behaviour or decisions that are in our best interest, especially if these aren't immediately obvious, require more effort, or take longer to materialise. When implemented well, tweaks to our environment lead us to choices that can improve our financial health, physical activity and carbon footprint. This holds regardless of where we stand on the socioeconomic ladder. Thinking about examples from how we go about our own lives and get ourselves to do things that may not come naturally to us serves to relate to the effectiveness of nudges. And as the design of effective nudges requires a profound understanding of what makes a person do the things they do, one might argue that empathy lies at their core.

However, when we consider how they are implemented within the realm of poverty reduction, we realise that nudges are often strikingly devoid of empathy. While the installation of washing machines could help make low-income parents' lives much easier and motivate them to take part in advisory services, most support services actively denounce such positive prods. In contrast to what's available to the middle classes, interventions are used to push people away rather than invite them in. Hostile architecture is employed to act as a barrier. Welfare policies aren't designed to help as many people to the best extent possible, but rather to limit their support to those who will grovel and grind. Nudges are deployed as a deterrent, not an encouragement, and empathy becomes missing in action.

7

SELF-HELPING YOUR
WAY UP AND OUT

'Our residents are referred to us by—'

Sharon is mid-sentence when an alarm goes off. I, along with the other visitors in the room, jump up.

'Don't worry,' she says. 'It's just the door. An alarm sounds when it stays open for too long. It's to stop the young kids leaving the house without anyone noticing. We can't keep an eye out for the little ones all the time, you see.'

That makes a lot of sense. We just walked past a room filled with toddlers spread out across the floor drawing and painting. They weren't too far from the main entrance, and having seen the many balls and other toys scattered across the house's garden, I'm not surprised that the children might try and escape to go and play in the fresh air.

The noise ends as abruptly as it started. Someone must have closed the door.

'As I was saying,' Sharon continues, 'our residents get referred to us by the Massachusetts welfare agency. The state-run agency is the first port of call for homeless families. They are then referred to organisations offering emergency housing, like ours. Where they go depends on their personal circumstances. We run multiple shelters, but this one only takes in families, not individuals.'

I'm in northern Boston, in one of the city's homeless accommodations. It's run by a local nonprofit, which provides emergency housing across the city. Sharon is responsible for helping its clients become self-sufficient. Together with her team members, Bianca and Yolanda, she kindly invited me and my colleagues to visit one of their locations. So here we are, sitting around a large dining table in what looks like the shelter's reception room. There's a generous spread of warm coffee, chilled juice, and sugar-coated doughnuts in front of us.

'Homelessness is a big problem. Public housing is taboo in the US and legislation to ensure affordable housing is available doesn't work. Housing support in Massachusetts is relatively well organised because of the way in which the state works with the nonprofit sector. But capacity is an issue.'

Bianca explains the basics of how their organisation operates. This shelter caters specifically to women with children. Located in a large detached wood-clad corner house on a quiet residential street, there's a real homely feel to it. Walking up the front porch steps and into the house, I admit I was positively surprised by how warm, cosy and welcoming it felt.

The house has eight rooms, each with its own bathroom. 'Staff are present 24 hours per day, and there are strict rules,' says Yolanda, 'This is for the residents' benefit, to create a safe environment. It also helps with acceptance in the neighbour-hood, as we're in the middle of a quiet residential area.'

'Would you like a tour of the house?' Sharon asks as she takes a last sip of coffee. Curious, we all agree.

First stop is the kitchen. It's big, and dominated by a large counter stacked with fresh fruit, vegetables and bread. 'They're mostly donations from the local community,' explains Yolanda as she notices our surprise at so much fresh and expensive-looking produce. There are two cooking stoves, one at either end of the kitchen. The walls are lined with four fridges, each to be shared by two families. Labels on the doors make sure there's no confusion, and no cause for a potential argument.

Sharon opens a door in the corner that leads into the basement. Walking down the stairs, I realise it's set up as a computer room. 'Adults can come here to write their job applications, or access other online services. Children use the computers for their homework. It's not open all the time, though. There's a sign-in sheet and the warden holds the key,' says Sharon.

We're ushered back up the stairs, along the corridor and up another flight of steps to the first floor. There's a laundry room in the corner, with a washing machine and tumble dryer. Each family has one day a week allocated to do their laundry.

Most of the bedrooms are on this floor as well. Bianca knocks on one of the doors, asking the occupant if we can have a peek inside. My colleague taps her on her shoulder to indicate that it's not necessary. It feels like too much of an imposition. But the woman behind the door has already agreed, and the door swings open. The room is basic but spacious. It holds a double bed, cot and wardrobe. The woman explains that she shares the room with her two young daughters. It's not ideal, but it will do for now. 'I feel safe. For myself and my daughters, that's most important,' she says.

A few minutes later, we're back in the living room. I pour another coffee as Sharon starts telling us about the specific approach taken by her organisation. In refreshing contrast to many other interventions I've come across, it has empathy written all over it.

'We try to do things differently. We don't simply provide emergency housing. We look at the situation that families and individuals find themselves in, and then consider how they can be best served. Would they benefit from education? Are there any issues with their immigration status? Do they need a work permit?'

There's a knock, and the door is pushed ajar. A staff member pops her head in and waves at Sharon, asking her to step out. Bianca takes over.

'Each client gets assigned a case manager, and they meet weekly. Together they identify the main issues that are holding them back, and how they can be addressed. The focus is on what individuals themselves can do to move forward. To get out of emergency housing and become self-sufficient. They may have big dreams, but goals need to be SMART.'

I scribble down 'SMART goals' in my notepad, underlining it. I'm struck by the adoption of an acronym I learned about in a management course as part of my undergraduate degree, describing the criteria that homeless people need to adopt when setting objectives for themselves: specific, measurable, achievable, relevant and time-bound.

'Dreaming big is great, but goals have to be realistic,' Bianca continues. 'Our case managers help clients to break down large areas for improvement into small and manageable steps. And they emphasise that goals need to be flexible. Life happens, but even small setbacks can be demotivating, and for some this creates barriers to trying again.'

Sharon has quietly made her way back into the room. Taking her seat, she instantly picks up from where Bianca left off.

'You have to understand, this is a temporary shelter. We won't push people out if they have nowhere to go, but it's vital for our clients to become self-reliant. For them to earn enough income to be able to afford a place of their own.' Yolande and Bianca nod in agreement. 'That's not possible if we do things for them. All we can do is guide them. We need to prevent learned helplessness. Teaching them how to plan their budgets, search for work and hold their own during a job interview, these are vital skills.'

She pauses and looks around the room. Her energy is one of hope and determination mixed with frustration and a sense of resignation.

'At the end of the day, we can't change the system. Our clients are responsible for building their own stable and financially independent futures.'

Graduating out of poverty

Is it possible to 'graduate' out of poverty? To move up the socioeconomic ladder to become self-sufficient, without needing any more support from anyone else? Most of us will associate the notion of graduation with college degrees or other forms of education. The idea of it applying to people moving out of poverty might seem odd. Yet it has been a hot topic amongst the anti-poverty policy and research swots for decades.

The concept originates from Bangladesh, in a remarkable tale of resilience, ingenuity and bottom-up community development. At the end of 1971, the country emerged from a relatively short-lived but gruelling liberation war with Pakistan. Scarred but determined to build an independent Bangladesh, local initiatives started popping up everywhere. The Bangladesh Rehabilitation Assistance Committee, now known by its acronym, BRAC, was one of those.

Initially established to provide relief and rehabilitation to returning refugees in northern Bangladesh, it quickly turned its hand to community projects before focusing on the much larger goal of rural development. It famously taught millions of people how to prepare oral rehydration solutions and treat diarrhoea,[1] a leading cause of child mortality at the time. Schools were set up, health insurance was offered, poultry vaccination was initiated and loans were provided. A whole host of education and livelihood initiatives have touched lives across rural Bangladesh. Testament to its success, BRAC is the largest NGO in the country, and has expanded its operations to countries across Asia and Africa. It's against this backdrop that the ultra-poor graduation approach was born.

'What the research and evidence began to show fairly clearly was that BRAC was failing to meet those who are living in the most extreme forms of poverty. Many of the traditional anti-poverty programmes were working for many, but there were large pockets of people being left out.' This is Greg Chen speaking, managing director of the BRAC Ultra-Poor Initiative at the organisation's international arm. He joined me on the Poverty Unpacked podcast to mark the 20-year anniversary of the graduation approach.[2]

'First is meeting basic needs. If people are hungry, or they have some very urgent matter, they can't plan for the future,' he explains.

Decades of working to relieve poverty across the country led to the realisation that the combination of economic, social and psychological barriers made it impossible for extremely poor families to benefit from the interventions provided by BRAC. Lack of access to land or capital prevented them from reaping benefits from agricultural inputs, craft cooperatives or micro-credit. After a period of trial and error, BRAC eventually landed on a holistic approach with multiple components, providing support over a period of about two years.

'Then there's a transition to a new kind of income-generating asset or activity, an opportunity to increase their income,' Greg continues. 'There is a link to some regular savings. This is an important thing to do not just for the amount of money that's put aside, but as a psychological activity. Because I'm setting aside something that I have a plan for. Throughout all of this, there is an ongoing coaching element. Someone shows up at the doorstep of participants at least once a week. Regular interaction that has a lot to do with momentum and self-confidence.'

The graduation approach is rooted in the economic concepts of poverty traps and asset thresholds.[3] The idea that there's an imaginary poverty barrier that needs to be broken down or pushed through. The only way to do this is by accumulating ample resources that constitute a big push upwards and onwards. If you're extremely poor and have hardly any assets, whether that's land, a house or livestock, obtaining some of these resources will help you to become slightly better off. But it's not enough to break through the barrier. Your single goat may get ill and die. A drought could prevent you from growing crops from your one batch of seeds. Earnings may be low and inconsistent. Any setback will push you back to where you were before.

Build up enough assets, though, and over and above the threshold you go. The milk and eggs produced by your goat and chickens offer healthy nutrition to your children, lowering costs for health care. The sale of excess produce allows you to save up and buy fertiliser to increase your harvest, or to buy a bicycle to transport your produce to markets where prices are higher. You've entered the virtuous spiral of accumulation. It's only a matter of time before you graduate out of poverty.

No wonder then that initiatives underpinned by this approach can be found all over the world, especially in low- and middle-income countries. A recent count includes 219 programmes across 75 countries, serving an estimated 92 million people.[4] With large proportions of the population in poverty and most governments operating modest budgets, the premise that a programme offering sizeable support over a short period of time will see families move into self-sufficiency is an attractive one. Governments are always worried about creating dependency, so a programme that helps families off welfare is incredibly appealing. This is true in the UK as much as it is in Bangladesh.

A few years ago, an unexpected email landed in my inbox. It was from a TV producer, not the type of person I tend to have regular encounters with. Their company was developing a new programme about poverty and was looking for advice. Having heard about the potential of giving a big economic boost to families in poorer countries, they wanted to see whether it might work in a rich country like the UK. Could the provision of a large cash transfer to the working poor kick-start a better life and help lift them out of poverty for good? An exciting idea, they said, and not yet tried in this country.

Alarm bells started ringing as soon as I read their message. So-called 'poverty porn' is an all too familiar occurrence on British television. Programmes like *Benefits Street* or *Can't Pay? We'll Take It Away!* – to name a few – feed off the misery and misfortune of their protagonists, portraying poverty as a lifestyle choice. I had no appetite to be part of anything like this. The producer understood my concerns, but this programme wasn't going to be like that, I was assured. Rather than using poor people as a conduit for entertainment – just to make 'good telly', as they put it – it was going to be a serious attempt to test a new approach for tackling the intractable problem of poverty.

Following a careful selection and vetting process, three families were each to receive a lump sum of £26,000, equating to the maximum annual entitlement of benefits at the time. In return, they would agree to give up any welfare payments for that year. The idea was that the transfer might constitute the financial push to help them transform their lives, to come off welfare and be independent, and if that was the case, the public needed to know about it.

Questions the producer asked me included whether there should be any restrictions on how the funds were spent (I said no), whether any misuse – such as on alcohol, drugs, gambling or foreign holidays – should be penalised (I strongly objected), whether the families should receive support throughout the three months of filming and beyond until the end of year (yes and yes), and whether they should spend all their money in the three months during which the programme was recorded (certainly not). I emphasised that, given the substantial size of the transfer, sound financial advice was going to be vital to weigh up the potential benefits, costs and risks. Could they ensure engaging a financial adviser to help families think through the various options they have in mind?

I didn't hear back from the producers until the programme aired more than a year later. Watching it on TV at home, I was relieved to see the makers had gone to some effort to give it an informative spin, rather than reverting to the attractive option of delivering cheap entertainment. Expert commentators offered nuanced reflections and the voice-over stayed away from judgemental commentary. The families received some advice as to how to handle the money, although it was minimal. As one reviewer poignantly observed: 'Why on earth weren't these lovely families given good financial advice from day 1, including education in realistic budgeting, counselling on easy record-keeping, instruction on planning ahead for future bills, etc., etc.??? This would not only have set them all on good, realistic pathways but it would have also educated many viewers in these crucial aspects of daily living.'[5]

Despite limited support, the experiment did bring some success to the families. As anticipated, the large lump sum helped them set up new business ventures and get rid of long-standing debt. This mirrors the wider evidence of the impact of these types of 'big push' programmes. They can prove life-changing, and quite literally life-saving for some participants, notably helping them to break through the magical barrier and go from strength to strength. For others, it constitutes a temporary uptick before falling back down the poverty ladder.

There are many reasons why interventions deliver success for some but not for others. Context is crucial. Economic, social and environmental factors all need to work together to provide favourable conditions. Markets must be able to absorb new supply; communities need to be accepting of changes in socioeconomic hierarchies; and infrastructure has to be in place to both facilitate and cope with increased economic activity. Family situation and individual characteristics also matter: it's far easier for a woman to set up and run a new business if she's literate, has a supportive partner and is able to leave her children in the care of a trustworthy neighbour.[6]

Progress can be fragile. When returning to Burundi a few years after the Concern Worldwide programme that we came across in Chapter 5 had come to an end, I found that many participants experienced levels of deprivation similar to when they started engaging in the project. A political crisis had taken place in the intervening period, driving people from their homes, selling anything of value along the way. Not the result the NGO had hoped for. But as my colleagues and I argued in the analysis of our results, the programme might well have prevented families from being even worse off, as it afforded them a financial buffer to deal with the shock of conflict.[7]

Sustainability of the income-generating activity supported by the intervention may also prove to be less promising than initially anticipated. There's an infamous example from Honduras where families were given chickens to be reared for their eggs, but many of the hens died. The breed wasn't local, required special feed and took too long to lay their eggs, causing the chickens to fall ill or to be slaughtered for their meat instead[8].

The viability of businesses is a concern for anyone anywhere investing in a new venture. Transporting ourselves back to the UK, about 7 per cent of new businesses don't make it past their first year, while almost half don't survive the first three years.[9] Indeed, one of the families participating in the TV show had to stop trading after 18 months as their business was no longer viable.

And this is where things can go awry when it comes to programmes trying to provide a big bang to shoot people out of poverty into economic prosperity. If these families had used their own money or taken out a loan, their business failure would probably have been brushed off as unfortunate. Their efforts to think big and act bold would have been applauded. 'At least they tried' captures the sense of admiration at entrepreneurial courage and ingenuity, even if unsuccessful.

In the case of those relying on external support, however, the narrative very easily gets flipped on its head. 'They've blown it!' read one tabloid headline in reporting on the TV show's family's demise.[10]

It isn't just the press looking for scapegoats. I've sat in high-level policy forums attended by hundreds of people with government ministers wagging their fingers at recipients of income support, telling them it's their fault and their fault alone if they are unable to move out of poverty. After all, they've been given all the tools required to become self-sufficient.

Yet when you aren't flush with cash, you're likely to invest at least as much effort and energy in living an autonomous life as someone with more to spend, because the consequences of things not working out or plans coming undone will be far greater. There's no back-up option, no easily achievable second chance. There can be many reasons why ideas or initiatives to earn more money don't pay off, many of which are beyond individual control. However, that's not how it's perceived in the public eye. It's far easier to condemn the person unable to live up to expectations than it is to take a more nuanced view of the complexities that hold them back from achieving economic independence. Once more, those on tighter budgets are held to different standards than those with larger bank accounts.

The fallacy of self-reliance

The Ancient Greek philosopher Epicurus once said: 'Self-sufficiency is the greatest of all wealth' and 'Freedom is the greatest fruit of self-sufficiency.'[11] Centuries on, self-reliance – being independent and able to provide for oneself – remains a prevailing value across societies. 'Standing on your own two feet' is a common phrase in English. The Dutch speak about '*je eigen boontjes doppen*' – which quite neatly translates into 'podding your own beans' – or '*je eigen broek ophouden*' – 'holding up your own trousers'. They are sayings ingrained into our collective psyche, emphasising the importance of earning one's own keep, of making it yourself.

Cue Patricia, a poverty activist with ATD Fourth World in London and in receipt of Universal Credit, a means-tested social assistance benefit. Rolled out across the UK over the last decade to replace six existing benefit and tax credit schemes, it aimed to simplify the benefit system, help people get into work and ultimately get them off welfare.

'When they started, they kept saying it would make sure that "work always pays" by making sure we didn't lose benefits by working extra hours. But as someone who has always worked, including all the way through the pandemic when I was working in train stations to help travellers, I can tell you that Universal Credit is a bloody nightmare!'

Patricia is speaking at a conference on social protection, co-organised by myself and colleagues,[12] a space usually reserved for academics and policy experts. She is part of a panel shining light on welfare recipients' lived experience. As she talks, it soon becomes clear that reforms that were introduced to the UK welfare system to promote self-reliance, as opposed to dependence or helplessness, seem to have achieved anything but that.

'The next problem is that when your agency needs you to cover extra shifts, your Universal Credit will go down – but not until the following month, when you might not get assigned many shifts at work. So you have to try to save money from the extra shifts or you'll be completely broke the next month.'

In order to ensure that welfare payments don't serve to top up earnings beyond a certain threshold, the amount of income support is recalculated every month. However, as Patricia explained, while calculations are based on this month's wages, they don't take effect until the next month. With many low-wage jobs offering piecemeal and insecure employment, this can cause great fluctuations in income levels from one month to the next. Meanwhile, monthly outgoings on rent or utilities don't change, nor does the need to feed one's children or heat the house.

'Another problem is that every time you get a Universal Credit statement, the numbers are different, depending on the shifts you or your partner have worked. Why does the government send us such a complicated statement? It makes people feel like we have no power over our own budget.'

Frustration and exasperation ring through in Patricia's voice. Used to hearing about these issues in abstract terms, the audience is listening intently.

Patricia's contribution highlights the catch-22 so many people in poverty find themselves in. They want to earn their keep and be independent as much as the next person. They don't take any pleasure in relying on others for support – whether that's the state, charities or generous community members – but the system keeps them trapped. Complementing welfare payments with work doesn't pay, not really. The combination of benefits and wages may turn out slightly higher, on balance. But the backdating of welfare deductions, the insecurity of how things will pan out, and the mere complexity of it all work to disempower rather than stimulate self-reliance.

But what does self-reliance mean anyway? And do we apply the same standards to all?

The notion of self-reliance is as much an illusion as it is an aspiration. Complete independence is a fallacy. We live in an interconnected world, relying on each other for care, comfort and support. To quote Aristotle, another Ancient Greek philosopher: 'He who is unable to live in society, or who has no need because he is sufficient for himself, must be either a beast or a god.'[13] Aristotle may have been referring to our human need for love and companionship, but the sentiment extends to the much more mundane: getting our hair cut, having our car serviced or ordering a hot meal to be delivered to our doorstep. Unless we're a recluse, we rely on others to get through life.

What, then, is the key to moving from a state of dependence into a life of self-reliance? You guessed it: money. When you have cash to spare, you no longer receive help or rely on external support. No, you buy a service. A product carefully procured and paid for. Need help with looking after your child while you go to work? Get childcare. Prefer not to wash and iron your shirts yourself to save some precious time? Outsource it. Can't be bothered to handle your financial affairs? Hire an accountant.

Having a larger budget doesn't make us less reliant on others, or less dependent. We merely have the financial means to turn a request for help into a monetary transaction. Money allows for buying into the false idea of independence. Paying for someone else to do the things we don't like, don't want to spend time on or lack skills for doesn't make us self-sufficient per se. Rather, it gives us power over others to facilitate our independence.

Ironically, it's the very people struggling to obtain the coveted 'self-reliant' label who make this happen. Cleaners, care workers, delivery drivers are the engine underneath the bonnet of our personal and national economies. Yet while they allow those with money in their pockets to claim their independence, many workers in the care and service industry are hardly able to keep their heads above water. Low pay, lack of job security and counterproductive welfare make the goal of self-sufficiency impossible for those from whom it's demanded the most. While hungry families are sent from welfare office to local charity to obtain a voucher so they can collect a parcel from their local food bank, UK members of

Parliament get to enjoy subsidised meals in Westminster's bars and restaurants.[14] Self-reliance comes a lot easier to those who already enjoy it.

The increased emphasis on self-reliance has helped fuel austerity and a hollowing-out of social services in most wealthy countries. The financial crisis that crashed economies in 2008 put considerable strain on governments' coffers the world over. In many places, the knee-jerk reaction was to consolidate public service provision.

Take the Netherlands. The population was explicitly roped in and made to share in the responsibility to balance the books. The liberal-right prime minister and centre-right coalition government embraced self-reliance – or 'zelfredzaamheid' – and placed it at the core of national policy. It drummed home the message that the country relied on its people to increase their problem-solving capacities, and to work together with their nearest and dearest, neighbours and willing volunteers to find solutions for social problems. Only if the population took more responsibility for themselves and relied less on the government to do it for them would the country as a whole get back on track and flourish again.

Vulnerable groups bore the brunt of this narrative. After all, they were the ones leaning on the state the most. For too long those in need of care or in receipt of income support, and often both at the same time, had been coddled and cosseted. No more. What was needed was for the elderly, disabled, chronically ill, unemployed and poor to take back control of their own lives. To be empowered. Instead of the state taking them by the hand, the onus was on people themselves to think creatively, reach out to others and be independent.

The implications reached far and wide. Care homes for the elderly were closed; it was now up to families and community networks to help their older relatives to live at home for as long as humanly possible. Youth services were cut to the bone, with many young people left to their own devices.[15] The policy shift to self-sufficiency might have created a greater sense of ownership, but it has been at the expense of many unable to receive the care they need and informal carers driven to despair by the emotional, physical and financial toll of the responsibilities transferred onto their plates.[16]

The self-reliance dogma has left its mark elsewhere as well. In 2010, David Cameron, the then UK prime minister, pitched his idea for the 'Big Society'.[17] Attempting to divert attention away from the inevitable pain that was to follow proposed public sector budget cuts, he announced, 'There are the things you do because it's your passion. The things that fire you up in the morning, that drive you, that you truly believe will make a real difference to the country you love. And my great passion is building the Big Society.'

Cameron had travelled from London to Liverpool for his big speech. Standing at a lectern in front of a select audience and with cameras rolling, he turned the logic of austerity upside down. Budget cuts didn't represent a lost opportunity; they were a chance for people to finally 'feel both powerful and free enough to help themselves and their own communities'. To reclaim ownership, and to redistribute power away from government elites to everyday people. Apart from this logic leading to the dismantling of vital services, it conveniently allowed for reshaping the narrative. Soup kitchens, food pantries and 'warm banks' are no longer examples of stopgaps in the glaring holes of service provision that might be expected from a responsible state caring for its citizens. They are beacons of hope, laudable efforts of communities coming together and caring for each other. Proof that the Big Society works.

Further afield, residents of one of the top five richest countries in the world, Singapore,[18] are no strangers to self-reliance either.[19] Considered as much a value as a character trait, self-reliance is core to being a good citizen. The importance of personal responsibility is a deep-seated narrative, rooted in the country's rise to economic power and perpetuated through messaging in the national curriculum. Rhetoric zooms in on combining individual responsibility – being gainfully employed so you can afford anything you and your family might need, from housing to health care and education – with collective responsibility, with communities coming together and society taking care of its weakest. In the words of Deputy Prime Minister and Minister of Finance Lawrence Wong: 'A social compact is not just about what Government will do for the people; it is also about what Singaporeans will do for one another.'[20] He lists philanthropy and volunteering as key to this compact.

The world over, governments have latched on to a discourse of personal responsibility and self-sufficiency. A charitable interpretation of this is that they're trying to do the best they can with limited resources. A more cynical but possibly more truthful telling of the tale is that states seek to absolve themselves of the responsibility to provide their citizens with adequate safety nets and solid springboards for success. The American Dream is predicated on a 'do it yourself' mentality, on the idea of individuals taking matters into their own hands and pulling themselves up by their bootstraps. Traditionally more generous European welfare states have shifted from their post-war objective of providing social protection for all to delivering highly targeted and limited support to some, much of it justified under the guise of empowering their people.

In poorer countries, the starting point is different. Social services and safety nets are being developed and often expanded. The COVID-19 pandemic gave rise to an unprecedented and rapid rollout of cash transfers across low- and middle-income countries,[21] evidencing the possibility of expanding support if appetite for it exists. Yet tight government budgets and large populations in poverty give rise to the almost irrefutable argument that self-reliance is the only route out of poverty and towards greater well-being. Rather than serving as a reason for clawing back welfare support, the notion of self-sufficiency risks acting as a self-imposed limitation on the breadth and reach of services.

Ignore the pain, think happy

'What is the secret to money?' asks Rhonda Byrne in one of the short videos based on her audiobook *The Secret to Money Masterclass.*[22]

'Prosperity is your birthright and you hold the key to more abundance in every area of your life than you can possibly imagine,' she goes on against the backdrop of mystical-sounding music. 'Think positive thoughts about money and you magnetise positive circumstances, people and events that bring more money to you. Think negative thoughts about money and you magnetise negative circumstances, people and events that cause you to have a lack of money.'

The Secret has been a self-help success ever since it was first published in 2006, selling more than 35 million copies worldwide.[23] The secret that *The Secret* espouses to reveal is the so-called law of attraction. The idea that we can have everything we want if only we put our mind to it and direct our positive thoughts and energies to what we wish to achieve. In other words, it's 'like for like'. From our health and careers to personal wealth, if we send positive waves into the universe, they will be met with a positive response.

Although there's no scientific base to the claims made by Byrne, millions swear by them. Oprah Winfrey is possibly one of *The Secret's* most famous supporters. In a CNN interview with talk show host Larry King, she reveals that 'the message of *The Secret* is the message I've been trying to share with the world on my show for the past 21 years. The message is that you're really responsible for your life. YOU are responsible for your life.'[24] She then goes on to share the story of how she got her first big acting role, in the 1985 movie *The Color Purple*, attributing her success to her obsession with the eponymous book from when she was little.

The Secret, in line with most self-help books, claims to put forward a revolutionary new method for achieving inner peace and happiness. However, when taking a step back and looking beyond the detail of individual approaches or methods, we can see that much of the rhetoric of these books revolves around one central message: our happiness is in our own hands. All we need to do is reach for it.

It's such an appealing idea: think positively and good things come to you. Think rich and you'll be rich. Focus your attention on earning lots of money, and lots of money will come your way.

Of course, we all know it doesn't work like this. While the internet has no shortage of glowing reviews and rave testimonies of how fortune has befallen believers of *The Secret*, we only have to look around us or think about our own situation to realise that reality is very different. If positive thinking was all it took, most of us would probably have a lot more money at our disposal than we currently have. If manifesting the idea of wealth attracts wealth, surely there would be far less poverty than is the case.

Even though this logic isn't borne out by reality, the mere promise of something bigger and better is enough. Personal growth is a booming business. In the US alone, the self-help industry amounted to a whopping $9.9 billion in 2016.[25] This is more than the annual income of many smaller countries. Take the Maldives: its national income in 2016 was just over $8 billion.[26] Through a myriad of books, speeches and courses, the industry offers to help overcome negative thinking, self-blame and overwhelm, and cultivate self-confidence and a 'can-do' attitude, inspiring us to take control of our own thoughts, feelings and behaviour to set us free and live a better life.

However fuzzy, warm and harmless all this may sound, self-help narratives can quickly turn sour. Author and activist Barbara Ehrenreich draws a direct link between the exponential growth of the motivational and positive thinking industry in the US in the 1990s and the economic trend of downsizing and outsourcing that led to 30 million workers losing their jobs. To encourage staff who didn't get culled, companies invested big money in motivational speakers and career coaches. Large businesses bought books and CDs in bulk to stop their remaining workforce from ruminating about what had happened to their less fortunate colleagues and move on.[27]

Meanwhile, the self-help industry gratefully seized upon the newly unemployed, helping them to put a positive spin on their bad luck and to market themselves to the rest of the world. Their change in circumstances was to be embraced: free from the shackles of a boss dictating their every move, it was finally possible to embark on the process of self-transformation. No more losing or trailing behind others: job loss was an opportunity for personal growth, and was to be grabbed by the horns. By overcoming negative thinking and adopting a 'winners' mentality', a new and improved life was now within reach.

I came across a striking example of similar logic at a conference a few years back. US-based public management scholar Elizabeth Linos was presenting findings from her work on how to reduce burnout among front-line workers, zooming in on her research with 911 emergency call-takers.[28] These are the people who pick up the phone when there's been an accident, when someone's having a heart attack or when a shooting is taking place, and who must then decide what happens next. It's an incredibly stressful job, and this is reflected in the statistics, with high rates of sick leave and job turnover.

In a bid to reduce burnout and improve levels of well-being among the workforce, Linos and her team sent call-takers regular emails over a period of six weeks. They included messages asking staff to reflect on how important they were to each other, what advice they might give to junior colleagues, or what characteristics they identified in people they respected. Rather than emphasising the significance of the call-takers' service to the wider community, the emails tried to instil a sense of social belonging, to make staff aware that they weren't alone and could reach out to each other.

And it worked. When the researchers followed up after four months and compared results with call-takers who hadn't received the emails, they found that reports of burnout had sharply reduced. Not just that, the number of workers who resigned from their jobs had also decreased.

These are great results, of course. If sending a few emails can improve staff well-being to such an extent, it sounds like an initiative every HR department should consider. But it was something that Linos said about the nature of the job and the context within which this experiment was framed that had me shaking my head.

Being a 911 call-taker isn't just a stressful job, it's also poorly paid and comes with mandatory overtime. Relatedly, and most crucially, call-takers aren't considered first responders. This means they don't have access to mental health services or support to deal with trauma and stress as a result of their job. Nor do they have the social status of being a first responder. Despite being the first to hear about and quickly having to respond to someone being trapped in a fire or attacked on the streets, call-takers are classed as call-centre workers. How's that for a kick in the teeth?

To be fair to Linos, she acknowledged these systemic issues upfront, and called the audience's attention to them again at the end of the presentation. Trying to change the nature of the call-takers' jobs was beyond her remit. She was asked to think about a solution within the structural boundaries of the 911 call-taker job profile, and she did so successfully. But it's difficult to get past the absurdity of the situation. Surely the obvious route to reducing burnout and improving job retention is by improving work conditions?

As political economist William Davies put it so poignantly in his book *The Happiness Industry*: 'If lifting weights becomes too painful, you're faced with a choice: reduce the size of the weight, or pay less attention to the pain. In the early twenty-first century, there is a growing body of experts in "resilience" training, mindfulness, and cognitive behavioural therapy whose advice is to opt for the latter strategy.'[29] It is even being adopted as a mechanism to reduce poverty.

Based on the knowledge that mental ill-health is widespread among those living on little, combined with the logic of social drift, which – as we saw in Chapter 3 – draws a causal link between mental distress and poverty, the thinking is that exposing the poor to counselling will help them break the reinforcing cycle. In Ghana, participants in an anti-poverty programme received 12 weekly sessions of 90 minutes each, and were asked to complete homework assignments in between. The course covered topics such as healthy thinking, goal-setting and problem-solving, aiming to help participants move away from 'catastrophising' over small problems and increase their bandwidth to improve decision-making. The intervention was successful in reducing psychological distress and improving participants' results in cognitive tests, such as the Raven's matrices we saw in Chapter 2. This improved mental state, the researchers argued, would subsequently lead to improved economic outcomes.[30]

A similar intervention in Kenya, however, found no discernible impact of psychotherapy on mental health or – crucially – economic outcomes. By contrast, it was the provision of cash that did the trick. A year after the intervention had come to an end, researchers did not detect any notable improvements for those who had been exposed to counselling sessions only. However, when looking at the effects of cash transfers on a similar group of poor individuals in rural Kenya, they found improvements in consumption and assets as well as psychological well-being.[31]

With the link between poor mental health and economic hardship well established, tackling poverty by intervening at the psychological end of things is an attractive proposition. Not unlike Rhonda Byrne's *The Secret* or self-help discourse more broadly, the thinking is that moving out of poverty is possible if only low-income individuals adopted the right mindset. While I'm a fervent proponent of therapy for supporting mental health, its potential for alleviating poverty strikes me as dubious at best. Linking back to William Davies' words, this approach asks people to ignore the pain of poverty, rather than helping them reduce the weight of it.

Beyond its ineffectiveness, the flipside of suggesting that we all have the power to improve our lives is that if life looks less glorious, it's our own fault. The primary premise underpinning self-help is that the problem lies with the individual. By extension, this means the power for overcoming the problem is also located within the individual. It isn't called 'self-help' for nothing.

Feeding the toxic narrative

Self-helping one's way out of poverty is predicated on the notion that we live in a meritocracy. A system within which everyone has equal opportunities, and effort and achievements are rewarded equally, regardless of who you are. Wealth, class, race, religion, gender, age, health and family background don't play a role. Take responsibility and put the effort in, and you can achieve anything you want. Success comes to those who want it, those who put in the grit and graft.

We don't live in a meritocracy. This much is clear. Opportunities aren't accessible to all. Grit and graft aren't equally rewarded. Yet the pull of the meritocratic ideal is strong. Not only does it allow us to dream of a better future, it also affords a feeling of ownership and control to achieve it. A sense that we're in charge of our destiny. It's the stuff that aspirations are made of.

But if we believe we can work our way to success and claim we got there on merit, the corollary also holds: if we're unsuccessful, it is our own fault. If we fail, it's because we haven't put in the effort, we haven't worked hard enough. If we're poor, we only have ourselves to blame.

Our steadfast belief in the value of a meritocracy drives the individualisation of poverty. It's the fuel that feeds the toxic narrative that suggests being skint, struggling to make ends meet and living on little is due to individual fault. 'The notion that the system rewards talent and hard work encourages the winners to consider their success their own doing, a measure of their virtue – and to look down upon those less fortunate than themselves,' writes political philosopher Michael J. Sandel in his book *The Tyranny of Merit*.[32] The meritocratic model brings hubris to the wealthy and successful, affording them a moral high ground from which to point the finger at those worse off and shun them for their self-inflicted failure.

The ideology that poor people only have themselves to blame doesn't just serve to offer the wealthy a moral high ground, it also gives rise to a politics of humiliation. To the weaponisation of blame and shame. Pervasive emphasis on ideas of self-reliance and self-help allows for pushing through policies that benefit the rich and disadvantage the poor, and blaming the poor for any fallout.

Take welfare. Decisions about who should get support are framed around deservingness, which in turn is determined by whether someone's struggle to make ends meet is due to factors deemed inside or outside their control. If you're severely ill or very old, your inability to earn your own keep is beyond your realm of influence. You're a victim of circumstance, and redistribution of resources is justified. But if you're of working age and unable to find a job, ideas about your deservingness become far less lenient. 'They must not be looking hard enough', 'They're picky in choosing a job' or 'They just don't want to work' are likely opinions you'll be confronted with. No longer is your need determined by bad luck. Bad choices and poor behaviour are the cause of your misfortune, and this disqualifies you from receiving taxpayers' money or charitable support.

The inevitable result of this line of thought is that failure becomes internalised. As we saw in Chapter 3, blame drives shame and poverty undermines mental health. The peddling of the false narrative that lack of success is a direct result of lack of effort robs people at the lower end of the socio-economic ladder of their voice. Repeated messaging about their failure and lack of deservingness puts them in their place and keeps them small. It's no coincidence that this facilitates the pursuit of policies that help the wealthy to accumulate more wealth while at the same time disempower poorer segments of society.

'Now, the dynamic is basically that if you shame someone, if you blame them for circumstances beyond their control, then it's easier to keep those circumstances as they are.' This is journalist Mary O'Hara speaking on my podcast. She describes the effects of repeated messaging that lack of success is because you don't try hard enough or aren't doing the right things: '[It] solidifies the negative attitudes toward poorer people and low-income people. And it reduces the appetite for policies and action that would make people's lives better. It justifies things like de-unionisation, precarious work, low wages.'

Despite these far-reaching political implications, the self-help rhetoric is remarkably devoid of critical engagement with the disadvantages that many face in achieving a better life, no matter how strongly they believe or how hard they work at it. Let's return to Oprah Winfrey. She has inspired and motivated millions, encouraging them to seek out their own path, believe in themselves and pursue their dreams. Her personal journey, life experiences and charisma make her uniquely capable of helping people believe in their inner strengths. She has broken down taboos and pushed boundaries around speaking about personal and sensitive subjects.

Yet at the same time, she is decisively apolitical.[33] Her discourse steers clear of engaging with economic, social or political realities that facilitate or prevent socioeconomic success. This isn't a coincidence. Quite the opposite. It's precisely because Oprah avoids thorny discussions about who is more or less likely to achieve their goals that she's so popular. It helps her fans to hold firm to the idea they so desperately want to believe: just fix yourself and you can achieve anything you want. A life of abundance and prosperity can be yours if only you want it enough. And this is exactly what makes it so dangerous.

There are undoubtedly benefits to be gained from reading self-help books, watching mindfulness videos or employing the many tools and methods for self-exploration. Available at no or low cost, these can help cut through engrained personal and societal patterns. In my own life I have certainly benefited from the principles of mindfulness to calm my chattering brain, and Brené Brown's teachings about the power of vulnerability to make me more receptive to my own and others' emotions. A shift towards more positive thinking, self-compassion and kindness has also helped me to feel more settled and content. Somewhat paradoxically, it also sowed the seeds for this book.

But think of the last person you witnessed buying a glossy self-help magazine, saw walking down the street with a yoga mat slung across their shoulder or heard professing the power of positive thinking. There's every likelihood they were middle-class. Someone relatively well off. Someone with personal issues to address or internal conflicts to resolve, but financial insecurity probably not one of them. Their efforts to cope with stress, live in the moment and improve their well-being can take place in relative comfort. They can fold themselves into downward dog or sit in the lotus position unperturbed by worries about how to pay the utility bill. Stomach rumbles might interrupt their flow and make them think, 'What shall I have for dinner tonight?', not 'Will I be able to afford anything to eat this evening?'

While positive thinking and self-help methods can provide a boost to mental well-being and bring a spring to our step, it's vital to realise that seemingly benign narratives about how self-care and fixing ourselves can help us do better across all aspects of life often tip over into toxic positivity. Masquerading as empathy, it is anything but a kind and compassionate approach to reducing disadvantage and hardship. It feeds off the self-sufficiency adage; a virtue that is held in the highest esteem yet is only achievable when money is no obstacle. It's a further twist of the knife in the individualisation of the problem of poverty and the responsibility to overcome it.

8

―――――

THE BIGGER PICTURE

'Order! Order!'

The chair looks up from his papers, takes off his reading glasses and turns his head towards the screen as he announces the start of the meeting.

I start searching for clues about his demeanour and what style he'll adopt as chair, but online meetings make it hard to read body language and facial expressions. As my eyes dart around the screen, I'm distracted by the vertically striped wallpaper behind the man's head. For a moment I think it's one of those template backgrounds to hide one's actual surroundings when video conferencing, but then I notice the room's clutter. Shelves stacked with books, boxes and bags. Papers and letters poking out from each, suggesting an arrangement that only the person who created it would be able to decipher. If I didn't know this person was a member of the UK Parliament, I certainly wouldn't have guessed it from his virtual whereabouts.

'A warm welcome, everybody, to this meeting for our inquiry on children in poverty. I particularly welcome the witnesses who join us this morning.'

Relieved to hear these friendly words, I look down at the notes in front of me. I'm well prepared, but a last glance won't hurt. Experience has taught me that a good start will greatly decrease the chances of me losing my train of thought or becoming lost for words when speaking. Uttering a few well-crafted sentences with confidence early on will also help settle my nerves and make the whole experience more enjoyable.

'Can I ask, first of all, how child poverty is defined in international work?'

Here we go, I think to myself as I start my response.

It's early 2021 and I'm giving evidence to the Select Committee on Work and Pensions.[1] Made up of MPs from various political parties, every government department has such a committee. They serve as an internal accountability mechanism, publicly examining policies implemented by their respective departments. Holding inquiries on topical issues, committee members cast their eye over evidence gathered from a wide range of experts before making recommendations to government.

The inquiry I'm taking part in looks into how child poverty in the UK is measured and monitored. In the previous decade, the UK changed its approach to measuring child poverty. In 2010, under the terms of the Child Poverty Act, the government enshrined four measures and accompanying targets in law. The Act obligated the government to meet those targets by 2020, notably reducing the proportion of children living in households with absolute low income to below 5 per cent.[2]

However, in 2016 – following the 2015 general election – politicians changed their tune. Instead of looking at whether children were living in families with adequate income or other types of material deprivation, the focus shifted to monitoring whether parents were in work or children were in school. Income poverty as a measure of child poverty was abandoned.

'The argument you both make, as I understand it, is that the development of a metric goes hand-in-hand with the development of the policy, and how to respond to poverty itself. Because how you choose what's inside the metric is driven by what your priorities are, and how you define areas you want to change.'

I can't help but smile inwardly when one of the MPs offers his reflections on what the other witness and I have just said. I'm glad our responses are well received. But mostly I'm struck by the irony of the committee member's comment. In gathering his thoughts, he – probably unwittingly – offered a poignant reflection of the issue at the heart of this inquiry. The change in metrics used to monitor child poverty doesn't merely have implications for number-crunchers. It has far-reaching and real consequences for children and families in poverty.

Another MP chimes in with her reflections. Unfortunately, this time around, my words seem to have been misinterpreted, as becomes evident when she elaborates.

'What you're saying about worklessness … we know six out of ten families in work are in poverty. We know that three quarters of children in poverty are from working households. So perpetuating these stereotypes and unfortunate inaccuracies is really a dangerous and slippery slope.'

I'm nodding furiously. I couldn't agree more. I have just explained that worklessness can be an explanation for poverty, but didn't mean to suggest it's a leading cause of low income or deprivation – as the MP seems to have understood my comment. Parental worklessness might be a contributing factor to child poverty, but this certainly isn't always the case. In Britain, it doesn't hold true that having work means that children aren't in poverty. Quite the opposite, as the MP has just rightly pointed out.

Keen to emphasise our consensus before the chair moves the conversation on, I jump in.

'That's exactly why worklessness should not be a measure of child poverty. But at the moment, it is used as an indicator, and I think that's wrong.'

How we measure poverty isn't just a numbers issue. It's political. The indicators used are a direct reflection of how the problem is perceived, and who holds responsibility for solving it. The mere act of changing how child poverty is measured has helped government to distance itself from the responsibility to tackle it. By moving the focus away from the importance of an adequate standard of living and narrowly homing in on parental behaviour, politicians made it clear they no longer considered tackling child poverty a collective problem. Feeding on tropes about parents unwilling to work or too lazy to pursue education, it isn't poor parents but poor parenting that gets the blame.

To illustrate the consequences, consider benefits, which were increased for every additional child in low-income households until 2017, when the government introduced a cap. From then on, payments were limited to two children only. Ministers said it was time for families to realise that raising children cost money, and to stop expecting taxpayers to foot the bill for people having children they couldn't afford. Mothers of large families were cast as 'benefits broods', choosing to have more children to cash in on them through the welfare system.[3]

Fast-forward a few years and research[4] shows fertility rates among poor parents have hardly changed. What has happened instead is that poverty rates of families with more than two children have shot up. When the two-child limit was announced in 2015, 27 per cent of children living in larger families were in poverty. Five years later, this had increased to 37 per cent.[5] The poverty rate for children in smaller families was lower to begin with, at 17 per cent, and stayed at that level throughout the years.

The knock-on effects are considerable. Increased poverty tears families apart. Having too few resources to provide adequate care is often labelled as neglect, which is the most common reason for children in the UK being removed from their parents' custody and taken into care.[6] And while there's a clause in the policy exempting children born out of rape from the two-child limit, don't be deceived by its empathetic shine. As compassionate as it may seem, it means women having to divulge intimate details of a traumatic event to gain access to economic support. Some have called it an inhumane and barbaric practice.[7]

After an hour of responding to committee members' answers, the chair closes the meeting. 'Thank you for bringing some very useful international perspectives.'

Other witnesses provide further evidence in subsequent sessions, making similar points about the inadequacy of parental worklessness and educational attainment as a proxy for child poverty. The final report,[8] published about six months later, recommends that measures of worklessness and education aren't a substitute for measuring poverty and that the government would do well to broaden the scope of indicators to gauge the extent of deprivation. To date, these recommendations have not been taken forward by the government.

If we're serious about tackling poverty, for children and the population at large, we need radical change. Despite decades of interventions, poverty in poorer countries remains widespread. In richer countries, the prevalence of deprivation, and sometimes outright destitution, has plateaued at best but in many cases has shot up in recent years. Those in charge of policies to tackle poverty have increasingly taken to blaming lack of progress on poor people themselves, ignoring their own role in the matter. Measures police and punish those at the sharp end of disadvantage rather than support and collaborate with them. Such efforts are counterproductive at best and inhumane at worst, deepening hardship and heartbreak instead of lessening it.

So where does that leave us? In a world where the odds are stacked against people in poverty, where systematic barriers seem insurmountable, what can be done? And how can empathy make a difference?

Having explored issues in the previous chapters that help us *relate* to poverty and *realise* why it persists, it's time to look at the third R of empathy: *response*. We start by reflecting on the bigger picture and considering how a more empathetic way of shaping policies, delivering support, providing welfare and distributing resources could move the dial.

Descending from the ivory tower

'How can programmes to end poverty be impactful if they don't involve anyone with experience?'

The words bounce off the walls of the packed room. All seats are taken, and there's a row of people standing at the back. Seated at the front of the room behind the panellists' table, I can clearly see how the question has captured the audience's attention. Everyone is looking at the speaker, Toneva Munroe, a social justice activist from Boston in the US, listening intently as she talks with energy and passion.

Toneva and I are at an anti-poverty conference in her home city. We were both invited on to a panel to talk about how to change negative narratives surrounding poverty. It's a session run in parallel with others at the same time, which is why we're in a relatively small space. As it turns out, the topic is of greater interest than anticipated by the conference organisers.

While I and two other panellists have shared our thoughts about the origins and pervasiveness of poverty falsehoods based on what we know from research, Toneva is tapping into her own experiences. It's no surprise that her words capture attention in a way none of the other panellists managed to do. By sharing her journey of battling homelessness, fighting insurmountable levels of student debt and interacting with numerous service providers, she gives a highly personal account of her struggle to overcome poverty. Her story also provides unique insight into the perniciousness of negative narratives, and how they infiltrate and undermine the support for those who have fallen on hard times.

'Are you listening to share, or are you listening to understand?' she challenges the audience, many of whom are service providers themselves.

Toneva's recurrent experience with a wide range of services, from state welfare offices to homeless shelters, like the one we visited in the previous chapter, and family support charities, is that despite her being asked to provide all sorts of information, very little of it is acted upon. Front-line staff often have good intentions, she says, but more often than not, the questions they ask serve as a platform for them to talk back at her rather than an opportunity to listen to what she really needs and find a solution accordingly. Instead of being offered alternative housing when voicing concerns about the safety of her young daughter in the shared accommodation she was in, she was told she was only eligible once there had been an actual incident. And when her application for housing support was rejected on a technicality, her caseworker suggested there was nothing that could be done.

The frustration of these experiences is palpable. The room is filled with a collective sense of indignation, coupled with a hint of uncomfortable guilt at contributing to such practices. But Toneva isn't out to point the finger, or to place blame. Her message is simple: talk to those who live poverty, who know what it's like. Listen, hear what they have to say, and respond to what they're telling you.

Empathy is about taking perspective, trying to imagine the world through someone else's eyes. If it is to serve as a basis for tackling poverty, we can only do this by tapping into the knowledge and wisdom of someone with lived experience. Throughout this book, we've seen examples of how inherent distrust and suspicion of people in poverty results in them deliberately being kept at arm's length when it comes to creating policies. But even when interventions are well intended, too often they're developed top-down without meaningful integration of voices and perspectives from those with direct experience. Big ideas and innovative practices are developed without engagement with or consultation of prospective participants.

When policymakers are hungry for new ideas or seeking options for how they might be implemented, there's a vast register of consultants, advisers and researchers – myself included – ready to get their hands dirty. They busy themselves reviewing documentation, collecting data and writing reports before offering their advice. Sometimes lived-experience experts or prospective beneficiaries of support will have been consulted, but certainly not always. Ultimately it's the knowledge of those with prestigious job titles or academic degrees that counts, not the wisdom and experience of those who live the daily reality of poverty. This has consequences.

Public administration expert and publicist Tim 'S Jongers brilliantly captures the divide between expert and lived reality and its implications with the Dutch title of his book, *Beledigende Broccoli*, or 'Insulting Broccoli'.[9] It refers to a social worker who was providing nutritional advice at a school in a low-income neighbourhood in the Netherlands. Wanting to incentivise better diets, she waved around a piece of broccoli, telling children how healthy it was and that they should ask their parents to make it part of their meals. In doing so, 'S Jongers says, she was probably unaware that half of the children in front of her wouldn't even have had breakfast that morning. The advice might be well intentioned, but it was so far removed from the everyday realities of the children present that day that it was not only ineffective, but also insulting. Why not simply talk about the benefits of yoghurt and bananas, and give children something to eat at the end of their speech, notes 'S Jongers.

The notion that people in poverty need outside advice and support can also extend to poverty saviourism. In contrast to painting people in poverty as feckless and lazy, saviourism feeds off a victim narrative portraying them as needy and unable to help themselves. This may seem harmless, or even beneficial. It recognises that barriers to escape the poverty trap are too high to be overcome individually, and that there's a need for external intervention. People are more willing to pull out their wallet if it makes them feel like a saviour. No doubt you'll be familiar with campaigns that portray individuals in need as helpless and desperate, and that some of these compelled you to part with your money. A toddler with a pot belly and protruding ribs, peering into the camera with big eyes. An unkempt young woman sitting on the wet ground with a dirty sleeping bag wrapped around her, a wary and scared look on her face. The greater the misery and anguish, the more likely it will lead to donations, and therefore help for those who need it.

As benign as this narrative may seem, it objectifies poor people and portrays them as spineless and weak. It renders them voiceless in much the same way as policies that are predicated on the belief that poverty is the result of individual failure. Both narratives play into thinking about 'them' versus 'us', not only suggesting there are inherent differences between the two groups but also that 'we' are somehow superior to 'them'. Whether it's people in poverty being considered less capable, low in motivation or lacking determination – and therefore to blame for their situation – or desperate, helpless and needy, and therefore in need of saving, both stories suggest it's 'us' who are best placed to find solutions to resolve poverty.

These narratives involve finding solutions *for* people rather than *with* them. They lead to talking over them rather than speaking with them. An acknowledgement of the systemic nature of poverty and a backlash against its individualisation can easily overshoot into poor individuals being considered silent sufferers who need saving, rather than being partnered with to address their situation. Similar to policies predicated on the belief that poverty follows a character flaw, saviourism denies people in poverty the right to tell their own story, and to have a say about what happens in their lives.

As much as poverty can traumatise and paralyse, poor people are by no means silent sufferers. There's a long history of resistance by those disenfranchised and economically excluded. Take the US, where the struggle against economic deprivation and social exclusion has long been intertwined with the fight for racial justice. In the spring of 1968, thousands of protesters set up camp on the National Mall in Washington DC, near the iconic Lincoln Memorial. Part of the Poor People's Campaign, established by Martin Luther King and fellow civil rights leaders following frustration and anger at the lack of progress on President Johnson's 'War on Poverty', it was a multi-racial social movement, with poor Americans coming together in an act of non-violent civil disobedience to protest prevailing socioeconomic injustice.[10]

The camp was in place for 42 days, until its occupants were evicted. Towards the end of that six-week period, on 19 June, Solidarity Day, an estimated 50,000 demonstrators marched through the streets of Washington demanding employment, higher wages, housing and anti-poverty programmes. While many demands were left unmet, the campaign remains one of the most powerful examples of people in poverty coming together in defiance and seeking emancipation. Building on its powerful legacy, the campaign was revived in 2018, carrying on the fight against prevailing and interconnected injustices including poverty, systemic racism and denial of health care.

But it's not just large-scale actions that attest to the pushback against the systems that keep people trapped in poverty. Acts of resistance, big and small, take place every day, everywhere. From withstanding the incessant onslaught of demeaning looks and micro-aggressions and taking sound decisions regardless of advice to the contrary, to following through on dreams despite a lack of role models or being told not to bother.

Whether they follow negative narratives, well-intentioned but ill-advised decision-making or poverty saviourism, top-down approaches without taking account of lived experience do a disservice to people in poverty. They undermine the agency and voice of those living on little, underestimating their power and ignoring their wisdom. Ultimately, they render interventions less effective than they could be.

Fixing poverty requires bureaucrats, public administrators, civil servants and academics to descend from their ivory towers. To become familiar with the world they're trying to influence and change. Visit a night shelter, volunteer at a food bank. Talk to the users of those services – and those who are excluded from them – and involve them in the decision-making process. Better still, make them part of the process. People in poverty can't share in the responsibility of resolving the problem if they're not involved in the process as equal partners whose wisdom, skills and experience are held in the same regard and whose agency and voice are meaningfully included.

Reclaiming connection

'I crossed the bridge to economic independence. I'm now managing my own small enterprise. I continue to grow. No mountain is too high.'

Haroun lives in Zaandam, a medium-sized town in the Netherlands. He's in his twenties when sharing his experience, but he has been struggling with crippling debt from an early age.[11]

'I have been supported by Jennifer and Mark. It's thanks to them I've been able to take the first steps to tackle my debt.'

Jennifer and Mark are youth workers, helping to resolve issues around housing, family conflict and financial insecurity. They also serve as mentors on the Get a Grip programme, an initiative targeted at young people with large debts. It's this scheme that marked a turning point for Haroun. By providing personalised support, Jennifer and Mark helped him to take control of his financial problems, pay off outstanding debt and get an education. He managed to start his own business, and is now working as a mentor himself. For Haroun, his participation in the programme was life-changing.

Also in the Netherlands, Patrick and Daisy, a couple with two young daughters, found themselves stuck in an untenable situation.[12] A combination of indebtedness, addiction and mental health issues had led to them losing their home, and they moved in with Daisy's parents. The intention was for it to be a short-term solution, but years later, they were still there. The house was too small to accommodate five adults, two children and multiple pets. Tensions ran high. Concerns were raised about the children's care and safety.

This was when the Uitvoeringsbrigade, or 'Implementation Brigade', entered the scene. The programme assigned a coach to help Daisy and Patrick manage their circumstances, from getting them signed up to social housing to dealing with their large loans. Instead of the couple having to navigate a myriad of services on their own – adding to already high stress levels – they developed a plan together with the coach. They were able to do things at their own pace, to take things one step at a time. Within months they had moved into their own home and started to repay their debts on a regular basis. They're not out of the woods yet, but the family has achieved an important level of stability and regained control over their own lives.

The initiatives Haroun, Daisy and Patrick took part in were based on the so-called Mobility Mentoring approach, which was developed in the US by Boston-based nonprofit EMPath. Beth Babcock, EMPath's previous CEO, refers to it as brain-science based mentoring.[13] The approach uses insights from behavioural and neurological sciences on how poverty affects mind and behaviour – as we've seen through-out this book – to help people navigate the prevailing system and find a route out of poverty within that system. However, in contrast to some of the 'quick fix' solutions we've come across in the preceding chapters, such as watching inspira-tional movies or receiving therapy sessions, the mentoring approach offers tailored advice and practical assistance.

EMPath is short for the organisation's full name, Economic Mobility Pathways, but the clever reference to empathy is hardly a coincidence. Consider the way in which Daisy and Patrick were supported. The programme allowed them to work with someone who paid close attention to their needs and who placed them front and centre. Their coach was avail-able for them any time, day or night, to offer calm during a crisis or lend a sympathetic ear. Struggles and stress don't stick to working hours, after all.

Although it may seem obvious for the client to be central to services that aim to improve their life, this certainly isn't self-evident. In fact, it's the exception rather than the rule. As will be clear by now, all too often services are guided by bureaucratic processes, with clients pushed into categories that trigger narrow and standardised responses. Rarely do those in need of support get asked what they need, or how they are coping. Solutions are imposed on clients rather than discussed with them. Service delivery is rigid and detached.

This is frustrating for service users as much as it is for front-line workers delivering those services. I have sat across from social workers in Botswana who felt their work on child protection was compromised after having been made responsible for the administration of cash support for poor families. Instead of working with children to understand the intricacies of their complex situation and keep them safe, they were asked to spend most of their time checking whether forms had been filled correctly and processing applications for welfare benefits. Similarly in Ethiopia, the intentions of young and energetic caseworkers were scuppered by their caseload being far too high, making it impossible to spend meaningful amounts of time with the families they were responsible for.

Don't let these two examples tempt you into thinking this is a problem limited to poorer countries. When talking to coaches working with Mobility Mentoring in the US, I learned that most had previously worked in traditional social service provision, and their experiences were often the reason they jumped ship. They got into the business of human services – the bucket term used in the US to denote public and social services – to do human-centred work, but it was the lack of human centredness that made them decide to change course.

Go anywhere and you'll find that much of the support provided to vulnerable groups, including people in poverty, is provided transactionally. Whether it's housing, workforce development or financial services, service delivery is treated as a box-ticking exercise. Front-line staff's engagement with clients is governed by risk assessments, monitoring templates and achievement checklists. The increased role of private companies, who place profit ahead of people, has further compounded the drive to efficiency, mostly at the expense of the quality of human interaction and the trust and respect that follows from it. Meanwhile, clients are forced to jump through all sorts of hoops to gain access to support. Unemployment, debt, housing and mental health – if services are available, they come with their own processes, rules and regulations. Applicants have to verify their eligibility time and time again, only to receive standardised support that may not be what they really need.

In a world increasingly driven by optimising rates of return and increasing profits, reclaiming connection is one of the most radical and transformative things we can do to address poverty. Nowhere have I witnessed the impact and potential of human interaction grounded in mutual trust and respect more than in my own work in Bangladesh.

Recall Raisa and community mobiliser Shakil from Dhaka, who we met in Chapter 1? They were part of an anti-poverty intervention that explicitly sought to test what it takes to place people and their needs front and centre, and what benefits such an approach brings. Rather than relying on protocols or manuals with standard step-by-step action plans, we equipped the front-line team with the relational, conversational and mediation skills to sit with residents of the low-income neighbourhood we were working in and pay attention. Instead of building their technical knowledge or teaching them to deliver a fixed list of messages about how to set up a business or why it's important to build up savings, training focused on how to engage deeply, without prejudice or judgement. There weren't any predefined goals or objectives. Repeated conversations were the starting point for a longer-term engagement, and ultimately action towards meeting people's needs.

The approach relied on being open-ended, letting issues emerge and bubble up to the surface and finding ways to address them. At its core, it was based on empathy. It led to women starting their own businesses, children getting the health care they needed, and local leaders becoming open to tricky conversations about highly contentious issues such as young girls getting married and children working in dangerous conditions.

For the sceptics among you, let me say I was one of you. As someone who is wary of losing control and therefore naturally inclined to make plans and create structure, the idea of letting go of the reins felt uncomfortable at best and terrifying at worst. While the idea sounded intuitive and theoretically appealing, I was far less convinced when it came to putting it into practice. If we didn't tell the team what to discuss with the community members, how would they know what to do? Without a checklist to guide the conversation or a manual to hold on to, how would we ensure that meaningful interactions were developed?

Fortunately, I had confident and persuasive colleagues with an unquestionable belief in our team's capacity to establish and connect. This has led to innumerable interactions like the one between Shakil and Raisa, and reports of community members feeling seen, heard and supported in ways they never were before – despite multiple organisations having worked in the community previously. Of course, such an approach needs to be implemented with care. It involves a lot of investment in staff capacity, and ongoing support and feedback, not least to process the trauma that front-line workers are inevitably confronted with.

The power of human interaction is increasingly recognised, or rediscovered, in anti-poverty policies. Returning to EMPath in Boston, the organisation works with hundreds of nonprofits and government departments as part of its Mobility Mentoring network, in the US and elsewhere – including the Netherlands. More generally, coaching and mentoring as part of wider interventions to tackle poverty have gained popularity in countries across the world. In Paraguay, the nonprofit Fundación Paraguaya pioneered the Poverty Stoplight programme, providing women in poverty not only with a package of economic support but also with a mentor to assess their needs and find a way forward. In countries across Asia, Africa and Latin America, initiatives aiming to boost poor families' economic inclusion include coaching components.

In the search for cost-effective ways to tackle poverty, the risk of the relational element getting squeezed is real. How often do clients need to meet their coaches for it to take effect? How long do they need to meet for, what needs to be discussed, and can it be done at group level rather than through individual home visits? Privy to conversations about design and development of schemes that include coaching, especially in poorer countries, I'm often frustrated by the questions that dominate the conversation. The human side of things is afforded a back seat while excitement about maximising impact on pre-defined indicators using the least number of resources takes over. I'm not suggesting these conversations shouldn't be had; resource constraints are real and it would be naïve and self-defeating to suggest otherwise. But in doing so, it's vital we don't lose sight of people being at the heart of the endeavour.

What leaves me more encouraged is that somewhat paradoxically, or perhaps unsurprisingly, the more the search for cost-effective interventions to reduce poverty continues, the more the need to maintain and reinstate human connection moves towards the top of the list of priorities. And the impetus towards greater human connection in how to deliver services to and care for vulnerable groups in our societies isn't limited to the confines of anti-poverty policies.

Initiatives in youth work and community empowerment in the UK pioneered by social innovator Hilary Cottam and presented in her book *Radical Help*[14] emphasise the importance of relationships, putting them forward as one of the six pillars of a twenty-first-century revolution of the welfare state. She writes, 'Without strong bonds with others, or with unhealthy relationships, very few of us can feel fulfilled – or even function,' highlighting the importance of social interventions using the power of human connection to support people in building their capacities, as well as seeing relationships as integral to those capacities. She also makes an important point about power, noting that relational work requires a shift away from hierarchical service delivery towards a practice of reflection and action.

Dutch-born initiative Buurtzorg[15] – 'Neighbourhood Care' – is perhaps one of the most popular examples showing that change is possible. 'Humanity above bureaucracy' reads the slogan on the organisation's website. By doing away with large top-down management structures and working in small local teams, it pushes back against big conglomerates selling care as a profitable product. Instead of treating its nurses and care workers as pawns in a money-making venture, it trusts them to manage their work locally and tap into their expertise and compassion to interact with their clients in the most appropriate and human way possible. It's nothing short of a revolution in the provision of home care in the Netherlands. Starting with just a single team of 10 nurses in the small city of Almelo in the east of the country, it now employs more than 1,000. The model proves popular well beyond the country's borders, with initiatives from Brazil to Belgium and Japan. It's not hard to see the appeal. Buurtzorg's approach takes care back to its core: a human interaction premised on trust, respect and – ultimately – empathy.

Put your money where your mouth is

Responding to poverty from a place of empathy makes it impossible to ignore that while a shift from pejorative and punitive policies to positive and constructive engagement is crucial, breaking the cycle requires the creation of favourable and fair conditions to ensure that people's efforts pay off. While initiatives to get participants to think more positively, build self-esteem and take action have their merit, it's the root causes of hardship and deprivation that need tackling. These are systematic, not individual. After all, if the science tells us that the strain of making ends meet taxes the brain, causes shame and takes its toll on mental health, why not simply make it easier to have a decent income?

As straightforward as it may sound, making enough money to keep one's head above water doesn't come easy. Take the UK. Average weekly earnings in real terms – meaning they've been adjusted for price increases over time – have remained mostly stagnant since the financial crisis in 2008. The think tank Resolution Foundation calculated that if wage growth hadn't been disrupted, real earnings would be about £11,000 per year higher than they currently are.[16] Brits on the lowest incomes experienced the most sluggish increase in their wages, with their earnings growing at only 0.3 per cent per year in the last decade.[17] Between 2021 and 2022, median income fell by almost 4 per cent for the poorest fifth of the population.

These trends are mirrored in the figures on in-work poverty, which has increased every year since the late 1990s.[18] In 1996/97, 44 per cent of all children and working-age adults in poverty were in families where at least one adult was working. By 2019/20, this had gone up to 66 per cent. Given these statistics, it's no surprise that the use of parents' worklessness as an indicator of child poverty received so much scrutiny in the parliamentary committee's inquiry. Work doesn't give any guarantee of a decent standard of living.

This is despite the UK having adopted a living wage in 2016. Following a 15-year grassroots campaign, instigated by community members in London who identified low pay as the single most pressing issue they struggled with, the government increased the national minimum wage and rebranded it the national living wage. Employers are legally bound to pay their workers the living wage.

The problem is, the national living wage isn't high enough to live on. The government took the opportunity to co-opt the concept of a living wage and appear to be supporting a decent standard of living without pushing for earnings that actually enable this. And so the campaign continues, asking employers to join the movement and become accredited living wage employers, because in the words of the Living Wage Foundation,[19] 'a hard day's work deserves a fair day's pay'.

Working for a fair wage is only a first step towards a more systemic solution to poverty. Equally important is a radical reshape of employment conditions. Over a period of decades, the mantra that a more flexible and dynamic labour market is vital for economic growth has led to the rolling-back of workers' rights and the removal of job security. The thinking is that businesses are better able to grow and thrive if it's easier for workers to shift, and be shifted, between employers. While we might have heard our grandparents talk nostalgically about having worked at the same company or the same factory from when they left school until they retired, our grandchildren certainly won't be sharing those stories.

A dynamic labour market isn't necessarily a bad thing. The ability to change jobs, find new careers and develop new skills throughout one's working life is likely a more appealing outlook for most compared to working for the same boss for 40 years. However, it's the erosion of workers' rights accompanying the introduction of a more flexible labour market that makes it problematic. This is especially true for low-wage work. The types of jobs that keep the economy going but that few want to do and even fewer want to see. Warehouse workers, cleaners, rubbish collectors, home carers – their work is indispensable to our societies, yet mostly invisible and systematically undervalued.

In his book *Hired*, author James Bloodworth goes under-cover in some of Britain's most widespread low-paid jobs, from telesales to on-demand drivers. He paints a grim picture of workers doing back-breaking work for little pay and without any certainty about the number of hours they might clock up in a week. All the while, they're supervised, scrutinised and messed around without limits, unable to take a toilet break when needed, penalised when ill, and made to wait for hours until an income-generating assignment comes along. Ken Loach's film *Sorry We Missed You* tells the heartbreaking and infuriating tale of Ricky, husband and father-of-two, who sells the family car to purchase a van and become a delivery driver. Enthusiasm and optimism over the opportunity to pay off accumulating debt soon turn into anguish and despair when faced with the reality of the job. Unrealistic delivery targets, penalty payments when calling in sick, and a total lack of humanity on the part of his superiors take a toll on Ricky's mental and physical health. Family relations are strained, and the cycle of debt only grows deeper.

If work is to pave a way out of poverty, it won't be through jobs like these. While the gig economy might offer a vibrant career to some, chasing new and exciting opportunities as they become available, for most it has meant a life of irregular earnings without any prospect of a steady and better-paid job in future. Zero-hour contracts and self-employment are further mechanisms through which responsibility for making ends meet is individualised, adding fuel to the fire of poverty blame and shame. Casting our minds back to the conversation about aspirations, it shows just how ludicrous it is for young people to be simultaneously criticised for failing to have high aspirations and admonished for not achieving more modest objectives for a 'simple life'.

This unravelling of workers' rights and job security doesn't just need to stop, it also needs to be reversed. Unions are vital to this. Large-scale strikes in the UK and across Europe in the last few years testify to the power of collective action.

Workers joining forces to get employers to pay a decent wage, contribute to fair pensions or commit to a level of job security can be incredibly effective. However, there's no doubt that in a world where work has become more of an individual affair, the appetite for unionisation has dissipated. The curtailing of union members' right to strike, as happened in the UK, or workers being denied the right to unionise altogether isn't challenged nearly as much as it should be. Politicians are quick to point out the inconvenience of disruptions to the lives of hard-working individuals, but fall silent when asked to address the real issue at hand. Job security and dignified working conditions aren't a luxury, but a priority in creating the conditions to end poverty.

Well-paid, secure and dignified employment will significantly lower barriers to making ends meet. It will move the needle on in-work poverty, making it far less likely for families to experience deprivation if one or more of their members work.

But what do we actually mean when we talk about 'work'?

If I asked you that question, you'd probably give me an answer that refers to money changing hands in exchange for labour. A paid job. Remunerated employment. Cash in hand for services provided.

But what about all the work that has no money attached to it? All the cooking, cleaning and washing that takes place everywhere every second of every day. The hours of caring for children by mothers, fathers and grandparents around the world. The many acts of voluntary service that bring to life soup kitchens, homeless shelters, libraries and sports clubs across our cities, villages and communities. It's these activities that underpin families' functioning, form the glue of our societies and fill the gaps left by inadequate public services. Without them, our social fabric would unravel and our economies fall apart.

Despite their importance, these activities aren't counted. We don't attach an economic value to them the way we would if they were undertaken for pay. As a result, they're not taken into consideration when we gauge the size of our countries' economies. Think about it, it's mad. If you take your child to nursery before you head off for work and pay a hefty monthly bill for someone else to look after them, your expense counts towards the size of the economy. If instead one of your parents settles themselves at the kitchen table ready for a day with their grandchild as you're on your way out, it counts for nothing. In both cases your child is cared for, but it's only valued economically if you pay for it. The contribution made by your mother or father is just as important as the one made by professional carers, but without money changing hands it's like it never happened.

Failing to attach a monetary value to the many forms of unpaid work that are the backbone of our collective functioning isn't just about underestimating the size of our economies. It sends a signal that such work has no value. Paid jobs tend to be central to our identity and how we are perceived by others. And the better they pay, the more status they afford. Work that comes without pay – no matter how hard, vital or lifesaving it may be – is dismissed as dispensable, or simply overlooked altogether. With women carrying the bulk of care and family responsibilities, they draw the short straw in this wherever you go.

The emphasis on self-reliance coupled with lack of investment in public service provision has made non-remunerated care and support even more important. People are to take care of themselves and each other rather than look to the government, as exemplified by the UK's Big Society and the Dutch '*zelfredzaamheid*' self-reliance policy we came across in Chapter 7. The drudgery that follows, especially when trying to combine it with multiple poorly paid and insecure jobs, adds to the stress and strain of poverty. But much to the convenience of politicians pushing the self-sufficiency logic, the toil is uncounted and thereby rendered invisible.

More for the many, less for the few

'People should have the power to say NO to what is undesirable in their lives, and the power to say YES to what they desire.'

This is Sarath Davala speaking on my podcast.[20] Sarath is president of the Basic Income Earth Network, a global collective of organisations and individuals working on basic income.

Basic income represents a radical alternative to the current provision of welfare and government support around the world. Also sometimes referred to as guaranteed income, it constitutes regular provision of cash without conditions. It's often advocated to be provided to everyone, regardless of who they are, what they do or how much wealth they have, in the form of universal basic income, or UBI.

It's a radical idea that has the potential to transform our societies, as Sarath so passionately explains. Instead of judging someone's worth on their employment or the size of their salary, it places value on contributions of all kinds – paid or unpaid, skilled or unskilled, big or small. Crucially, it allows for individuals to contribute to the economy and their communities by tapping into their skills, interests and expertise in the best way possible, and to walk away from work that is poorly paid and unfulfilling or harmful to mental and physical health.

'People are entering the workforce. People are finding work that pays the living wage, people are going back to school, people are finding ways to integrate in a way that works for them.' These are the words of Melody Valdes, taking part in the same podcast conversation. When we speak, she's in charge of leading a guaranteed income intervention in Boston in the US.

A basic income acknowledges that merit isn't individually determined but a product of our joint efforts and interconnectedness. And its impact cuts across many areas of life, especially for those struggling with financial insecurity.

Giving people money for free releases the constraints imposed by poverty, as we saw in Chapter 5. It opens up space to think, offers a platform for taking new initiatives and serves as a safety net when things don't quite work out. With everyone receiving the payments, this approach stands in stark contrast to current forms of welfare provision, dominated by rules, conditions and sanctions. Providing cash unconditionally and universally dissipates the stigma of being singled out and silences the voices of blame and shame.

The idea of a basic income isn't new. While mostly a fringe idea in the 1980s and 90s, the notion that governments could be paying all their citizens a basic income has steadily been gaining momentum. In 2016, Switzerland held a referendum, putting the idea of a guaranteed basic income to a public vote. A majority voted against the proposal, but the fact that a referendum was held at all is a sign that the idea of a basic income is no longer a far-fetched policy ideal. In the US, universal basic income was central to presidential candidate Andrew Yang's campaign in the lead-up to the 2020 elections, firmly placing it in the public consciousness and moving it away from a mere utopian ideal to an achievable policy objective. Building on the legacy of the civil rights movement, Mayors for Guaranteed Income brings together city leaders advocating for an income floor for all Americans.

Basic income isn't only relevant in high-income countries. One of the fastest-growing nonprofits in the world, GiveDirectly,[21] has already reached thousands of people in countries such as Liberia, Malawi and Mozambique, paying everyone in selected communities a monthly cash transfer. In Kenya, they started doing so in 2016 for a period of 12 years, evidencing what happens to recipients and helping to make a compelling case for the benefits of such programmes. Other initiatives can be found in Bangladesh, China and India, with enthusiasm for universal and unconditional models of support building.

'We don't believe this to be the be all and end all. This is something that we want to give families in addition to what they're already receiving,' Melody says.

Both she and Sarath are clear that basic income in itself is not an anti-poverty policy. Offering everyone an income floor does just that: it provides a minimum standard of living for all. It isn't a permission slip for the depression of wages, replacement of other support, or services such as health care or education to be left to the mercy of the market. This is in contrast to the reason why those on the right of the political spectrum and business tycoons such as Mark Zuckerberg lend their support to basic income. They see it as a way of rolling back all types of state support; permission for doing away with existing public provision, welfare services and workers' rights. Clearly, basic income can only play a role in tackling poverty if it is part of the transition to a more progressive system of support, not a route towards clamping it down.

A common argument against universal basic income is its cost. I can hear you thinking, 'Sounds nice, but isn't this far too expensive?' Of course, paying everyone a meaningful minimum amount every month doesn't come cheap, there's no doubt about it. But the resources needed aren't necessarily prohibitive, certainly not everywhere. A study looking at the UK,[22] for example, estimates that the cost of providing a level of income that would lift everyone out of poverty would total roughly 2 per cent of GDP. The calculations take account of the fact that although transfers are provided to all, those paid to higher-income earners would flow back into the government's coffers through taxation. In this scenario, a universal basic income would add only 25 per cent to the cost of the existing benefit system. Public services, including national health care, would be maintained.

If you think about it, that's a bargain when comparing the potential of an income floor for all against the current form of highly targeted and conditional welfare provision. It allows for a completely different starting point. Instead of asking 'How can we avoid people taking advantage of the system?' we can make the empathetic shift to 'How can we support people taking advantage of the support on offer?'

Since we're on the topic of redistribution, changes to address poverty shouldn't merely focus on the bottom layer of our socioeconomic pyramid. They should also consider the top. Having learned that the experience of poverty isn't simply about lacking the resources to make ends meet but is shaped by the depth of inequality, where we stand in the hierarchy and who we hold up as role models of success, what is the point of raising the floor for the poor if the rich at the top can keep growing their wealth unfettered? How can poverty be tackled meaningfully if more and more wealth becomes concentrated amongst an ever smaller minority, inequality is allowed to increase without limit and crazy rich lifestyles are held up as models to aspire to?

Philosopher and political scientist Ingrid Robeyns asks herself the same question, and puts forward a radical proposal in her book *Limitarianism*.[23] The unencumbered accumulation of wealth has to stop, she argues. Being unimaginably rich isn't only unnecessary, as it doesn't make you happier; it's also bad for the planet and its people. What's more, there's a moral case to answer, especially when it comes to 'old money' and wealth rolling over from one generation to the next, growing in size along the way. Economist Thomas Piketty caused quite a stir a decade ago when his calculations showed that without interference in the generational capture of long-term returns on private wealth, such as through inheritance tax, the schism between 'haves' and 'have-nots' will only grow deeper.[24]

Even some millionaires seem to find it hard to square this circle, with 250 of them signing an open letter at the occasion of the 2024 World Economic Forum in Davos calling on the world's political leaders to tax them.[24] Marlene Engelhorn, an Austrian-born heiress of millions, was one of them, and didn't make herself popular walking around at the swanky annual get-together of the economically powerful with a large placard reading 'Tax the Rich'. But, she says, 'Millionaires should not get to decide whether or not they contribute in a just way to the societies they live in, and without which they never would have become millionaires. Social justice is in everybody's best interest. Wealth taxes are the least we can do to take responsibility. Tax us!'[25]

In this vein, Robeyns makes the case for a radical reform of taxation and a substantial redistribution of wealth. A limit on excessive wealth will improve our physical and mental health, enhance social cohesion and be better for the planet. Also, she says, 'there is so much more we could do with the money'.[26]

My point exactly.

9

———

SMALL ACTIONS, BIG CHANGE

A bottle of water in one hand and a small cardboard box in the other, I try to gently lower myself to the ground. I bend my knees and crouch down, but without arms available to steady myself, I land in the dusty grass a bit harder and far less elegantly than I had hoped. I look around to see if anyone has noticed, but my colleagues are busy collecting their own lunch packets from the car. I cross my legs to find a comfortable position on the open patch of land where we're taking a break. Only once I'm properly settled do I realise the scenic quality of our location. The view in front of me is spectacular, and any soreness following my ungainly descent is quickly forgotten.

I'm in Rwanda, the land of a thousand hills. The country is small – about the size of Hawaii – but its landscape is majestic. With its rolling mountains, green valleys and foggy peaks, a stunning outlook is never far away, today included. We're in the south of the country, in a village near the city of

Butare, which houses Rwanda's main university. The many students give the mid-sized provincial town a surprisingly vibrant feel, quite unlike the rural tranquillity where I'm unwrapping my lunch. Even though it took less than an hour to get here this morning from our accommodation right next to the university campus, it feels like a world of difference. Apart from the occasional motorbike driving along the winding and dusty road, the clucking of chickens, and neighbourly greetings as villagers pass each other's houses, there's very little sound at all.

As I start unwrapping the sandwich in my lunchbox, Catherine, a member of our research team, approaches and asks if she can join me. 'Of course!' I respond. She sits down next to me, and I can't help but notice that her landing is much smoother than mine. 'Isn't it stunning?' I say to her as I nod in the direction of the view in front of us. 'It truly is,' she agrees. 'We don't have this at home,' she adds, sighing with appreciation.

Catherine travelled here from Tanzania, her home country, to join the team at the university in Butare to study the impact of interventions incentivising women to become more economically active.

In the last few decades there's been a big push behind efforts to promote women's economic empowerment, and it has come with questions about their effects. Apart from the economic benefits of women setting up businesses or earning an income of their own, it helps increase their status in the family and makes them more independent. But it can also be a double-edged sword. Women are often expected to combine newly acquired business skills or entrepreneurial activities with caring for their children and keeping their households going, often without help from anyone else. It can take its toll.

'How was your visit?' I ask Catherine. We had split up into two teams, visiting a different family each.

She briefly looks up before quietly continuing to peel the egg that was in her lunchbox. Thinking she might not have heard me, I wonder whether I should repeat the question.

'It was tough,' she suddenly responds, her eyes still tracing the movements of her hands. 'The woman we spoke to – her name is Ineza – doesn't have it easy. She's been able to earn some money through the employment programme. But despite having a small income, she struggles to provide for her three children.'

Catherine is visibly emotional as she recounts the conversation.

'Her husband is away most of the time. She thinks he stays with another family. When he comes back, he doesn't have anything to contribute. He doesn't bring any money. He doesn't help at home. But he complains to Ineza that his children aren't properly fed. He blames her for not taking proper care of them. She got quite upset when she was telling me all this, understandably.'

I don't know what to say in response. Ineza's experience isn't unusual, unfortunately. So many mothers struggle in the same way. But that doesn't make their individual stories any less impactful. The woman I went to visit did have a supportive husband, but she was still left to do all the household chores and childcare. And despite both of them being engaged in paid work, they still weren't making enough money to feed their children three times a day. As I sat in front of the family's modest one-room house, I couldn't help but think how lucky I am in my life.

'I mean, what is she supposed to do?' Catherine's rhetorical question brings me back to our conversation. 'The work provided through the programme may increase her income, but it's not enough. If anything, it's making things worse. The husband thinks he no longer has a responsibility to contribute to the family, and Ineza needs to do everything on her own.' She shakes her head in frustration.

Our colleagues have come over to join us, and it feels inappropriate for Catherine and me to continue our conversation. We're in a semicircle, with the shade from a large tree protecting us from the midday sun high above our heads. Despite the scene lending itself to social chit-chat, everyone seems too preoccupied, or simply too hungry, to engage in conversation. So we sit in silence, concentrating on our food and gazing at the view, each lost in our own thoughts.

It isn't long before we've all finished eating. We have a busy afternoon ahead and need to get going. Having collected our belongings and disposed of our rubbish, we're about to climb into the car when I spot someone running across the open field. It's a woman, waving and yelling something, presumably wanting us to wait.

'That's her,' says Catherine in surprise. Having realised we're not driving off, Ineza slows her pace. Breathing heavily, she walks straight up to Catherine, takes her hands and starts speaking, uttering words in rapid succession. It sounds urgent. Catherine looks a bit bewildered.

'I'm sorry, I don't understand what you're saying,' she responds, but one of our Rwandan colleagues is quick to translate. 'She came up here because she wanted to thank you.' Still holding Catherine's hands, Ineza is nodding her head as if to lend extra weight to her words as they are translated for us. 'It was the first time anyone made the effort to ask her how she was doing, and listened to what she had to say. She's very happy you came to visit. She wanted to make sure to thank you before leaving,' says our colleague.

I see Catherine tear up. 'It's me who's grateful,' she says to Ineza. 'Thank you for trusting me with your story. I'll try my best to do it justice.' Ineza looks at our colleague for the words to be translated, before turning to Catherine again. She smiles, and squeezes Catherine's hands before letting them go.

'Let's go!' the driver calls out to us. We need to get a move on if we want to complete our afternoon plans. 'I'm sorry, we have to leave now,' Catherine explains to Ineza, shaking her head apologetically. Ineza smiles back, indicating it's okay. Slowly we all get into the car. Catherine is last to take her seat.

As we drive off, Ineza is still there, waving. Her face seems to be full of joy and sadness at the same time. We all wave back.

As I catch a last glimpse of the scenic view in the rear-view mirror, Catherine reminds us of the reason we were there in the first place. 'We must tell Ineza's story, and that of all the other women. Their words and our work have to make a difference.'

Empathy for change

Having considered what a more empathetic response to poverty might look like at a societal and structural level, we now move to what we – each of us – can do to respond to poverty.

If you're reading this, I assume you're interested in wanting, just like Catherine, to be part of positive change. To tap into empathy and help tackle the hardship and deprivation that plays out on our doorstep as it does across the world.

'But how?' I hear you ask. Poverty and socioeconomic injustice are such big problems, how can any one person make a difference?

It's a valid question, and one I ask myself almost every day. But as small as our individual contributions may be, together we constitute the communities we live in and shape the society we inhabit. They aren't external forces bestowed upon us. No matter how tiny or seemingly insignificant, the ways we engage with the people and the world around us make a difference. Cultivating our empathy skills and putting them to good use can make us all part of breaking the poverty deadlock.

The three Rs of empathy – *relate, realise* and *respond* – are the practical steps by which we can make this large and arguably abstract task more tangible and concrete.

If we've never been in a situation of socioeconomic disadvantage or injustice, relating to the experience of poverty is the first step towards creating a response grounded in empathy. By exploiting our capacity for curiosity, open-mindedness and non-judgement, we can gain an awareness of the struggle and its implications. Relating to the grind of living on little can trigger a feeling of frustration and injustice that serves as a basis for further action.

Next, we need to realise why poverty exists and persists. To consider the structures and policies that poor people need to navigate, the hoops they're made to jump through, and reflect on how these may do more harm than good. It also calls for asking ourselves some tough questions about our own role in maintaining the status quo, and how we might be implicated in perpetuating the problem. It requires us to understand the barriers that hold individuals and families back and see options for change.

You'll now have laid a foundation for the first two Rs of empathy. The stories and evidence from around the world will – I hope – have evoked an embodied sense of the daily struggle and a cognitive understanding of its causes and implications, to help you relate to the experience of poverty and realise how the current responses are ineffective at best and harmful at worst. In this chapter, I offer practical suggestions as to how you can further cultivate the first two Rs of empathy.

This brings us to *respond*. As noted in Chapter 1, I only consider empathy complete when it includes action. Take Ineza's story, and how it touched Catherine. It evoked a mix of emotions, including sadness and frustration. It gave rise to a sense of injustice, and triggered the desire to act. Catherine wanted Ineza's story, and those of so many other women in similar situations, to be put out into the world, for people to pay attention, and for those who hold the power to change things for the better.

No matter who we are, what job we do or what position we occupy on the socioeconomic ladder, we can all be part of positive change. Actions are plentiful, ranging from large in focus to small in scale, from the practical to the political, and from vocal to quieter forms of resistance. There's space for all types of contributions, and a need for everyone to chip in. Towards the end of this chapter, I provide some ideas of steps you might take, and encourage you to add your own.

I have no doubt that empathy is a catalyst for change. When we connect to others' experiences, we feel the struggles and challenges faced by those around us. Empathy helps us reflect on the implications of those struggles – mentally, physically, socially – and to realise how society stacks the odds against those on the lower end of the socioeconomic ladder. It compels us to respond, and to counteract the injustice faced by people in poverty.

Relate

The first R – relating to poverty – involves stepping out of our own bubble and becoming curious about what's going on in the bubbles of those around us. Philosopher Roman Krznaric proposes the attractive idea of becoming 'empathic travellers', to embark on unexpected empathetic journeys. These may involve actual travel to places unknown, or in-person conversations with people outside of our social circles. Or they can entail journeys of the mind, from the comfort of your own armchair, by reading books or watching films.

It's all about taking the 'imaginative leap', as Krznaric puts it. About stepping into someone else's world and being willing to relate to others' experiences from their point of view.

Reading is one of the most accessible ways to stimulate imaginative thinking. Books offer a unique window into someone else's world, or more crucially, how others experience the world. Rather than being a factual representation of circumstance, they give space to the protagonist to speak their mind, to unpack their emotions and let us feel what's happening to them. This person could be very different from you. They could be a different gender, age, race or political affiliation, and represent someone from a social circle far removed from your own. Yet by reading the words that describe what's important to them, you're offered a perspective that wouldn't otherwise be available to you. It will engage your emotions, and can help you identify with being in situations very different from your own. As psychologist and novelist Keith Oatley points out,[1] because reading allow you to be vicariously connected to others' emotions and hone your empathy skills in a safe space, it can serve as effective preparation for practising empathy in the real world.

Memoirs are an especially apt vehicle for taking a deep dive into someone else's lived reality. Author Natasha Carthew is a staunch champion of writers from disadvantaged backgrounds whose voices have for far too long been underrepresented. From a rural working-class background herself, she emphasises the need for moving away from the overrepresentation of middle-class experiences and giving space to overlooked, ignored and diverse voices. Speaking on my podcast, she says: 'The lived experience is so important. And it's important for people to read those stories, to get a truthful telling.'[2]

Fortunately, books about and written by working-class authors or those with experience of poverty are an increasingly common sight on bookshop shelves. In her own memoir, *Undercurrent,* Natasha shares her experience of growing up in rural poverty. Set in a small town on the stunning Cornish coast, her book exposes how young people from less affluent families are cut off from opportunities to help them thrive. Her raw and honest way of writing brings to life the issues that stifle opportunity, and the frustration and anger at the injustice of it all. The effects of lack of education beyond primary school, a dearth of well-paid jobs, and poor public transport become tangible.

The wider availability of books by lived-experience writers also affords exposure to their unique circumstances, and the different ways in which they navigate hardship and forge opportunity. Natasha's memoir carefully unpicks the idyll of coastal life and shows its readers the often hidden reality of rural poverty. Contrast this with Scotland-born Kerry Hudson and her memoir *Lowborn,* in which she describes a childhood spent traversing the UK with her mother and sister, moving from one form of temporary accommodation to another. She paints a poignant picture of life in homeless hostels and social housing, making palpable the stress of the arrangements' impermanence, especially for a young girl who has no control over when they might come to an end and what might be next. Both Natasha and Kerry tell unique stories of the struggle that is poverty, taking the reader by the hand and giving them the privilege of seeing the world through their eyes.

If books aren't your thing – although the fact that you're reading this one suggests otherwise – there are many other ways to cultivate your empathy. Watching movies is an obvious alternative. The very point of films is to invite the viewer into a world that isn't their own, and to make them feel as if they're right there with the main characters, living their experience with them. Who hasn't sat in the cinema or at home in front of the television overcome with emotion? Who hasn't felt anger, frustration or despair as they're immersed in stories of deprivation, discrimination or other forms of injustice? As much as *Queen of Katwe* inspired young girls in Kampala to do well in school, films such as *Sorry We Missed You* and *I, Daniel Blake* by Ken Loach can help us feel the stress and worry of precarious work and the anguish and shame of having to queue at the food bank.

The list goes on. Theatre, music and visual art can also instigate empathy. While the science on this is still relatively nascent,[3] all art forms have the potential to make us more prosocial, and to relate to situations or experiences unlike our own. What moves us is ultimately very personal, and different sensory experiences might appeal to our emotive or cognitive empathic abilities in different ways.

Technological advances offer more immersive ways of relating. Virtual reality is a relatively new but promising gateway to another world. The virtual reality film *Clouds Over Sidra* is a case in point. Made using a 360-degree camera in a Syrian refugee camp in Jordan, it gives people who would never set foot in such surroundings a glimpse of what life is like as a refugee. World leaders, policymakers and entrepreneurs attending the annual World Economic Forum in Davos in 2015 were invited to put on headsets and immerse themselves. Within an instant, they were transported from the glitzy Swiss mountain resort to the home of 12-year-old Sidra, sitting opposite her on the floor. 'It connects humans to other humans in a profound way I've never seen before,' according to the film's maker, Chris Milk.[4]

Unlike watching the world unfold in a two-dimensional manner, as is the case with books, movies or visual art, virtual reality offers a three-dimensional immersive experience. It quite literally helps you to step into someone else's shoes. Look down and you'll see the ground they and you are standing on. Instead of peering into another world, you're inhabiting it. No wonder virtual reality is also dubbed the 'empathy machine'. As with other forms of arts exposure, the scientific jury is still out about the measurable impact of virtual reality on empathy,[5] but the way in which it allows you to transplant yourself into a different space suggests great promise for relating to others' experiences. It's another tool in the empathy instigator toolkit.

Finally, and possibly the most obvious way to relate to the experience of poverty: talk to those with first-hand insight. Books, films, art and virtual reality are wonderful tools for allowing an insight into someone else's life, but there's nothing like an actual conversation. To sit across from someone and hear how they experience their lives, what they struggle with and why, and what their hopes, dreams and expectations are. Rather than being presented with a genuine but carefully crafted and curated story, a conversation also allows for interaction. It gives you the opportunity to follow up on things that are puzzling, and – crucially – for the person opposite to ask you questions.

Making such conversations happen takes effort. Unlike Catherine, not many people are in a position to travel to another country to have a face-to-face conversation with someone about their struggles and challenges. But even closer to home, most of us tend to live in quite separate social bubbles, with little mixing across socioeconomic strata. And with much of our lives now playing out in online spaces, the opportunity for everyday personal interaction has reduced even further.

All that said, there are still ample ways to reach out and have a conversation. They may be brief encounters, but they can be enough to give you a glimpse into how others navigate life. Like the taxi driver who is forced to accept unfavourable rides, because if he doesn't, the algorithm of the taxi app will push him down the list when future jobs come along. Or the food delivery courier who has just spent hours waiting in the rain for this one assignment, even though it will hardly earn them enough to afford a meal for themselves. Or the child who joined the school trip without a lunchbox because there wasn't anything in the fridge or kitchen cupboards for them to pack. Understanding such experiences through direct conversation are likely to bring home their human aspect unlike anything else.

Whichever way you to choose to cultivate your empathy, the most important thing is to be curious. If you're serious about wanting to connect with the world as others experience it, expose yourself to alternative realities lived by millions around you in any way you can.

Read, watch, listen. Take in, absorb and be moved. By relating to experiences of disadvantage, exclusion and hardship, you're working the empathy muscle and taking the first step towards contributing to the fight against poverty.

Realise

'I was so stressed out trying to find out how to get bills paid and grocery money.'

Char Christenson is a county commissioner in Minnesota, US. She offers her feedback after having participated in an in-person poverty role play, the Community Action Poverty Simulation (CAPS).[6] Developed by the Missouri Community Action Network, it aims to challenge misconceptions around poverty.[7] As noted on their website, it 'bridges that gap from misconception to understanding'.

Char was assigned one of more than 20 roles that feature in the interactive group exercise. She was asked to represent a mother with two children who had just been left by her husband and only had $10 to spare. Like other poverty simulations, CAPS places participants in the hypothetical situation of being poor, and having to deal with the dilemmas and impossible choices that are inherent to life on a low income.

'I just couldn't believe how angry I got and how helpless I felt,' Char says.

In the case of CAPS, each of the fictional families faces a unique set of circumstances, but they all struggle to get by. They are asked to make ends meet during a hypothetical one-month period, availing themselves of the shops, schools, moneylenders and social services that are set up around the room in which the exercise takes place. But just like in real life, participants find themselves held back by ill health, broken-down cars, bureaucratic services, and the mere stress of dealing with it all.

Over the years, thousands of nonprofit organisations, schools and communication action groups across the US have implemented CAPS. They ask their staff, volunteers and students to take part in the exercise not only to relate to the experience of poverty, but also to create awareness and shift mindsets about why people are poor and remain trapped.

'Lawmakers should be required to experience something like this so they can vote with knowledge of the situation rather than just numbers and charts,' says a student who took part in a simulation exercise at the University of Mississippi.[8] Developed with lived-experience experts, simulations like CAPS can be incredibly powerful in challenging preconceived ideas or assumptions about why people experience disadvantage and are unable to escape. They can help change attitudes and practice, which is especially welcome if simulation participants are already or will in future be involved in the design or delivery of services.

You don't have to be a member of an organisation, work in the social sector, be part of a group or even leave your home to take part in a simulation. Developed by nonprofits and charities, individual simulations are available online and are often free to use.[9] They provide a potent and interactive method of engaging with everyday decisions and the impossible trade-offs they entail. They can help us realise the ways in which policies trap poor people in a merry-go-round of proving their eligibility and evidencing their deservingness. Having to weigh up one bad option against another makes tangible the frustration and injustice of being sent from pillar to post, only to be left with limited support or advice that does little to address the predicament.

Developing a realisation of the daily conundrums inherent to poverty and the counterproductive nature of many anti-poverty policies in addressing them constitutes the second R of an empathy-induced foundation for change. Becoming aware of the structures and power dynamics that produce and perpetuate poverty is fundamental for disrupting the status quo.

Yet empathy doesn't merely require us to look out towards others; it also calls on us to hold up a mirror and look at ourselves. To examine our attitudes to poverty, and our role in perpetuating stereotypes or falsehoods. To consider our everyday actions and how we might be implicated in reinforcing disadvantage and deprivation.

Doing so entails an honest reflection about the extent to which common myths about poverty have infiltrated our own belief system, whether we realise it or not. We may think we aren't prejudiced against people in poverty, but is that really true? We may at an intellectual level know there are insurmountable barriers that hold people back, but how does this knowledge hold up against ingrained perceptions or stereotypes? And we might be convinced that our personal actions don't harm individuals or families in low-income situations, but to what extent is that a tenable position?

As we've seen throughout this book, negative narratives and damaging tropes about those at the lower end of the socioeconomic ladder are everywhere. Persistent messaging about people in poverty being lazy, dependent or unwilling to change their lifestyle are inescapable and will leave their mark, whether we realise it or not. As an indication of how hard-wired these perceptions are, ask ChatGPT about the personal traits of someone in poverty and it will point you to criminal behaviour, drug abuse and poor decision-making.[10]

We're socialised to believe that disparities in socioeconomic outcomes are a result of effort and behaviour rather than systemic failure to offer equal opportunity to all. Political philosopher Michael J. Sandel writes, 'In an unequal society, those who land on top want to believe their success is morally justified. In a meritocratic society, this means the winners must believe they have earned their success through their own talent and hard work.'[11]

This widespread and persistent discourse leads to inevitable unconscious bias, guiding gut reactions and everyday actions. Even if at a theoretical level you believe there should be greater equality and less poverty, ask yourself the following:

How happy are you about paying taxes? Or do you take part in the widespread social exercise of complaining about how much of your hard-earned income or inheritance gets sucked into the government's coffers?

How willing are you to give cash to someone who tells you they're hungry? Or would you rather buy them some fruit and bread yourself, so you can quell your concern about the money being spent on something other than what you deem essential?

And what about this one: If you were faced with socio-economic disadvantage, do you think you would struggle like others living on little, or do you believe you would make smarter decisions and cope better?

Empathy requires us all to face up to the inconsistencies between our values, beliefs and behaviour. Not to trigger an exercise of finger-pointing, but rather so that we own up and act in accordance with our values. Greater equality is only possible if those of us in comfortable socioeconomic positions honestly reflect on how wedded we are to the idea that our success and the things we've achieved are down to our own hard work and graft. If we're willing to admit how much our lives may have been positively influenced by the wealth of our parents, our gender, our skin colour, or the neighbourhood we happened to grow up in. If we commit to asking ourselves questions about our own role in the perpetuation of socio-economic disadvantage playing out all around us, and the lens through which we seek to address it. If we consider the assumptions and perceptions we bring to bear when wishing to connect to the lived reality of those in poverty.

There's no merit in occupying a moral high ground by making reference to a set of ethical or political principles if we don't abide by them, and even less so if doing so prevents us from being honest with ourselves about how our actions might implicate us in the perpetuation of poverty. The second R of empathy requires us to come face-to-face with our own privileges and attitudes, and to be self-critical about the extent to which our ideology and moral values align with our everyday actions. Only once we come to terms with our hypocrisies, and are willing to concede their existence and prepared to address them, can we begin to be part of positive change.

Respond

Breaking the cycle of poverty demands action. Relating to the emotive side of hardship and cultivating an understanding of why poverty persists forms the foundation for our own contributions towards change. Response is the third R of empathy.

Fundamental to whatever role we wish to play in the fight against poverty is a belief that change is possible. This may sound obvious, but it's all too easy to get overwhelmed by the scale of the problem or the seeming futility of swimming against the tide. We've seen the numbers of women, men and children around the globe living in deprivation, and it's easy to feel powerless in the face of those figures.

But as historian Rutger Bregman reminds us in his book *Utopia for Realists*, we shouldn't be afraid to imagine and strive for a different world. We need to be able to see beyond the way in which the world is currently structured, including the dominance of economic neoliberalism, and consider alternative socioeconomic constellations in which everyone can thrive. However hard it can be at times, we need to hold on to the idea that the status quo can be challenged, and our vision of what a different society might look like.

Part and parcel of a vision for change is a move away from the potent but unhelpful narrative that helping those in hardship is a zero-sum game. It's easy to portray redistribution as a dichotomous take-and-give evocative of a Robin Hood scenario, with the poor heralded as winners and the rich demonised as losers. This might make an appealing story, but it plays into false and polarising suggestions that those better off need to become worse off to lift the living standards for those on lower incomes. While a fairer society inevitably means those with more wealth parting with more of their money to level the playing field, they also stand to benefit.

Supporting each other is a win–win situation. We all benefit from greater equality. We all do better if we can be certain that something and someone has our backs if we go through a rough patch in life. We're all much more likely to do the things we like and lead the lives we want in societies that equally value all of us instead of just some of us. With narratives made up of individual stories, it's up to each one of us to challenge the discourse.

As I mentioned in Chapter 1, a few years ago, I asked readers of my blog on Poverty Unpacked to share widely used terms that refer to people in poverty or in receipt of social welfare. I received responses from all over the world, from the UK to Pakistan and Zimbabwe. I asked those who responded to explain the connotations that came with the use of those terms, whether there were any explicit or hidden meanings.

Some were outright offensive, intended to insult and paint people in poverty in a bad light. 'Skivers', 'scroungers' and 'benefit broods', or versions thereof, are commonplace and serve no other purpose than to demonise and dehumanise.

The most obvious and easy empathetic step in challenging the status quo on poverty and avoiding the perpetuation of these stereotypes is to not use them, and to disengage from media that employ them as catchy headlines or clickbait. Go one step further and you might call out those who do make these terms part of their vocabulary. Make sure to pick your battles, though. Challenging a friend on their use of a derogatory term and engaging them in a conversation about its hurtful and harmful nature is probably more challenging than engaging in an anonymous online debate, but it is also likely to be more constructive and have greater success in moving the needle.

A response to poverty requires us to do more than denounce tropes and labels that are obviously intended to put people down. Terms that refer to people in poverty or receiving support are by no means all explicitly negative. In fact, many responses to my request suggested that terms are mostly technical, used in a neutral manner. They could be translated as 'a person with little money' or 'someone needing support to get by'. They might be used as a statement of fact, or as a label to identify individuals in need.

Yet as pointed out by late social scientist Santi Kusumaningrum, no words are value-neutral in and of themselves. Instead, it depends on who uses them, in what context and for what purpose. As Santi noted: 'I think we need to admit that as researchers or policy thinkers, we might not assign any degrading meaning to the words "poor" and "vulnerable". But once we use that in a conversation with bureaucrats or politicians, what we thought of as neutral might not be the case anymore.' Without reflecting on the audience or context of our use of words, seemingly innocent terms may take on a meaning we didn't intend.

While it's important to reflect on how certain language may be received by those in the higher echelons of the decision-making hierarchy, first and foremost we should ask how lived-experience experts feel about the use of certain language, and what terms they prefer. It's for this reason that in this book I have made reference to 'the poor' sparingly.

Over the years, conversations with poverty activists have impressed on me the understanding that speaking of 'the poor' can be both unhelpful and undignified. It serves as a label, defining individuals by their socioeconomic status, as if that's all there is to them. It suggests the experience of poverty is a singular, static and self-imposed state rather than a complex, ever-changing and enforced part of life. But most of all, it feeds into the pervasive discourse of 'them' and 'us', and that we are somehow fundamentally different from each other.

In a bid to counteract this narrative, anti-poverty organisation ATD Fourth World has actively denounced the notion of 'intergenerational transmission of poverty', widely used to point to the perpetuation of poverty across multiple genera-tions. The word 'transmission' carries with it the suggestion that parents somehow infect their children. As if poverty is a disease or a personal default that is carried over from one generation into the next.

Even if we steer clear of denigrating terms, the seemingly innocent labelling of people experiencing poverty as a single group can leave its mark. Whether we like it or not, many of us are implicated, deliberately or subconsciously, in shaping the rhetoric of those living on little. Responding to poverty from a place of empathy, it's imperative we use our words wisely and with care, reflecting not only on how we might understand their meaning, but also on how others might interpret them.

A second and more direct way for us to take action is to volunteer. To give our time to be of service to others. Not as a way of endorsing the idea that charitable service should replace or offer a stopgap for holes in a country's welfare system, but rather as acknowledgement of the real needs and disadvantage that exist across our communities and everyone's responsibility in meeting those needs. Volunteering is an immediate and tangible way of getting involved, and to come face-to-face with the structural inequalities that create the need for charity-based service provision in the first place.

Probably one of the first activities that comes to mind when thinking about volunteering to help tackle poverty is to get involved in direct delivery of services. To serve meals in a soup kitchen, make beds in a night shelter or put together parcels in a food bank. Such activities have the added benefit of human interaction. You get to have those conversations that are crucial for creating an understanding of the experience of poverty, to realise that there's more that binds us together than divides us.

If such people-facing and often quite physical activities aren't for you for whatever reason – maybe you're home-bound, you can't commit to regular shifts or the hours available, you prefer working in non-personal activities, you don't live in the vicinity of such types of facilities or they don't have volunteering vacancies – there's a lot more to be done and get engaged with. Desk-based work, such as helping people challenge decisions on their welfare claims or working with charities on their social media or fundraising events, tends to be more flexible and might be a more accessible option for some.

Wanting to contribute some of my free time but unable to commit to a fixed schedule due to the demands of my day job, I found a position as community representative for a grant-giving charity in Milton Keynes. The voluntary role entails serving on a panel that assesses applications for funding of community projects, ranging from setting up mental health support in schools to providing meals to disadvantaged community members. The role allows me to contribute my time and expertise on issues of poverty in a way that's helpful to the charity and fits with my irregular work commitments. As a bonus, it has given me deep appreciation of the many and varied initiatives set up across the city, with people from different backgrounds coming together to create more inclusive and thriving communities.

In short, all sorts of activities are available, and it should be possible to find something that fits your schedule, that you enjoy doing, and that makes best use of your skills. If you don't know where to start, look for portals or platforms that combine and list volunteer opportunities in your local area. They offer a helpful starting point to get a sense of what type of volunteering is available and how you can get engaged. If something sounds of interest but you're not sure, reach out. Don't be discouraged if you don't receive an immediate response: serving people in need is an organisations' priority. Be assured that they will want to hear from individuals willing to share their time and energy. With a little effort and some patience, you will find a role that offers benefits to everyone involved.

In addition to the choice of our words or any volunteering we might do, our response – empathy's third R – means we must also be willing to examine and change our everyday behaviour. Not least in terms of how we spend our money, and whether it might reinforce economic inequality.

As we saw in the previous chapter, paid work commonly doesn't pay enough. Employees are asked to provide their labour cheaply. Most people in poverty have some sort of job – this is true in both richer and poorer countries. With work widely considered the route to prosperity, the fact that toiling for money is hardly a way out of deprivation is frustrating at best and infuriating at worst.

But let me ask you this: how often do you wonder about the origins of the products you buy? About who made the clothes you're wearing, assembled the car you're driving or picked the strawberries you're eating. Whether they received a fair wage, or were given adequate equipment to keep them safe while doing their jobs. They're not easy questions to answer and can be difficult to engage with, but it's vital we try.

The gig economy and flexible employment opportunities have brought benefit to some, pulling them into the realm of economic opportunity. Yet they have also led to widespread evaporation of job security and fair pay. As much as this may seem an inevitable shift in our economies and a force beyond our control, we must own up to the fact that we are all a piece of the puzzle, and together we made it happen.

It's our desire for fast fashion, cheap deals and the convenience of having meals delivered to our doorstep that has led to an army of low-wage workers, many of whom struggle to get by. The collective shift in our consumption patterns, away from durable but more expensive to short-lived and cheaper products, has played into the hands of business tycoons trying to make big money off the back of low-paid workers. And it's become a catch-22: being a more ethical consumer has become unaffordable for many.

For those of us who can, resist the urge to visit that large online retailer and choose a smaller chain or independent seller. Buy better quality for a price that you know is both reasonable and can sustain a well-paid job. Better still, venture out and shop local, investing in your community rather than filling the pockets of greedy millionaires. I won't pretend I get this right all the time, or even most of the time. But the truth is that what we buy and from whom signals our preferences and priorities. Our everyday consumption behaviour allows us to vote with our feet. The more we look beyond our busy lives and resist the pull of convenience and the appeal of low prices, the better we're able to do this.

But we also have a direct way of telling those in power about how we would like our societies to be shaped, and that's by exercising our right to vote. Sadly, faith in our political systems is at a low in many places, especially in richer countries.[12] In Australia, UK and the US, trust in the legislature has steadily declined in the last three decades. In the US, confidence in Congress fell from 53 per cent in 1982 to 15 per cent in 2017. In the UK, only one in five trust Parliament, while trust in political parties is even lower, at 13 per cent. In an era where political leaders such as Donald Trump and Boris Johnson can act brazenly without impunity, many have grown suspicious of politicians and the political system as a whole.

Despite this suspicion, or perhaps because of it, it's imperative for each of us to use the vote we have. The right to vote and ability to exercise it underpins democracy. It has been hard-fought, and in many places continues to be, and should therefore never be taken for granted. It wasn't until 1928, less than a century ago, that all women in the UK were allowed to vote. In Kuwait, women had to wait until 2005, casting their ballots for the first time a year later. But even with a legal right to vote, there's no guarantee that everyone can exercise it. Lack of identification documents, for example, are a common barrier, especially for already disenfranchised groups. This includes people in poverty.

While politicians may not live up to their promises, or change plans as they go along, they do hold the reins when it comes to big decisions about the shape of our society. Our individual vote may seem an insignificant drop in the ocean, and there's no guarantee that election outcomes are respected, or parties abide by their manifestos once in power. But one thing is for sure: if we don't go to the ballot box, we acquiesce. If we don't cast a vote when we have the opportunity to do so, we forgo an opportunity for change.

Fortunately, you don't have to wait for elections to come round for your voice to be heard. There are more ways to get politicians, and other decision-makers for that matter, to pay attention.

Take campaigning. It can be a potent mechanism to shine a light on injustice and call for a change in policy or legislation. Petitions have long been a campaigner's tool, drawing attention to public support for a particular cause. Their use has become much easier due to the rise of online platforms such as Change.org and openPetition, which allow anyone to raise an issue and collect signatures in support of their cause. A quick browse reveals there are petitions calling for exempting menstrual products from VAT in a bid to reduce period poverty in Austria, and abolishing co-payments on medical bills for children with disabilities in low-income families in the US.

If you're wondering whether petitions ever make any difference, consider the case of school meals in the UK. A decision by the government not to extend free school meals into the holiday period during the height of the COVID-19 pandemic caused a public uproar. At a time of national crisis that hit vulnerable families the hardest, there was strong public support for making sure children didn't go hungry over

Christmas. When high-profile celebrities started lending their weight to the cause, politicians could no longer ignore the widespread outrage at their decision.

The famous footballer Marcus Rashford launched a petition on the government's own e-petition website calling for free school meals to be extended into the holiday period, and it gained more than a quarter of a million signatures within days.[13] In the six-month period it was open for, more than 1.1 million people lent their support.[14] With success. Reading the mood of the British public, the government made a U-turn and continued to provide meals to eligible children during the next few holiday periods. The then prime minister, Boris Johnson, even picked up the phone to personally inform Marcus Rashford about his change of heart.[15]

Whether you're the one launching the petition or one of thousands adding their signature, the point is they're both forms of poverty activism. And there are many more. Join a rally and demonstrate against injustice. Write to your political representative and demand change. Engage in 'craftivism' and join the ranks of gentle activists who draw attention to injustice in kind and creative ways. In a remarkable act of calm and generous protest by the Craftivist Collective, a dozen hand-stitched handkerchiefs with personal messages convinced board members at Marks & Spencer – one of Britain's most iconic retailers – that the company should become an accredited living wage employer.[16] How's that for making change happen?

Choosing our words with care, volunteering our time, thinking twice about where we part with our money, using our vote, and raising our voice as well as amplifying others' are actions each of us can take. Rather than these suggestions being seen as a definitive list, they should serve as inspiration to add your own. They are all part of the response, of the third R of empathy.

It's easy to get swept up in the sentiment that taking small steps leads to nothing. But seeing value in individual action, whatever shape or size it takes, allows for bringing many more people into the fold. Actions might be small, but their ripple effects can engender large impact. They inspire others, building belief that change is possible and growing the movement. And as the saying goes: small drops make a mighty ocean. We can all be change-makers, and be so with empathy.

CONCLUSION

In an interview with the *Catholic Herald* in 1978, Margaret Thatcher infamously claimed that poverty is a flaw of character. Opposition leader at the time, a year before becoming Britain's first female prime minister, she made her inflammatory comment when reflecting on poverty and the work of missionaries in poorer countries. 'In Western countries we are left with the problems which aren't poverty. All right, there may be poverty because people don't know how to budget, don't know how to spend their earnings, but now you are left with the really hard fundamental character – personality defect.'[1]

Thatcher voiced her opinion at a time when the proportion of Brits in relative low income was at its lowest since the 1960s. If her stance was ignorant, pejorative and insulting in prosperous times, it can only be considered outrageous now. Yet in an era when levels of deprivation and destitution remain widespread and stubbornly stagnant – in the UK and across the world – the suggestion that poverty is the result of personal failure is still very much alive. The narrative has become ingrained in our collective psyche, causing shame and stigma among those in poverty, and disdain and a sense of superiority among the wealthy.

Inevitably, this attitude infiltrates the ways in which we think poverty should be tackled, and the policies that are implemented to address the problem. The poor are pushed and policed to ensure any support is put to good use, and punished if it isn't. Help might be available, but only if you're considered deserving enough, and with strings attached. Trust isn't part of the vocabulary. Dignity and respect don't enter the equation. Empathy is nowhere in sight.

Psychological explanations for why poverty persists have grown incredibly popular in the last decade. They have shed light on the debilitating effects of living on little, and how poverty reproduces itself. The so-called psychology of poverty helps us see how the cognitive strain of financial precarity makes it harder to think straight. An understanding of the shame and trauma of poverty points us to the devastating effects on self-esteem and mental health. A lack of role models, low societal expectations and the large gap between ambition and opportunity explain aspiration failure. This has all led to great enthusiasm for interventions that seek to directly impact poor people's attitudes, knowledge and behaviour, often with the notion that real change starts with people in poverty themselves.

As much as these insights and interventions are predicated on a recognition that it's not the choices that people make that keep them poor, but the state of poverty that leads to difficult decisions and impossible trade-offs, it has also firmly placed the focus on people in poverty and their individual actions. Although easily afforded the empathy label, behavioural explanations of and solutions to poverty have fed the individualisation of the problem, whether intentionally or not. They offer an escape route for those of us in more privileged positions to say 'it's them, not us', and for us to absolve ourselves from our responsibility.

Let me be clear. This book isn't about fixing people in poverty. It's about fixing the problem of poverty.

To do that, we have to make the causes and consequences of poverty visible. To create an understanding of the reality of living on little so that everyone can become involved in counteracting it. Because if your life isn't defined by the struggle to get by, it's hard to imagine what that's like and what it does.

If you have a surplus on your bank account, how will you know about the financial, mental, physical and psychological costs imposed on those with smaller budgets? How would you be aware of the mental strain of the constant financial accounting required to make ends meet? Realise that life is more expensive if you're only able to buy in small quantities or take out high-risk loans? Or appreciate the anxiety of having to comply with an impenetrable web of rules and regulations to receive welfare support, and the shame of being confronted with the relentless flow of negative stereotypes and pejorative treatment?

If ever there was a time to challenge the harmful discourse surrounding poverty and the policies that feed off it, it's now. The fact that billions of people on this planet are struggling to satisfy their basic needs every single day while a select few are enjoying unimaginable wealth isn't just morally wrong, it makes everyone worse off. The suggestion that deprivation is a problem that affects only those who experience it, and are therefore responsible for solving it, is a fallacy.

Interventions grounded in positive psychology can build inner strength and motivate change. Raising aspirations, incentivising beneficial behaviours and instilling confidence have their role in breaking the negative cycle of poverty. But they shouldn't be peddled as a quick fix or adopted in isolation, without taking account of the wider context in which people are making ends meet. More fundamentally, such efforts shouldn't be hijacked by a meritocratic agenda and neoliberal narrative that ultimately leaves people worse off. What we need is an overhaul of the way we understand and tackle poverty, and to do it from the perspective of those who experience it. We need an empathy fix.

Although this is easily dismissed as a soft and fuzzy concept, I hope to have conveyed that tackling poverty through the prism of empathy isn't for the faint-hearted. The three Rs – *relate, realise, respond* – require us to become familiar with and challenge uncomfortable truths about the world we live in, the society we're part of and the positions we occupy and strive for. In doing so, the power of empathy in addressing the persistent and pernicious problem of poverty is twofold.

First, it shifts the emphasis in terms of whose perspectives count when it comes to understanding the situation and formulating a solution. Rather than relying on the knowledge and skills of those in high places, it locates the wisdom surrounding poverty and how to tackle the issue with those who experience it.

Second, it allows for making everyone part of the solution. For someone financially secure but without direct engagement with anti-poverty efforts, it can be hard to know how to get involved. Relating to the problem of poverty and realising its causes and consequences, including your own role in it, can be done by anyone, and form the starting point for positive action – individual and collective.

Empathy also warrants caution. We need to acknowledge that it isn't inherently benign. We're biologically programmed to feel with those who are like us, and to put up barriers against anyone who might be considered a threat. Tapping into our capacity for empathy without due care risks reinforcing existing inequalities, and deepening divisions between the haves and have-nots. We need to keep ourselves in check, and own up to the biases that inevitably emerge. Who stands to benefit from our empathy? Who do we withhold it from? Empathy requires openness to the perspectives of all lived-experience experts, even – or especially – if they challenge our own world views.

Importantly, taking perspective and stepping into the shoes of someone with lived experience is decisively not about shoving them aside and taking their place. A desire to highlight the plight of people in poverty shouldn't overshoot into tropes of suffering and victimhood. An empathy-driven approach to poverty reduction is about standing with and walking alongside lived-experience experts. It requires continuous examination of our intentions, and a willingness to change course if necessary. What's more, an empathetic response to poverty also requires us to confront beliefs about our own success. To come face to face with any privileges that have contributed to it, and to be honest about the way in which systemic advantages may have served socio-economic fortitude.

Finally, a word about the book's geographical remit. In my two decades of working on issues of poverty across the world, I have been struck by the many similarities in how poverty is experienced, how those experiences and the people living them are misunderstood, ignored and undermined, and how policies explicitly or inadvertently perpetuate and reinforce vicious cycles of poverty.

That said, of course there are also important differences. The scale of the problem is many times bigger in poorer countries than it is in richer countries. Tackling an issue that affects more than half the population versus 10 or 20 per cent of society brings its own moral dilemmas and practical considerations in deciding who to support and how. In addition, development aid and its colonial legacy bring an international power dynamic to poverty reduction in lower-income countries that isn't unlike the unequal relationship between poorer individuals and their wealthier counterparts. In those countries, choices about poverty reduction and anti-poverty policies aren't national affairs. Instead, they're tied to, constrained by and conditioned on the priorities of rich nations.

Nevertheless, despite, or perhaps because of, international meddling in poverty-reduction policies in poorer countries, the similarities in discourses and narratives underpinning those policies are larger than their differences. There might be wider recognition that deprivation and hardship is a structural problem – countries themselves are labelled as 'poor' or 'low-income', after all – but the desire to tackle such a pervasive issue in a context where the environment is unfavourable at best makes the appeal to individuals' own responsibility even more attractive. The range of examples drawn upon in this book – whether they reflect long-standing state-run welfare policies or more recent nonprofit and smaller-scale anti-poverty policy interventions – shows that the dominant discourse that poverty is a predominantly individual problem that can be tackled through behavioural solutions prevails the world over.

If we stay stuck in the current loop of blame and shame, focusing almost exclusively on poor people's character and behaviour, the cycle of poverty will only deepen and become further entrenched. If we fail to widen the lens and cast light on how our social policies and welfare schemes place the responsibility of moving out of poverty with individuals and their families, the scale of deprivation will increase. If we ignore how big businesses inflate costs and suppress wages to maximise their profits at the expense of the working population, the gap between the 'haves' and 'have nots' will expand. And if we discount the role of governments in maintaining a lower class that can be othered, shamed and blamed for the ills in society instead of taking responsibility for fixing those ills, poverty will never be eradicated.

No one sums it up better than lived-experience expert and anti-poverty activist Maryann Broxton: 'People in poverty are constantly held accountable for their level of poverty, as if their personal choices/actions alone are responsible for it. But yet governments are not held accountable for the deliberate choices that push people into and maintain poverty, or deepen the level for others. When we talk about eradicating poverty, we tend to talk about a lack of political will. But this is misleading. Poverty does not exist simply because of a lack of political will. In our world today poverty exists because of deliberate political choices. Poverty does not affect vulnerable people like a natural disaster. Poverty is man-made.'[2]

And that's the good news. We got ourselves into this mess, and we can get ourselves out of it. We're all capable of empathy. This is a call to tap into it, use it wisely, and fix poverty.

ACKNOWLEDGEMENTS

This book has been a long time in the making and wouldn't have happened without the support of many people along the way.

I am most indebted to everyone who over the last two decades so kindly and generously shared their experiences, views and insights with me. At the heart of this book are the adults and children from around the world who agreed to give up their time and open up to me or my research colleagues about their struggles, strategies and dreams in pursuit of a better life. It's these conversations that gave rise to the idea for this book, and I will never take their gift for granted.

I'm also immensely grateful to the many guests on my podcast, Poverty Unpacked, for sparking new ideas, and in so doing helping me develop the narrative for this book. Some guests are featured in its pages; others have left their mark in less visible but no less important ways. Similarly, I have greatly benefited from countless conversations with colleagues and students alike, whose own work and critical reflection of mine was indispensable in sharpening my ideas and honing my argument.

Thank you to Ciara Finan at Curtis Brown, who believed in my idea from the get-go and whose tireless enthusiasm and encouragement were invaluable in navigating the world of non-fiction publishing. Many thanks to Erika Koljonen at Allen & Unwin UK and Atlantic Books for understanding what I was trying to do with this book, and helping to shape and reshape it into its current form. Thanks also to Jane Selley for multiple rounds of meticulous copy-editing and to the team at Allen & Unwin UK and Atlantic Books for their support in getting this book out into the world.

Lots of gratitude to my amazing friends and family, who have been a massive support, whether they realised it or not. Debating title options and cover designs, offering feedback on problematic chapters, providing much-needed moral support, or simply putting up with relative silence as I was typing away in the corner of my study at home – thank you for sticking with it!

A special word of thanks to my parents, who imparted to me the importance of empathy in their own understated but steadfast manner. From an early age, I realised that their refusal to judge others by their cover or place themselves above anyone else were valuable lessons to take to heart.

And finally, to my husband, Bart, for his unwavering support and unconditional belief in my ability to pull this off. His optimism simply knows no bounds. Fortunately, as I've learned in the process of writing this book, nor does his patience. Thank you for being by my side.

NOTES

Introduction

1. Figures from JRF (2024). *UK Poverty. The essential guide to understanding poverty in the UK.* York: Joseph Rowntree Foundation.
2. Based on IMF estimates of 2023 GDP, current prices at IMF World Economic Outlook Database, accessed 21 January 2024.
3. Estimates from Eurostat: Living conditions in Europe – poverty and social exclusion – Statistics Explained (europa.eu), published June 2023, accessed 26 January 2024.
4. Estimates from United States Census Bureau: Poverty in the United States: 2022 (census.gov), published September 2023, accessed 25 January 2024.
5. Estimates from World Bank 2019 poverty estimates: https://pip. worldbank.org/home, accessed 21 January 2024; and World Bank (2022). *Poverty and Shared Prosperity 2022. Correcting Course.* Washington DC: World Bank.
6. Estimates from United Nations Population Fund: https://www. unfpa.org/data/world-population-dashboard, accessed 25 January 2024.
7. Estimates from https://ourworldindata.org/extreme-poverty, accessed 12 November 2021.
8. Based on 2023 Joint Malnutrition Estimates by UNICEF, WHO and the World Bank: Joint Malnutrition Estimates (2023 Edition) | Tableau Public, accessed 21 January 2024.
9. Estimates from https://ourworldindata.org/child-mortality#child-

mortality-around-the-world-since-1800, accessed 12 November 2021.

10. Based on 2022 estimates by UNICEF and World Bank as reported in Salmeron-Gomez, D., et al. (2023). *Global Trends in Child Monetary Poverty According to International Poverty Lines*. Policy Research Working Paper 10525. Washington DC: World Bank.

11. Figures based on JRF (2024). *UK Poverty. The essential guide to understanding poverty in the UK*. York: Joseph Rowntree Foundation.

12. Estimates by CPB Netherlands Bureau for Economic Policy Analysis: Raming Augustus 2023 (concept-Macro Economische Verkenning 2024) | CPB.nl, published in August 2023, accessed 26 January 2024.

13. Yusuf, A. A., et al. (2023). *Will economic growth be sufficient to end global poverty? New projections of the UN Sustainable Development Goals*. WIDER Working Paper 2023/123. Helsinki: UNU-WIDER.

14. Based on Oxfam (2024). *Inequality Inc. How corporate power divides our world and the need for a new era of public action*. Oxford: Oxfam.

15. See UNICEF's *Adjustment with a Human Face*, first published 1985, for critique of structural adjustment policies and their consequences for people in poverty.

16. For effect on child mortality and child malnutrition, see: Thomson, M., Kentikelenis, A., and Stubbs, T. (2017). 'Structural adjustment programmes adversely affect vulnerable populations: a systematic-narrative review of their effect on child and maternal health'. *Public Health Review* 38(13); and for effect on excess deaths from tuberculosis and respiratory disease, see: Nosrati, E., et al. (2022). 'Structural adjustment programmes and infectious disease mortality'. *PLoS One* 17(7).

17. Gladwell, Malcolm (2006). 'Million-Dollar Murray'. *New Yorker*, Vol. 82, Issue 1, published 13 February 2006.

18. Figures based on Geraghty, Liam (2021). 'Homelessness could cost the government £2.6bn a year without action'. *The Big Issue*, published 22 November 2021.

19. Hirsch, D. (2021). *The cost of child poverty in 2021*. Loughborough: Centre for Research in Social Policy. Loughborough University.

Chapter 1: Getting to Grips with Empathy

1. Estimates from Dhaka Population 2023 (worldpopulationreview. com), accessed 30 December 2023.
2. Roelen, K., et al. (2023). *CLARISSA Cash Plus: Innovative Social Protection in Bangladesh*, CLARISSA Design Note 1, Brighton: Institute of Development Studies.
3. As discussed in Coplan, Amy, and Goldie, Peter (eds.) (2011). *Empathy: Philosophical and Psychological Perspectives*. Oxford: Oxford Academic.
4. As discussed in Stueber, Karsten (2019). 'Empathy'. *The Stanford Encyclopedia of Philosophy* (Fall 2019 Edition), ed. Edward N. Zalta: https://plato.stanford.edu/archives/fall2019/entries/empathy/, accessed 2 August 2023.
5. Based on Google Trends, accessed 3 August 2023.
6. Geoff Blackwell (2020). 'Jacinda Ardern: "Political leaders can be both empathetic and strong"'. *The Guardian*, published 30 May 2020.
7. See Cohen, S. (2012). *Zero Degrees of Empathy. A new theory of human cruelty and kindness*. London: Penguin, p.12, and Krznaric, R. (2015). *Empathy. Why it matters and how to get it*. London: Rider Books, p.x.
8. Chakrabarti, Bhismadev, and Baron-Cohen, Simon (2006). 'Empathizing: neurocognitive developmental mechanisms and individual differences'. *Progress in Brain Research*, Vol. 156, pp.403–17.
9. Ibid.
10. The power of empathy: Helen Riess at TEDxMiddlebury, December 2013.
11. Singer, Tania, et al. (2004). 'Empathy for Pain Involves the Affective but not Sensory Components of Pain'. *Science* 303,1157–1162.
12. Baron-Cohen, S. (2012). *Zero Degrees of Empathy. A new theory of human cruelty and kindness*. London: Penguin, p.12.
13. Krznaric, R. (2015). *Empathy. Why it matters and how to get it*. London: Rider Books, p.xix.
14. Horner, V., et al. (2011). 'Spontaneous prosocial choice by chimpanzees'. *PNAS* 108 (33) 13847–13851.

15. Moral behavior in animals: Frans de Waal at TEDxPeachtree, November 2011.

16. Suntsova, M. V., and Buzdin, A. A. (2020). 'Differences between human and chimpanzee genomes and their implications in gene expression, protein functions and biochemical properties of the two species'. *BMC Genomics* 21 (Suppl 7), 535.

17. Based on Great Apes and the Gift of Empathy: Frans de Waal in Monologue, published May 2018 by Topic, and Do Animals Have Morals?: Frans de Waal on TED Radio Hour, published September 2014 by NPR.

18. Zaki, Jamil (2019). *The War for Kindness. Building Empathy in a Fractured World*. London: Little, Brown: https://www. warforkindness.com/introduction-claims, claim 0.2.

19. The power of empathy: Helen Riess at TEDxMiddlebury, December 2013.

20. Interview with Sigrid Kaag, NOS *Met het Oog op Nederland*, 15 December 2023, by NPO Radio 1.

21. Konrath, S. H., O'Brien, E. H., and Hsing, C. (2011). 'Changes in Dispositional Empathy in American College Students Over Time: A Meta-Analysis'. *Personality and Social Psychology Review*, 15(2), 180–98.

22. Based on Edelman (2023). 2023 Edelman Trust Barometer. Global Report. Edelman Trust.

23. Cohen, S. (2012). *Zero Degrees of Empathy. A new theory of human cruelty and kindness*. London: Penguin, p.5.

24. Speaking of Psychology: The decline of empathy and the rise of narcissism: Sara Konrath, Speaking of Psychology podcast, Episode 95, by American Psychological Association (APA).

25. Leatherby, Lauren (2017). 'Five charts show why millennials are worse off than their parents'. FT Data. *Financial Times*, published 29 August 2017.

26. Cameron, C. D., et al. (2019). 'Empathy is hard work: People choose to avoid empathy because of its cognitive costs'. *Journal of Experimental Psychology: General*, 148(6), 962–976.

27. Hein, Grit, et al. (2010). 'Neural Responses to Ingroup and Outgroup Members' Suffering Predict Individual Differences in Costly Helping'. *Neuron*, 68(1): 149–160.

28. Fourie, Melike M., Subramoney, Sivenesi, and Goboda-Madikizela, Pumla (2017). 'A Less Attractive Feature of Empathy: Intergroup Empathy Bias'. In Makiko Kondo (ed.). *Empathy – An Evidence-based Interdisciplinary Perspective*, Chapter 3. IntechOpen.

29. Ali, Lorraine (2022). 'In Ukraine reporting, Western press reveals grim bias toward "people like us"'. *Los Angeles Times*, published 2 March 2022.

30. See Twitter/X feed Alan MacLeod, 27 February 2022: https://x.com/AlanRMacLeod/status/1497974245737050120.

31. See Bayoumi, Moustafa (2022). 'They are "civilised" and "look like us": the racist coverage of Ukraine'. *The Guardian*, published 2 May 2022; and Ali, Lorraine (2022). 'In Ukraine reporting, Western press reveals grim bias toward "people like us"'. *Los Angeles Times*, published 2 March 2022.

32. Roelen, Keetie (2021). Poverty has a language. Poverty Unpacked podcast, published 28 March 2021.

33. Hochfeld, Tessa, and Plagerson, Sophie (2011). 'Dignity and Stigma among South African Female Cash Transfer Recipients'. *IDS Bulletin* 42(6): 53–59.

34. Armoede. Lex Bohlmeijer in gesprek met Vanessa Umboh. Podcast: interview. *De Correspondent*, published 17 April 2023.

Chapter 2: Cognitive Costs and Poverty Premiums

1. See https://commonslibrary.parliament.uk/the-furlough-scheme-one-year-on/, accessed 20 February 2024.

2. Korducki, Kelli Maria (2021). 'I have "pandemic brain". Will I ever be able to concentrate again?'. *The Guardian*, published 24 June 2021.

3. Mullainathan, S., and Shafir, E. (2013). *Scarcity. The True Cost of Not Having Enough*. London: Penguin.

4. Mani, Anandi, et al. (2013). 'Poverty Impedes Cognitive Function'. *Science* 341, 976–80.

5. Ibid.

6. Mullainathan, S., and Shafir, E. (2013). *Scarcity. The True Cost of Not Having Enough*. London: Penguin.

7. See O'Shea, Ruairi (2022). 'Buy now pay later preys on the poorest consumers'. *Consumer*, published 1 November 2022.

8. Gilbert, Aaron, and Scott, Ayesha (2023). 'If it looks like debt, let's treat it like debt – "buy now, pay later" schemes need firmer regulation in NZ'. *The Conversation*, published 6 September 2023.

9. Edwards, Jean (2023). 'Struggling families "stuck" using buy now pay later for essentials'. Radio New Zealand, published 8 May 2023.

10. Haushofer, J., and Fehr, E. (2014). 'On the psychology of poverty'. *Science* 344 (6186), 862–7.

11. See Hamid and Khadeja's household profile from Collins, D., et al. (2009). *Portfolios of the Poor*. Princeton: Princeton University Press: http://www.portfoliosofthepoor.com/.

12. Dillon, Brian, De Weerdt, Joachim, and O'Donoghue, Ted (2021). 'Paying More for Less: Why Don't Households in Tanzania Take Advantage of Bulk Discounts?'. *The World Bank Economic Review*, Vol. 35, Issue 1: 148–79

13. Citizens Advice (2023). 'Millions left in the cold and dark as someone on a prepayment meter cut off every 10 seconds, reveals Citizens Advice'. Citizens Advice, published 12 January 2023.

14. Gayle, Vicky (2022). 'Thousands of Vulnerable People Cut Off from Gas and Electricity for Days at a Time'. Bureau of Investigative Journalism, published 16 December 2022.

15. Balfour, Reuben, and Allen, Jessica (2014). *Local action on health inequalities: Fuel poverty and cold home-related health problems*. Health equity briefing 7: September 2014. London: UCL Institute of Health Equity and Public Health England.

16. Marmot, M., Sinha, I. and Lee, A. (2022). 'Millions of children face a "humanitarian crisis" of fuel poverty'. *BMJ* 378: o2129.

17. Ibid.

18. Davies, Sara, and Evans, J. (2023). *The poverty premium in 2022 – Progress & problems*. Personal Finance Research Centre. Bristol: University of Bristol.

19. Fair By Design (2024). *Fair By Design Manifesto. Eliminating the poverty premium by 2028*. Fair By Design.

20. Saner, Emine (2022). '"It's just so easy, isn't it?" How buy now, pay later can leave Britons struggling with debt'. *The Guardian*, published 3 October 2022.

21. Carrns, Ann (2022). 'The Downsides of Using "Buy Now, Pay Later"'. *The New York Times*, published 29 December 2022.
22. Pratt, Kevin (2022). *Buy Now Pay Later Usage Soars As Cost-Of-Living Crisis Bites*. Forbes, published 30 November 2022.
23. Carrns, Ann (2022). 'The Downsides of Using "Buy Now, Pay Later"'. *The New York Times*, published 29 December 2022.

Chapter 3: Caught in the Web of Shame

1. Brown, Brené (2012). Listening to Shame. TED talk, March 2012.
2. Smith, A. (1776). *An Inquiry into the Nature and Causes of the Wealth of Nations*. Oxford: Clarendon, pp.351–2.
3. Recounted by Imogen Tyler in her book *Stigma: The Machinery of Inequality*. London: Zed Books (2020).
4. Tyler, I., and Campbell, S. (2024). *Poverty stigma: a glue that holds poverty in place*. York: Joseph Rowntree Foundation.
5. See the following references for these examples. Girl in Uganda – Bantebya-Kyomuhendo, G., Chase, E., and Kyoheirwe, F. (2019). 'Children and Young People's Experiences of Managing Poverty-Related Shame in Uganda and the UK'. In Roelen, K., Morgan, R., and Tafere, Y. (eds.), *Putting Children First: New Frontiers in the Fight Against Child Poverty in Africa*. Stuttgart: Ibidem Verlag, p.63. Parents in Guinea-Bissau – Narayan, D. (1999). *Can Anyone Hear Us? Voices from 47 Countries. Voices of the Poor*. Washington DC: World Bank.
6. Many will remember the 2010 earthquake that devastated the capital city of Port-au-Prince and killed more than 250,000 people.
7. OPHI (2023). Multidimensional Poverty Index 2023. Haiti. Unstacking global poverty: data for high impact action. New York: UNDP.
8. IHE and ICF (2018). *Enquête Mortalité, Morbidité et Utilisation des Services en Haïti 2016-2017: Rapport de synthèse*. Rockville, Maryland, USA, Institut Haïtien de l'Enfance (IHE) et ICF.
9. Walker, S. P., et al. (2011). 'Inequality in early childhood:

risk and protective factors for early child development'. *The Lancet* 378:1325–38; and Walker, S. P., et al. (2007). 'Child development: risk factors for adverse outcomes in developing countries'. *The Lancet* 369:145–57.

10. Roelen, K. and Saha, A. (2021). Pathways to stronger futures? The role of social protection in reducing psychological risk factors for child development in Haiti. *World Development* 142: 105423.

11. See Public Health England (2019). Mental Health and Wellbeing: JSNA toolkit. Guidance 2. Mental health: environmental factors. 3. Poverty and financial security, updated 25 October 2019, accessed 14 May 2024.

12. Ridley, Matthew, et al. (2020). 'Poverty, depression, and anxiety: Causal evidence and Mechanisms'. *Science* 370, Issue 6522.

13. Hicks, D. (2011). *Dignity: The Essential Role It Plays in Resolving Conflict*. New Haven: Yale University Press.

14. Chase, E., and Bantebya-Kyomuhendo, G. (2014). *Poverty and Shame: Global Experiences*. Oxford: Oxford University Press.

15. Mathew, L. (2010). 'Coping with Shame of Poverty: Analysis of Farmers in Distress'. *Psychology and Developing Societies* 22(2) 385–407.

16. Merriott, D. (2016). 'Factors associated with the farmer suicide crisis in India'. *Journal of Epidemiology and Global Health* 6(4): 217–27.

17. Schwarz, N., et al. (2009). 'Reasons for non-adherence to vaccination at mother and child care clinics (MCCs) in Lambaréné, Gabon'. *Vaccine* 27(39): 5371–5.

18. Bregman, R. (2020). *Human Kind. A Hopeful History*. London: Bloomsbury Publishing.

19. Jacquet, J. (2015). *Is Shame Necessary? New Uses for an Old Tool*. London: Penguin.

20. Lawrence, J. J., et al. (2016). 'Beliefs, Behaviors, and Perceptions of Community-Led Total Sanitation and Their Relation to Improved Sanitation in Rural Zambia'. *The American Journal of Tropical Medicine and Hygiene* 94(3): 553–62.

21. Based on World Health Organisation 2017 data of people practising open defecation (% of population), accessed 31 December 2020.

22. Based on World Health Organization 2015 data of population practising open defecation (%), accessed 31 December 2020.
23. See CLTS Knowledge Hub: http://www.communityledtotal sanitation.org/.
24. Otieno, P. (2012). 'The "shame question" in CLTS'. CLTS Knowledge Hub, published 24 April 2012.
25. Bateman, M., and Engel, S. (2018). 'To shame or not to shame – that is the sanitation question'. *Development Policy Review* 36(2): 155–73.
26. Ibid, 162–3.
27. Brewis, A., and Wutich, A. (2019). 'Why we should never do it: stigma as a behaviour change tool in global health'. *BMJ Global Health* 4(5): e001911.
28. Goffman, Erving (1963). *Stigma: Notes on the Management of Spoiled Identity.* New York: Simon and Schuster.
29. Hrynkiw, Ivana (2016). '"I need lunch money", Alabama school stamps on child's arm'. *Advance Local*, published 13 June 2016.
30. elder.175 (2020). 'The No Shame at School Act: The Purpose and Need for Prohibition of Shaming Children for School Lunch Debt'. The Ohio State University, published 15 June 2020.
31. Tyler, I. (2020). *Stigma: The Machinery of Inequality.* London: Zed Books.
32. Poverty Unpacked podcast – Episode #4: Shifting the Blame and Shame of Poverty – Mary O'Hara, published June 2020.
33. Poverty Unpacked podcast – Episode #1: All Together in Dignity – Diana Skelton, published March 2020.

Chapter 4: Aspiring to Brighter Futures

1. El-Mofty, Nariman, and Michael, Maggie (2020). 'Determined: Ethiopian female migrants risk all for Saudi'. AP News, published 14 February 2020.
2. Ray, Debraj (2006). 'Aspirations, Poverty, and Economic Change'. In Banerjee, A. V., Bénabou, R. and Mookherjee, D. (eds.) *Understanding Poverty.* Oxford: Oxford University Press: pp.409–22.

3. Siddique, Omer, and Durr-e-Nayab (2020). *Aspirations and Behaviour: Future in the Mindset. The Link between Aspiration Failure and the Poverty Trap.* PIDE Working Papers No. 2020: 13. Islamabad: Pakistan Institute of Development Economics.
4. Poverty Unpacked podcast – Episode #17: Aspirations and poverty – a double-edged sword – Katrina Kosec, published July 2021.
5. Chattopadhyay, Raghabendra, and Duflo, Esther (2001). *Women as Policy Makers: Evidence from an India-wide randomized policy experiment.* NBER Working Paper 8615. Massachusetts: National Bureau of Economic Research, p.7.
6. Beaman, L., et al. (2012). 'Female leadership raises aspirations and educational attainment for girls: a policy experiment in India'. *Science* 335(6068): 582–6.
7. Poverty Unpacked podcast – Episode #12: Working-class writers – voices to be heard – Mahsuda Snaith, published February 2021.
8. Sellgren, Katherine (2020). 'Warning over youth career aspiration-reality disconnect'. *BBC News*, published 22 January 2020.
9. See https://dictionary.cambridge.org/dictionary/english/aspiration, accessed 20 May 2021.
10. Lybbert, T. J., and Wydick B. (2018). 'Poverty, Aspirations and the Economics of Hope'. *Economic Development and Cultural Change*, Vol. 66, No.4.
11. La Ferrara, E. (2019). 'Presidential Address: Aspirations, Social Norms, and Development'. *Journal of the European Economic Association* 17(6), 1687–1722.
12. Riley, E. (2018). 'Role models in movies: the impact of *Queen of Katwe* on students' educational attainment'. CSAE Working Paper WPS/2017-13. Oxford: University of Oxford.
13. Morrison Gutman, L., and Akerman, R. (2008). 'Determinants of Aspirations'. Research Report 27. Centre for Research on the Wider Benefits of Learning. London: Institute of Education.
14. Lee, J. O., et al. (2012). 'The Role of Educational Aspirations and Expectations in the Discontinuity of Intergenerational Low-Income Status'. *Social Work Research* 36(2), 141–51.
15. Poverty Unpacked podcast – Episode #17: Aspirations and poverty – a double-edged sword – Katrina Kosec, published July 2021.
16. Ibid.

17. Brown, Gordon (2007). 2007 Speech on Education, held on 31 October 2007 at University of Greenwich.
18. 'Social mobility "still a problem in UK"', says Cameron'. BBC News, published 14 November 2013.
19. La Ferrara, E. (2019). 'Presidential Address: Aspirations, Social Norms, and Development'. *Journal of the European Economic Association* 17 (6) , 1687–1722.
20. Bernard, T., et al. (2011). 'The Future in Mind: Aspirations and Forward-Looking Behaviour in Rural Ethiopia'. Washington DC: World Bank.
21. See Platt, L., and Zuccotti, C. V. (2021). *Social Mobility and Ethnicity*. London: Institute for Fiscal Studies.
22. Crivello, Gina, and Morrow, Virginia (2019). 'Against the Odds: Why Some Children Fare Well in the Face of Adversity'. *The Journal of Development Studies* 56(5): 999–1016.
23. La Ferrara, E. (2019). 'Presidential Address: Aspirations, Social Norms, and Development'. *Journal of the European Economic Association* 17 (6): 1687–1722.
24. Poverty Unpacked podcast – Episode #18: Millennials, a generation of frustrated aspirations – Thomas Rochow, published August 2021.
25. The Prince's Trust (2020). *The aspiration gap: the lost hopes and ambitions of a generation*. London: The Prince's Trust.
26. Poverty Unpacked podcast – Episode #17: Aspirations and poverty – a double-edged sword – Cecilia Mo, published July 2021.
27. See ReviseSociology blog, 'Why do White Working Class Kids Lack Aspiration?', published 5 April 2016, and BBC Radio 4, Thinking Allowed, 'White Working Class Boys; French Thought', published 29 June 2015.

Chapter 5: The Other Side of the Coin

1. Fuhlrott, F. (2007). 'Burundi after the Civil War: Demobilising and Reintegrating Ex-Combatants'. *Africa Spectrum*, 42(2), 323–33.

2. Based on WFP Burundi country profile: https://www.wfp.org/countries/burundi, accessed 5 March 2021.

3. Roelen, Keetie, and Devereux, Stephen (2019). 'Money and the Message: The Role of Training and Coaching in Graduation Programming'. *The Journal of Development Studies*, 55:6, 1121–39.

4. Hanlon, J., Barrientos, A., and Hulme, D. (2010). *Just Give Money to the Poor: The Development Revolution From the Global South*. Boulder: Kumarian Press.

5. Social Assistance Explorer by the University of Manchester: http://www.social-assistance.manchester.ac.uk/map/, accessed 20 February 2021.

6. Based on United Nations Population Division 2020 data of ranking of countries based on population: https://www.worldometers.info/world-population/population-by-country/, accessed 19 February 2021.

7. Gentilini, U. (2022). *Cash Transfers in Pandemic Times. Evidence, Practices, and Implications from the Largest Scale Up in History*. Washington DC: World Bank.

8. Bastagli, F., et al. (2016). *Cash transfers: what does the evidence say? A rigorous review of impacts and the role of design and implementation features*. London: ODI.

9. Tiwari, S., et al. (2019). 'Impact of Cash Transfer programs on Food Security and Nutrition in sub-Saharan Africa: A Cross-Country Analysis'. *Global Food Security* 11: 72–83.

10. Haushofer, Johannes, and Shapiro, Jeremy (2016). 'The Short-Term Impact of Unconditional Cash Transfers to the Poor: Experimental Evidence from Kenya'. *The Quarterly Journal of Economics* 131 (4): 1973–2042.

11. Handa, S., et al., on behalf of the Transfer Project (2017). 'Myth-busting? Confronting Six Common Perceptions about Unconditional Cash Transfers as a Poverty Reduction Strategy in Africa'. Innocenti Working Paper 2017-11, UNICEF Office of Research, Florence.

12. Evans, D., and Popova, A. (2017). 'Cash Transfers and Temptation Goods'. *Economic Development and Cultural Change* 65(2): 189–221.

13. Attah, R., et al. (2016). 'Can Social Protection Affect Psychosocial

Wellbeing and Why Does This Matter? Lessons from Cash Transfers in Sub-Saharan Africa'. *The Journal of Development Studies* 52(8): 1115–1131.

14. Tran, A., Kidd, S., and Dean, K. (2020). *'I feel more loved.' Autonomy, self-worth and Kenya's universal pension*. Orpington: Development Pathways.

15. See Berhane, G., et al. (2015). 'Evaluation of the social cash transfer pilot programme: Tigray Region, Ethiopia: Endline report'. International Food Policy Research Institute (IFPRI); Institute of Development Studies (IDS); Mekelle University.

16. Gibson, Jennifer, and Watson, Carol (2009). Joint SCUK/UNICEF Study. Malawi Country Report. The Transfer Project. University of North Carolina.

17. An overview of evidence can be found in this systematic review: Yoshino, C. A., et al. (2023). 'Experiences of conditional and unconditional cash transfers intended for improving health outcomes and health service use: a qualitative evidence synthesis'. *Cochrane Database of Systematic Reviews*, Issue 3: 1465–1858.

18. Covert, Bryce (2019). 'The Myth of the Welfare Queen'. *The New Republic*, published 2 July 2019.

19. Tirado, L. (2014). *Hand to Mouth. The Truth about Being Poor in a Wealthy World*. London: Virago, p.34.

20. See research from Welfare Conditionality research project: http://www.welfareconditionality.ac.uk/, accessed 25 July 2021.

21. Wickham, S., et al. (2020). 'Effects on mental health of a UK welfare reform, Universal Credit: a longitudinal controlled study'. *The Lancet Public Health*, Vol. 5, Issue 3, e157–e164.

22. Williams, E. (2021). 'Unemployment, sanctions and mental health: The relationship between benefit sanctions and antidepressant prescribing'. *Journal of Social Policy*, 50(1), 1–20.

23. Disability Rights UK (2022). 'DWP ignored "hugely alarming" research that linked WCA with 600 suicides, MPs are told', published 27 June 2022, citing findings from Barr, B., et al. (2016). '"First, do no harm": are disability assessments associated with adverse trends in mental health? A longitudinal ecological study'. *Journal of Epidemiology and Community Health*, 70: 339–45.

24. Kurmelovs, Royce (2019). 'The nightmare of Australia's welfare

system: "At the push of a button, my working life was erased"'. *The Guardian*, 14 September 2019.

25. Ibid.
26. Henriques-Gomes, Luke (2019). 'Jobless suffering under "punitive" Jobactive program, says Senate report'. *The Guardian*, published 18 February 2019.
27. Fiszbein, A., and Schady, N. (2009). *Conditional Cash Transfers: Reducing Present and Future Poverty*. Washington DC: The World Bank.
28. Ibid.
29. Millán, T. M., et al. (2019). 'Long-Term Impacts of Conditional Cash Transfers: Review of the Evidence'. *The World Bank Research Observer*, Vol. 34, Issue 1, pp.119–59.
30. Baird, S., et al. (2013). 'Relative Effectiveness of Conditional and Unconditional Cash Transfers for Schooling Outcomes in Developing Countries: A Systematic Review'. *Campbell Systematic Reviews* 9:1, 1–59.
31. Akresh, Richard, de Walque, Damien, and Kazianga, Harounan (2016). 'Evidence from a Randomized Evaluation of the Household Welfare Impacts of Conditional and Unconditional Cash Transfers Given to Mothers or Fathers'. World Bank Policy Research Working Paper No. 7730. Washington DC: World Bank.
32. Baird, S., McIntosh, C., and Özler, B. (2010). 'Cash or Condition? Evidence from a Randomized Cash Transfer Program'. Impact Evaluation Series No. 45. Washington DC: World Bank.
33. Schüring, S. (2012). 'To condition or not – is that the question? An analysis of the effectiveness of ex-ante and ex-post conditionality in social cash transfer programs.' PhD dissertation. Maastricht: Boekenplan.
34. Marston, L. (2020). 'PATH to a 'better' life? Exploring the influence of conditional assistance from the Programme of Advancement through Health and Education (PATH) on the lives of its beneficiaries in Jamaica.' PhD thesis. Cambridge: University of Cambridge. p.146.
35. Ulrichs, M., and Roelen, K. (2012). 'Equal Opportunities for All? A Critical Analysis of Mexico's Oportunidades'. IDS Working Paper 413. Institute of Development Studies: Brighton.

36. Cookson, T. (2018). *Unjust Conditions. Women's Work and the Hidden Cost of Cash Transfer*. Oakland: University of California Press.
37. Ibid.
38. NRC (2021). 'Wiebes: geen schuldgevoel, maar affaire is "in mij gaan zitten"'. *NRC*, published 15 January 2021.
39. Henley, Jon (2021). 'Dutch government resigns over child benefits scandal'. *The Guardian*, 15 January 2021.
40. Ibid.
41. Frederik, Jesse (2020). 'Tienduizenden gedupeerden, maar geen daders: zo ontstond de tragedie achter de toeslagenaffaire'. *De Correspondent*, published 13 November 2020.
42. See Twitter/X feed Arre Zuurmond, Ombudsman Amsterdam, 17 June 2020 (link no longer available).
43. Henley, Jon (2021). 'Dutch government resigns over child benefits scandal'. *The Guardian*, 15 January 2021.
44. Garside, J. (2016). 'Benefit fraud or tax evasion: row over the Tories' targets'. *The Guardian*, 13 April 2016.
45. The Week (2016). 'Benefit fraud v tax evasion: Which costs more?'. *The Week*, published 14 April 2016.
46. Turner, George (2021). 'Comparing the prosecution of tax crime with benefits crime'. Taxwatch, 19 February 2021.
47. Butler, Patrick (2020). 'Family of mentally ill single mother accuse DWP of failing to protect her'. *The Guardian,* published 5 November 2020.
48. Butler, Patrick (2021). 'Capita pays compensation to family of woman who died after benefits cut'. *The Guardian*, published 3 November 2021.
49. Borrowed from the apt subtitle of Virginia Eubanks' book *Automating Inequality. How high-tech tools profile, police and punish the poor* (2018).

Chapter 6: A Nudge in the Wrong Direction

1. Kahneman, D. (2011). *Thinking, Fast and Slow*. London: Penguin.
2. Iyengar, S., and Lepper, M. (2000). 'When Choice is Demotivating:

Can One Desire Too Much of a Good Thing?'. *Personality Processes and Individual Differences* 79(6): 995–1006.

3. Dolan, P. (2015). *Happiness by Design. Finding pleasure and purpose in everyday life.* London: Penguin Books.

4. NHS England. 'Reducing did not attends (DNAs) in outpatient services'. Publication reference PR2012. NHS England, published 2 February 2023, last updated 15 August 2023.

5. See ideas42 (2022). 'Increasing Savings Among Cash Transfer Recipients in Tanzania. Encouraging Cash Transfer Recipients to Save'. ideas42,https://www.ideas42.org/wp-content/uploads/2022/08/Tanzania_Cash_Transfers.pdf and on the ideas42 website: https://www.cashtransfers.ideas42.org/.

6. Karlan, D., et al. (2014). 'Getting to the Top of Mind: How Reminders Increase Saving'. Washington DC: Innovations for Poverty Action.

7. Orkin, Kate, et al. (2023). 'Aspiring to a Better Future: Can a Simple Psychological Intervention Reduce Poverty?'. Oxford: University of Oxford.

8. Estimates from Children Count. Statistics on children in South Africa, 2023 data on Child Support Grants accessed 16 December 2023.

9. The Decision Lab (undated). 'How labeling cash transfers increased the likelihood of spending it on intended goods by 38%'. The Decision Lab, accessed 24 February 2024.

10. See guidance 'Electric vehicle chargepoint grant for renters and flat owners' on https://www.find-government-grants.service.gov.uk/grants/, accessed 24 February 2024.

11. See *pv magazine* (2022). 'Germany slashes VAT for residential PV to 0%'. *pv magazine* International, published 8 December 2022.

12. See guidance 'ISDE: Warmtepomp woningeigenaren' on https://www.rvo.nl/subsidies-financiering/isde/woningeigenaren/warmtepomp#meldcodelijst; and here: Meldcodelijst Warmtepompen 22 Januari 2024 (rvo.nl), accessed 25 February 2024.

13. See Booth, Robert (2022). 'Awaab Ishak death: Rochdale housing chair to quit after damning report'. *The Guardian*, published 15 December 2022; and Weaver, Christian (2022). 'Awaab Ishak's

death shed light on a social housing scandal. Now we have a brief chance to fix it'. *The Guardian*, published 23 November 2022.
14. Shelter (2017). 'More than 300,000 people in Britain homeless today'. Shelter England, published 8 November 2017.
15. Baker, Keiligh (2017). 'Milton Keynes becomes Tent City as homelessness soars'. MailOnline, published 21 November 2017.
16. Darlington, Emily (2023). 'Compassion, not cruelty, is the answer to rough sleeping – we have the proof in Milton Keynes'. *The Guardian*, published 7 November 2023.
17. Greenfield, Patrick (2018). 'Tented Britain: rise in rough sleepers taking shelter under canvas'. *The Guardian*, published 10 August 2018.

Chapter 7: Self-Helping Your Way Up and Out

1. Chowdhury, A. M. Raza, and Cash, Richard A. (1996). *A Simple Solution: Teaching Millions to Treat Diarrhoea at Home*. Dhaka, Bangladesh: University Press.
2. Poverty Unpacked podcast – Episode #27: Graduating out of poverty – can it be done? – Greg Chen, published September 2022.
3. See Barrett, C. B., and Carter, M. R. (2012). 'The Economics of Poverty Traps and Persistent Poverty: Policy and Empirical Implications'. Ithaca: Cornell University; Carter, M. C. and Barrett, C. B. (2005). 'The Economics of Poverty Traps and Persistent Poverty: An Asset-Based Approach'. SAGA Working Paper. Princeton: Cornell and Clark Atlanta Universities; and Carter, M. R., and Barrett, C. B. (2006). 'The economics of poverty traps and persistent poverty: An asset-based approach'. *The Journal of Development Studies*, 42(2), 178–99.
4. Andrews, Colin, et al. (2021). 'The State of Economic Inclusion Report 2021: The Potential to Scale. Overview'. Washington, DC: World Bank.
5. Review by lillightjc-85500 on IMDB, September 2023: 'The Great British Benefits Handout' (TV Series 2016–) – IMDb.
6. See Roelen, K., et al. (2019). *Pathways to Stronger Futures in Haiti:*

the role of graduation programming in promoting early childhood development. Brighton: Institute of Development Studies.

7. Roelen, K., et al. (2018). *Understanding post-programme graduation trajectories in Burundi.* Brighton: Institute of Development Studies.

8. See Banerjee, Abhijit, et al. (2015). 'A multifaceted program causes lasting progress for the very poor: Evidence from six countries'. *Science* 348, 1260799; and DeGiovanni, Frank, and Hashemi, Syed M. (2014). 'Graduation Model: Ready to Scale Up?'. CGAP blog, published 25 February 2014.

9. Based on Office of National Statistics (ONS) data on business survival rates between 2017 and 2022: Business demography, UK – Office for National Statistics (ons.gov.uk), published 22 November 2023.

10. French, Katie (2017). 'They've blown it! Benefits family who were handed £26,000 in TV experiment admit they've wound up their new business just 18 months later'. MailOnline, published 18 July 2017.

11. Konstan, David (2022). 'Epicurus'. *The Stanford Encyclopedia of Philosophy* (Fall 2022 edition), ed. Edward N. Zalta and Uri Nodelman: https://plato.stanford.edu/archives/fall2022/entries/epicurus/, accessed 20 November 2023.

12. ATD Fourth World UK (2023). 'Reimagining Universal Credit'. ATD Fourth World UK, published 15 September 2023.

13. Ratcliffe, S. (2017). 'Aristotle 384–322 BC'. In Ratcliffe, S. (ed.). *Oxford Essential Quotations* (5th edn). Oxford: Oxford University Press.

14. Full Fact (2019). 'What can MPs claim on expenses?'. Full Fact, published 17 July 2019.

15. Bredewold, F., et al. (2018). 'De Verhuizing van de Verzorgingsstaat'. *Tijdschrift voor Sociale Vraagstukken.* Uitgeverij van Gennep.

16. See here on the effect of closure of care homes on elderly relatives: Heijenga, Miriam (2020). 'Door verdwijnen verzorgingshuis moeten ouderen langer thuis blijven wonen: "Er is geen alternatief meer"'. *EenVandaag* (avrotros.nl), published 15 January 2020.

17. Cameron, David (2010). Big Society Speech, held on 19 July 2010 in Liverpool.

18. Based on Ventura, Luca (2024). 'Richest Countries in the World 2024'. *Global Finance Magazine*, published 3 May 2024.

19. See Kwek, Theophilus, and Siow, Stephanie (2018). 'Rethinking Responsibility'. ETHOS Digital Issue 2, Civil Service College, published April 2018; and Yenn, Teo You (2017). 'Poor People Don't Like Oats Either'. New Naratif, published 9 September 2017.

20. Wong, Lawrence (2023). Speech made by Deputy Prime Minister and Minister for Finance Lawrence Wong at the debate on President's address. *Forward Singapore*, published 17 April 2023.

21. Gentilini, U. (2022). *Cash Transfers in Pandemic Times. Evidence, Practices, and Implications from the Largest Scale Up in History.* Washington DC: World Bank.

22. Byrne, Rhonda (2022). 'The Secret to Money. An excerpt from the Rhonda Byrne Masterclass audiobook. The Secret book series'. YouTube, published 20 February 2022.

23. AP (2020). '"The Secret" author Rhonda Byrne has new release in November'. *The Washington Post*, published 14 August 2020.

24. CNN Larry King Live. Interview with Oprah Winfrey, aired 1 May 2007. Transcript retrieved from http://edition.cnn.com/TRANSCRIPTS/0705/01/lkl.01.html.

25. LaRosa, John (2018). 'The $10 Billion Self-Improvement Market Adjusts to a New Generation'. Market Research Blog, published 11 October 2018.

26. Estimates based on World Bank data of GDP PPP, using 2017 as base period: https://data.worldbank.org.

27. Ehrenreich, B. (2009). *Smile or Die. How Positive Thinking Fooled America and the World.* London: Granta Books.

28. Presentation on the Behavioural Insights Team website: 'Boosting diversity & inclusion' featuring Aneeta Rattan, Elizabeth Linos & Frank Douglas | The Behavioural Insights Team (bi.team); and research paper here: Linos, Elizabeth, Ruffini, Krista, and Wilcoxen, Stephanie (2021). 'Reducing Burnout and Resignations among Frontline Workers: A Field Experiment (July 5, 2021)'. *Journal of Public Administration Research and Theory*, forthcoming.

29. Davies, W. (2015). *The Happiness Industry.* London: Verso, p.35.

30. See 'The Impact of Cognitive Behavioral Therapy on Low-Income

Individuals in Rural Ghana' | The Abdul Latif Jameel Poverty Action Lab, accessed 9 June 2024; and Barker, Nathan, et al. (2021). 'Mental Health Therapy as a Core Strategy for Increasing Human Capital: Evidence from Ghana'. NBER Working Paper No. 29407.

31. Haushofer, Johannes, Mudida, Robert, and Shapiro, Jeremy P. (2020). 'The Comparative Impact of Cash Transfers and a Psychotherapy Program on Psychological and Economic Well-being'. NBER Working Paper No. 28106.

32. Sandel, M. J. (2020). *The Tyranny of Merit. What's Become of the Common Good?*. London: Allen Lane, p.25.

33. See Aschoff, N. (2015). *The New Prophets of Capital*. London: Verso.

Chapter 8: The Bigger Picture

1. The full recording of the evidence session can be found on: Parliamentlive.tv – Work and Pensions Committee, recorded 3 March 2021.

2. Timms, Stephen (undated). 'A new child poverty target'. Children's Commissioner for England (childrenscommissioner.gov.uk), accessed 18 May 2024.

3. Jensen, T., and Tyler, I. (2015). '"Benefits broods": The cultural and political crafting of anti-welfare commonsense'. *Critical Social Policy* 35(4), 470–91.

4. Reader, M., Portes, J. and Patrick, R. (2022). 'Does cutting child benefits reduce fertility in larger families? Evidence from the UK's two-child limit'. Larger Families project: https://largerfamilies.study/.

5. Chzhen, Yekaterina, and Bradshaw, Jonathan (2024). 'The UK's two-child limit on benefits is hurting the poorest families – poverty experts on why it should be abolished'. The Conversation, published 29 February 2024.

6. ATD Fourth World UK (2018). 'When the Right to Family Life Is Violated: "Trust Betrayed, Again and Again"'. ATD Fourth World UK, published 13 December 2018.

7. Walker, Peter, and Butler, Patrick (2017). 'Government under fire over new child tax credit form for rape victims'. *The Guardian*, 6 April 2017.

8. See Third Report on UK Parliament website, Work and Pensions Committee: Children in poverty: Measurement and targets – Committees – UK Parliament, published 22 September 2021.

9. See 'S Jongers, Tim (2022). *Beledigende Broccoli*. Amsterdam: Uitgeverij van Gennep; and Participatielezing 2022 Tim 'S Jongers: 'Jullie zouden me tien jaar geleden nog geen vijftig cent hebben gegeven', Movisie, 25 March 2022.

10. See Britannica (2024). 'Poor People's Campaign'. *Encyclopaedia Britannica*, last updated 12 June 2024; Diamond, Anna (2018). 'Remembering Resurrection City and the Poor People's Campaign of 1968'. *Smithsonian Magazine*, published May 2018; and website of Poor People's Campaign: Join us as We Build the Third Reconstruction – Poor People's Campaign (poorpeoplescampaign. org).

11. Podcast 31 – Episode #1: De cyclus van armoede en schulden doorbreken met Mobility Mentoring® – Platform 31, published January 2020.

12. Based on Smeets, Suzan (2020). 'Een gezin met multiproblematiek uit hun noodwoning helpen'. Platform 31, published September 2020.

13. Poverty Unpacked – Episode #23: Mobility mentoring to navigate the trauma of poverty – a brain-science based approach – Beth Babcock, published January 2022.

14. Cottam, Hillary (2018). *Radical Help. How We Can Remake the Relationships Between Us and Revolutionise the Welfare State*. London: Virago Press.

15. Website Buurtzorg: https://www.buurtzorgnederland.com/, accessed 5 February 2024.

16. Resolution Foundation (2023). '15 years of economic stagnation has left workers across Britain with an £11,000 a year lost wages gap'. Resolution Foundation, published March 2023.

17. Based on Office of National Statistics (ONS) data on average household income: Average household income, UK – Office for National Statistics (ons.gov.uk), published January 2023.

18. The Health Foundation (2022). 'In-work poverty trends'. The Health Foundation, published December 2022, accessed 2 February 2024.
19. Living Wage Foundation (2024). 'Our history'. Living Wage Foundation website: https://www.livingwage.org.uk/history, accessed 3 February 2024.
20. Poverty Unpacked podcast – Episode #30: Basic income - more than just cash – Sarath Davala, published March 2023.
21. See GiveDirectly website: https://www.givedirectly.org/ubi/, accessed 4 February 2024.
22. Widerquist, K., and Arndt, G. (2023). 'The Cost of Basic Income in the United Kingdom: A Microsimulation Analysis'. *International Journal of Microsimulation* 16(3), 1–18. DOI: 10.34196/IJM.00286.
23. Robeyns, I. (2024). *Limitarianism. The Case Against Extreme Wealth*. London: Allen Lane.
24. Piketty, T. (2014). *Capital in the Twenty-First Century*. Cambridge, MA: Harvard University Press.
25. Sharma, Shweta (2024). 'Most millionaires would pay more tax and see extreme wealth as a threat to democracy, campaigners say'. *The Independent*, published 17 January 2024.
26. Engelhorn, Marlene (undated). Marlene Engelhorn membership video. Millionaires for Humanity website: https://millionairesforhumanity.org/the-millionaires/marlene-engelhorn/, accessed 5 February 2024.
27. Robeyns, I. (2024). *Limitarianism. The Case Against Extreme Wealth*. London: Allen Lane; and as discussed in Adams, Tim (2024). '"No one should have more than €10m": the author of *Limitarianism* on why the super-rich need to level down radically'. *The Guardian*, published 21 January 2024.

Chapter 9: Small Actions, Big Change

1. See Oatley, Keith (2005). 'A Feeling for Fiction'. *Greater Good Magazine*, published 1 September 2005.
2. Poverty Unpacked podcast – Episode #12: Working-class writers

– voices to be heard – Natasha Carthew, published February 2021.

3. See Konrath, S., and Kisida, B. (2021). 'Does Arts Engagement Increase Empathy and Prosocial Behavior? A Review of the Literature'. In Hersey, L., and Bobick, B. (eds.). *Engagement in the City. How Arts and Culture Impact Development in Urban Areas.* Maryland: Lexington Books, pp.7–38.

4. UNICEF USA (2015). 'Clouds over Sidra: An Award-Winning Virtual Reality Experience'. UNICEF USA, published 18 December 2015.

5. See Sora-Domenjó, C. (2022). 'Disrupting the "empathy machine": The power and perils of virtual reality in addressing social issues'. *Frontiers in Psychology* 13:814565.

6. Geisen, Shannon (2023). 'Simulation opens eyes to realities of poverty'. Park Rapids Enterprise, published 16 May 2023.

7. See website of The Poverty Simulation: https://www.povertysimulation.net/about/, accessed 20 February 2024.

8. As reported in Stout, A. G. (2016). 'Perceptions of Poverty and the Community Action Poverty Simulation Experience.' Thesis. The University of Mississippi.

9. See the SPENT game website: https://playspent.org/, accessed 20 February 2024.

10. See Vargas, Ariadna, et al. (undated). 'Uncovering Hidden Biases in ChatGPT's Written Content and Preventing Them from Exacerbating Existing Inequalities'. ideas42 blog, accessed 12 February 2024.

11. Sandel, M. J. (2021). *The Tyranny of Merit. What's Become of the Common Good?.* London: Allen Lane/ Penguin, p.13.

12. See Duffy, Boggy (2023). 'Trust in trouble? UK and international confidence in institutions'. The UK in the World Values Survey. London: King's College London.

13. Savage, Michael (2020). 'Quarter of a million sign Marcus Rashford's free school meals petition'. *The Guardian*, published 17 October 2020.

14. Closed petition, End child food poverty – no child should be going hungry, on UK Government and Parliament Petitions website: https://petition.parliament.uk/petitions/554276/, accessed 16 February 2024.

15. BBC Newsround (2020). 'Marcus Rashford: Government changes decision on free school meals'. BBC Newsround, published 8 November 2020.

16. See The Art of Gentle Protest: Sarah Corbett at TEDxRoyalTunbridgeWellsWomen, November 2016; and Corbett, Sarah (2024). *The Craftivist Collective Handbook. Projects, Stories and Methods for your Gentle Protests*. London: Unbound.

Conclusion

1. Dowden, Richard (1978). Interview with Margaret Thatcher, *Catholic Herald*, published 5 December 1978.

2. Maryann Broxton, co-coordinator for the ATD-US research project on Hidden Dimensions of Poverty, quoted in ATD Fourth World International (2020). COVID-19 and the Human Rights of People Living in Poverty. ATD Fourth World International, published December 2020.